THERE'S NO SUCH THING
AS
Magic Blood

DAVID MATITYAHU BEN AVRAHAM

Jewish Learning Press

Jewish Learning Press

Paperback ISBN: 978-0-578-25148-6
Hardback ISBN: 978-0-578-25149-3

PRINTED IN THE UNITED STATES OF AMERICA

This book is dedicated to my children;
I love each of you intensely.
And to my sister,
who is proof that changing your life doesn't require magic blood.

TABLE OF CONTENTS

INTRODUCTION

I lay face up in tall, dead grasses, within short sight of the single-prop airplane which had crashed along the northern edge of my parents' property. The accident was decades old. The tart aroma of wild grapes lingered in the cool but sun-drenched September air. It smelled like Halloween. A jet-black crow circled high overhead, threatening. I was conscious of the earth beneath my back. Holding myself perfectly still, I imagined I could sense the rotation of the planet. *Perhaps someone had died, right here, on this very spot*, I wondered. It was possible. After all, what had happened to the pilot who crashed this plane into the trees, burning many of them down? No one could have survived this, could they?

When our religion proves fallible and its untouchable doctrines come crumbling to earth in flames, our psyche can unravel along with it, and it can feel as though it is the world around us that is spinning rather than our own mind, much like my ten-year-old self in my father's field. In fact, one might wonder how a person can even survive such a fall from the spiritual heavens.

Jesus is reported to have said, *"I am the living bread that came down from heaven. If anyone eats of this bread, he will live forever. And the bread that I will give for the life of the world is my flesh…* The Jews disputed amongst themselves, saying, *"How can this man give us his flesh to eat?"* Jesus doesn't answer them with, "Hey, it's for effect. Haven't you learned the Kabbalah?" No, John's Jesus doubles down on the macabre, saying,

"He who eats my flesh and drinks my blood has eternal life, and I will raise him up on the last day. For my flesh is true food, and my blood is true drink." (Jn.6:50-55)

These are projected ideas. Jesus is not a real human being here, but a spiritual avatar; like a wedding cake, which is admired and photographed before being cut up and stuffed into the face of the bride, to the applause of all. One might think, as most evangelicals do, that the only possible justification for such an exchange in the New Testament (put in the mouth of a Jewish rabbi no less, of all absurdities) is that he is employing metaphor. *He doesn't mean this literally*, they proclaim, laughing. Yet, it does not appear that this is how the Church fathers saw it at all. In fact, to this day, the Roman Catholic Church teaches that the eucharist at the Mass is the transubstantiated body of Jesus, and that the wine in the chalice is his actual blood; precisely because they do not view this exchange in the gospel of John as metaphorical language in any way, but categorically literal. The official Catechism of the Catholic Church leaves little doubt on this matter and has historically guarded this doctrine as sacred. The Catholic Church, for its part, views Jesus's blood as *magic*. Protestants mock this doctrine while at the same time clinging to the core theology of the idea. How else can the Protestants explain the Christian concept of atonement? Most evangelicals recoil from the Catholic interpretation of John chapter six and yet fail to recognize how critical such a reading is to their confession of salvation through *"nothing but the blood of Jesus"*, as the famous Baptist hymn proclaims:

"Nothing can for sin atone...nothing but the blood of Jesus..."

Truly, without this understanding of the literal application of Christ's *magic blood* to the problem of sin, all conceptions of Christian salvation fall apart. We read, for example, in Hebrews,

"But when Christ appeared as a high priest of the good things to come..."

and not through the blood of goats and calves, but through his own blood, he entered the holy place once and for all, having obtained eternal redemption." (Hebrews 9:11-12)

The *magic blood* of Jesus is the spinal column of all the many variations on Christian atonement theory posited through the centuries. If you take it away, the entire religion begins to ferment and stink, and will burst asunder like new wine erupting out of an old wine skin. It is notable, for instance, that the only ministry event of Jesus cited by Paul is the Last Supper, a ritual that is rehearsed by Christians across the globe as representing the ceremonial consumption of the Lord's body and blood.

"Is not the cup of blessing which we bless a sharing in the blood of Christ?" (1 Cor.10:16)

The *magic blood* of Jesus is central to Paul's theology, and it is Paul's writings that are responsible for most of the doctrines of the many varied branches of Christianity. These facts place the Jesus of Christian tradition far afield of any Jewish conception of redemption and atonement. (The Torah also, incidentally, expressly prohibits the consumption of blood in general, let alone the blood of other humans.) Rather, this situates Jesus very much in company with other pagan myths which incorporated salvation rituals in which the participants ate the proverbial or simulated "flesh and blood" of their deity. Religions popular in the day, such as Mithraism, had similar traditions, and were ubiquitous in the many provinces of the Roman Empire at the time the gospels were written. Such pagan parallels were unknown to me during most of my Christian years. The New Testament said that Jesus was the "lamb of God" who shed his blood and died for me and I believed it, not in small part because my very soul depended upon it, as I had been repeatedly told. To question such things was considered both reckless and unacceptable to everyone within the church communities to which I belonged. No one did so. Therefore, it was a given that Jesus needed to be filleted like a trout and grilled naked on the hot coals of God's wrath.

However, unwinding the theological part of the pretzel is only a small slice of the story for myself and many others precisely because belief involves far more than mere logic. There is no place you can go, ultimately, where you can escape the heart's inner journey; its avarice, moral deficiencies, driving desires and unexpected insights, or from the people and ideologies you meet along the way who share in these problems.

Many people are victimized by religious leaders and systems which hold them in bondage and suppress the spark of genius within them. Constrained by a sense of imposed duty and expectation, these precious souls are suffocated; their flame doused by dogmas, superstitions and traditions which add no real purpose to their life other than maintaining the proverbial machinery of method. Of course, all expressions of religion are subject to the whims of interpretation. And, at least in my opinion, no religious organization has any right whatsoever to rob you of your individual sovereignty and the human right you must vigilantly guard to manage your own affairs, not the least important of which is your very mind itself; your intellectual integrity.

By the same token, however, the disciplines of religious devotion have been healing and centering for many people; even rather stabilizing. It is untrue that everyone involved in religious practices is being stifled, suppressed, or manipulated. I believe, ultimately, that man is more than just an animal with an opposable thumb that craves socialization, and which experiences an existential need to buffer the fear of death. Religion, from a spiritual and psychological perspective, is not without positive potential or intrinsic value, but it is easily abused, and often in tragic ways.

I've found it's possible to have an expression of faith which is both personal, meaningful and social. However, when one's sense of independence is violated repeatedly, subversively, even violently, in a religious environment, then it is difficult to find value in such a community.

Religion in general, for many, is an elixir. It can offer a façade of personal relevance to the marginalized, but it can also lead to a dangerous intoxication which has the real, well-established potential to push aside human decency and ethics in favor of a "mission" which justifies nearly any means to accomplish a noble "end". This is the dark side of religion; a world in which narcissistic personalities manipulate others and play upon their insecurities to gain advantage and influence, all in the name of God.

However, this book is not a frontal attack upon religion or upon people who practice religion. I did not leave Christianity on purpose. To the contrary, it was the result of research which was intended to accomplish the exact opposite. I wanted to learn as much as I could about it; its origins, doctrines and how it changed over time, so that I could feel confident in the core message. Initially, this impulse was driven by a desire to justify and defend my beliefs. I never could have imagined that this inquisitiveness would result in my complete debunking of the entire structure of my faith. Yet, that is exactly what happened.

Further, this volume is not merely dedicated to explaining how I lost faith in the one called Jesus and in the religion which claims him as its author and founder. It is also an open-hearted confession of my own limitations and how my vulnerabilities and insecurities allowed me to become a victim to the avarice of others and their desire to establish power and control over me, and more subtly, how I unwittingly cooperated with their efforts. I am not alone in this problem. There are hundreds of thousands of others, like me, who have suffered in this manner.

It's not possible to get the years back that we've lost, but it *is* possible to make it to the other side of spiritual and emotional mistreatment and put together some semblance of a meaningful life that doesn't involve being angry all the time. It isn't easy, but it's *possible*. And since it's possible, we should try. We may not be able to guide each other home, but we might just be able to sing a hopeful tune that smooths the road and helps us find peace along the way.

When I first moved to Vermont, I was driving an ancient Toyota station wagon that I picked up for six hundred dollars and that had over three hundred fifty thousand miles on it, but it was getting very tired, and I was nervous about trusting it on the mountainous dirt roads of my new residence. I had been told of an antiques dealer up the road, a kind of icon of the community. He might be able to sell it for me. I found him arranging furnishings in the barn where he held his auctions.

"What can I do you for?"

"Well, I've got this car…"

"You're lucky…" he said, cutting me off with his deeply affected Vermont drawl, "Lots of folks aint got one."

Damn straight, I thought, smiling. Damn straight.

Chapter 1

LOST OR FOUND?

MY BIRTH OCCURRED in a military hospital in San Juan, Puerto Rico which is now a museum. My mother was left to endure ten hours of labor in a room alone, in a bed positioned to face a large clock which made an unrelenting ticking sound that echoed off the cement walls and floor, for her pleasure. The military nurses would not allow my father to be with her during her labor. It was 1967, in the afterbirth of the infamous Summer of Love. I would be officially registered as a member of humanity on New Year's Eve Day, at 1:11pm.

My parents were in Puerto Rico because my father was in the Navy. At the end of my father's tour of duty, they moved back home to Rhode Island and resumed civilian life. Eventually, they bought a large Victorian-styled home in the industrial-era textile town of Woonsocket, where both families were from. My mother was a homemaker and my father had begun a promising career selling insurance, having already lost steam in the pursuit of his original goal of becoming a professional jazz musician.

My father eventually walked away from his insurance career and bought a business in south-central Massachusetts in a manual, dying trade he knew nothing about and had no experience in, just so he could call his own shots, and moved our family there from Rhode Island. Looking back at my father's professional journey, it is so much like my own, that I wonder why he's always been so critical of my choices in life. Maybe, upon reflection, *that's exactly why.*

I was encouraged at this time to join the Boy Scouts. The troop I joined was active in the outdoors, a leader in expeditions, and led by a pedophile. He was a large, imposing German man, balding, well over six feet and of substantial build, and I was afraid of him. He used to command his wife like she was a criminal. She was gaunt, pale and had greasy, long, straight black hair and a terrified look in her eyes most of the time. I am not sure if he was ever arrested, but he should have been. I eventually shut the whole affair out of my mind so that I could pretend to be a normal kid in front of my peers.

My father's new business was in a town called Sutton, and our home was an old New England farmhouse which had been built in the 1850's. In this house, I lived through the infamous Blizzard of '78, after which our cat, Mittens, came inside by digging a tunnel to the *top* of our back door, from where she literally fell into the mud room after I opened it. One day, the Massachusetts legislature approved the expansion of Rt.146 and the construction of a new set of on/off ramps on our street. Any property within the zoning would either be demolished or relocated. This included the white house on the corner with the rose garden that I would mow once a week for summer cash. Wiped out. Also, the large blue farmhouse across the blacktop which had the strawberry rhubarb patch and the garden snakes and the smell of baking wafting from the window of the kitchen all the time. And the yellow house next to it with the retirees who would sit on their front porch and smile at the neighborhood kids while we played. They would ask us about our families and encourage us to do good in school. They were all bulldozed, and the lots leveled. Our house was different, though. We owned nearly twenty-five acres in a roughly rectangular

THERE'S NO SUCH THING AS MAGIC BLOOD

lot, with the house near the front. So, rather than be demolished, our house could be moved back on the property, which in fact is exactly what they did. They literally lifted the house off the old foundation with wooden beams and rolled it onto a flatbed trailer, which was driven a hundred or so yards to a new, waiting foundation, and plopped it into place. We even got to keep the big willow tree which used to be in our back yard but now was in front of the house. But the neighborhood kids were all gone. The neighborhood itself was gone. We found ourselves alone next to an exit ramp.

Both of my parents were raised in marginally observant Roman Catholic families; blue-collar folks, with no college degrees among them. That was the way back then. It was big news when blue-collar families sent a kid to college. Today, it's expected.

I was quite close to my grandfather on my mother's side as a young boy. We lived next door to my grandparents for the first several years of my life, while my father finished his tour in the Navy, and my grandfather served as my dad during that time. He was a machinist. A smart man who excelled in his trade (he was a Master Grinder for Gillette Company for decades and designed the mold for the now-defunct Atra razor), he seemed to me to have squandered his health and his life after retiring at 62. My grandparents took my sister and I to Lake George, NY one year. I remember, during the trip, my grandfather calling the Adirondack Mountains *nature's love bumps*.

He once told me, "If you have a trade, you'll always have work." Many young people today would do well to heed such advice. He also held onto old attitudes like a man who clings to the hand straps on a subway when the train isn't even moving. He told racist jokes which made me uncomfortable. Yet, he was a jovial, kindly man at his best. He used to scare my sister and I by thrusting his dentures out of his mouth in front of us. He was square-jawed, bald and flat-footed. But he was nimble and strong. And he was convinced he was going to hell. You could not talk him out of it. Two or three times after becoming *born-again*, I attempted to talk to him about God and about faith in

Jesus. I never got anywhere. Finally, the last time (I was in my early thirties by this point) he told me,

"David, I made my peace with God a long time ago. There's nothing to discuss."

"So, you believe in him?" I asked. "Is that what you mean by "making peace"?" He grimaced, then looked at me seriously. He was rarely serious, so I was careful to look him in the eyes as he spoke.

"No, I mean I told him I was happy to go to hell, and to leave me alone. I'll burn in hell, because I sure don't want anything to do with his church." He turned back in his chair and looked out the window, pensively, before characteristically changing the subject with an unrelated wisecrack. And that was that. I reflected on this conversation when he developed dementia. At the end of his life, he barely recognized me. Then, he was gone.

My grandmother was a gentle person of generous spirit, but not religious at all. She never spoke of God, and she seemed afraid of everything. She never obtained a driver's license, never learned to swim and would not venture into anything unknown. If she went to a restaurant, she wanted to sit in the corner in a booth, and never at a table in the middle where "everyone could see her". I think my father married my mother primarily so he could get permission to date her, since he wasn't able to do that until she walked the aisle, as my grandmother would hardly ever let her leave the house. She always remembered us and our children, however, on every meaningful occasion, usually with a handwritten card, even when no one else did. She lived to be over a hundred years old.

My father is the oldest of three brothers. The middle brother, Don, went to Vietnam. He saw infantry combat, killed men in battle, and watched many of his unit die. My uncle Don was the one who got drunk and started dancing on tables at my wedding reception. He is also the one who took a picture of a giant turd which he had deposited into his toilet with his instant Polaroid and then passed the picture around the dinner table as we were about to say grace before the

Thanksgiving meal. His psychotic grin was uncontainable as people passed the picture around the table. My Aunt Marie was furious with him. It came to me at last.

"Impressive." I stated. He beamed with glee.

"It broke the water line." He said proudly. Then he handed me the sweet potatoes.

I never really got to know the youngest of the three, my Uncle Lenny, but I remember him being very funny. Holidays at Uncle Lenny's house consisted of football, beer, peanuts, French meat pie with ketchup and lots of sarcasm and laughter. These were regular people, all of them, and none of them were religious. All of them eventually left Rhode Island and moved to Florida.

My father was, or is, religious in some sense, but in secret. Even in retirement, he took interest in theological books, which could be found on his bureau. He has a strong intellect and seems to consider the topic of religion moderately interesting at times, but he generally was never willing to discuss it, in the same way that he was similarly uninterested in discussing anything which he considered personal (he considered everything personal). And he did not value attending religious services. Once I gave up on the Catholic Church, I think my parents did too. At least, they stopped attending Mass. About the only subject my father talked about openly with me was sports, and since it was practically the only way for me to connect with him on a personal level as a youth, I took an interest in sports. My father is an intense person and was highly driven during his working life. He strove after and obtained positions of leadership no matter what circle he ran with, whether Rotary, the Chamber of Commerce, or Amway. He likes life and people on his terms: *at arm's length*. One of my lasting memories of growing up with my dad was him kicking me in the shins for fun when he was wearing dress shoes. I still have indents in my shin bones. I would drop to the floor, and he would laugh. It was terrific family bonding. He took us to Disney World once, and I started the trip off on a bad note when I led my sister into the Swiss Family Tree House while he bought food for us. Rather than hang on to it until we returned, he threw it all in the garbage can in disgust when we weren't *exactly* where he had left us. He refused to buy any more food that day until we got back to the hotel. I used to frustrate him so.

Among all the people on both my mother and father's sides, I became the only person who veered off the Catholic track and entered the glamorous and shiny world of evangelical Protestantism, in whose circles Catholics were not even regarded as Christians at all.

My 7th-grade English teacher was an aging Jewish hippie named David Zaidi. Mr. Z, as we called him, would host these incredible creative writing sessions. For an entire class, we'd all be sitting around at various places in the room, writing poetry and short stories or whatnot, to the accompanying music of Led Zeppelin or Lynyrd Skynyrd or whatever records the students brought in for that purpose. It was my first introduction to the creative process, and I would never be the same. Mr. Z was an eccentric and imposing man, well over six feet in height, with a shock of graying curly hair that acted as a sizzling halo around his hawk-like nose and sallow complexion. He wore blue jeans and a cowboy belt buckle with a seersucker preppy jacket over a tee-shirt. His voice was a never-ending bass note, and when he whispered the whole room stopped talking.

He called me to the front of the room one day after class and informed me that I had real talent; that my writing could "knock down walls". I was excited to hear this since he had inspired me already to be a writer. My father, however, didn't like this at all, and dismissed my excitement for the craft. For one thing, he did not like hippies, and seemed to resent that Mr. Zaidi had any meaningful influence on me. He viewed my teacher as a never-do-well and not a role model and expressed to me that I should focus my efforts on more practical pursuits. Over the years, my father repeatedly exhibited a low opinion of artists and writers and others who held what he considered low-end jobs; fields he felt were populated by non-achievers, drop-outs and pot smokers. But I wanted to be a writer.

THERE'S NO SUCH THING AS MAGIC BLOOD

Mr. Z passed away in his chair, alone in his apartment, in June of 2010, and was found by police who came to check on him after a friend complained of unreturned phone calls and emails. His wife had left him years earlier. He is marked as the first significant Jewish influence I was exposed to. He had taught in the public sector for over thirty years, and retired lamenting the state of public education in America.

One thing that was becoming a theme of my teen years was a search for meaning. I felt displaced and out of sync with popular culture and with most of my peers. I struggled to connect with them. I pondered philosophical concepts and felt increasing pressure to figure out what this life thing was all about. This would gnaw away at the margins of my mind until it erupted into a crisis at college. I did not understand what was happening to me until much later. In the meantime, I was in my room playing records and learning how to sing like Robert Plant. My father didn't approve of this either.

Chapter 2

———— ❧ ————

THE VIRGIN MOTHER
AND THE PEDOPHILE

I WAS PLACED in Catholic school as a lad, and attended long enough to complete my First Communion, which is a ritual through which a young Catholic girl or boy gets to have a taste of Jesus's flesh and blood for the first time. You wear white for the occasion.

Since I was only nine, I don't recall much of the event, save for one poignant scene as all of us were waiting to go out to the sanctuary and take our places in the front row in preparation for our big moment. All the virgin partakers in the *magic blood* of Jesus had been corralled like impetuous baby goats into the altar boy room, unsupervised. In this parish, the altar boy room was an ambitious carpeted expanse with all manner of ceremonial gear, from altar cloths to bronze crosses attached to staffs displaying the crucified Savior, to flags and sashes and altar boy gowns.

I'm not sure how it started, but our group began attempting to reenact the passion narrative of Christ. One boy had grabbed hold of an incense pole and hoisted it over his shoulder. Two lines of children formed behind him. I recall watching this from a detached distance, but I could have been involved. The boy with the incense pole trudged along, as though the weight of the pole was about to crush him under its weight. The two lines of boys began a chant. It started, as these things always do, with just a couple of boys, but soon all joined in: "Crucify him!" Quickly, the chant gained momentum, and the boy with the incense pole smiled and exaggerated his feigned struggle further as the chant intensified. Soon, everyone was bouncing up and down and marching behind the boy with the pole and chanting in unison, ever louder, *"Crucify him! Crucify him! Crucify him!!"* The room reverberated with the sound, which clearly carried into the hall and apparently even disturbed the service in the sanctuary. This continued until one of the rectory officials swung open the door to the room with violence and burned us alive with his eyes. It took a few moments, but he brought an embarrassed hush over our proceedings. I remember feeling a considerable amount of shame over this as I sat in the front row of the church, intuiting the wrath of the priest through his steely gaze. It was all rather inglorious and forgettable. But it was nothing compared to the experience of going to "confessional". This is when you step into a small wooden box, and sit on a thin, vinyl seat, staring ominously at a small screen which you could not see through, on the other side of which sat (you could only assume) the priest. Since I was a young boy, it was difficult to come up with much to pray about. After all, I didn't have a car, a credit card or even access to porn. But I did my best to sound contrite in any case.

After my father had moved our family to south-central Massachusetts to take over the business he bought, we left Our Lady Queen of Martyrs Church and joined St. Patrick's in Whitinsville. While I have vague and scattered memories of this church in general, I retain vivid recollections of the stained-glass windows in the sanctuary. During the Mass, as we alternatively kneeled and then sat and kneeled and stood and then sat again, I would stare at these translucent pictorials of the "passion" of the Christ in stations. Sunlight glistened prismatically through the vibrant colored portraits of the modestly robed Jesus carrying the enormous wooden cross on his shoulder, in seemingly effortless fashion. His face was perfect, with well-groomed beard and rosy cheeks, his eyes serene and steadfast. I remember wondering how it was possible he could look so glowingly relaxed and unfazed after having been scourged by a cat-of-nine-tails and allowed to bleed out practically to extinction. I wondered how he could even walk after such an ordeal, let alone carry a tree up a hill to his own death. Even his robe was untainted by blood or soil. This stood in stark relief to the humiliated and bloody body of Jesus hanging on the giant cross screwed to the wall behind the altar in effigy. In all of it, however, whether the abused, mostly naked Jesus on the wall facing our kneeling forms or the well-groomed altar-boy Jesus in the windows at our sides, what was being celebrated were not his teachings, but his *death*. Here was a man, the images portrayed, that suffered in a way no one would wish upon their worst enemy. My curiosity was peaked: Who was this person being glorified in these windows and in this Mass? And what did he have to do with me? How could this ancient event have any bearing on people alive today? These were questions that had started to form in my mind, and little of it made any sense at all.

One day, my father announced that we were switching parishes to the one in Manchaug, a little hamlet about ten minutes up the road. The switch was left unexplained, but I think I know why. My parents had noticed that I was struggling emotionally and socially and were concerned. My dad arranged for me to have a private counseling session with the priest at St. Patrick's. He dropped me off at the rectory office and left. I was supposed to call him when we were done. I was nervous and sat alone in the office waiting for the priest to show up. I was twelve, or maybe thirteen, and well beyond the bell curve of pubescent self-consciousness. I was still actively involved with the Boy Scouts at that time. The air in the room was stale and rank and smelled of nicotine tar. There was an ashtray a few feet away on the coffee table overflowing with cigarette butts, in variously grotesque states of disfigurement. The priest eventually entered the room from a door be-hind my left shoulder. I turned my head to look at him, but he failed to make eye contact as he brushed past, instead settling heavily into the chair across from me before crossing his legs, tapping a fresh smoke from the pack which rested in his flat-black shirt pocket and lighting it up. He inhaled deeply, then blew smoke off to one side, squinted and looked at me for the first time. The rotating table fan on his desk be-hind his head sent the smoke my way and it burned my eyes, blurring them. After a few more moments, he spoke.

"So, what's your damn problem kid? Why are you here?"

"I'm not sure," I replied, trying to hold my breath. He took another drag before leaning forward to tap ash into the tray, which ricocheted off the existing refuse and landed on the blonde veneer of the table. I stared at it, wondering if it would burn the glossy finish, and noticed that this had happened before, as there were several scars in it already.

"You don't know why you're here?" He asked, leaning even further towards me, with one hand on his thigh and the other holding the ciga-rette. "I can't help you if I don't know what I'm supposed to help you with." He then sat back and waited for me to respond. I didn't want to talk to him about anything. I wanted out of this disgusting pig's office. Additionally, I had a private agreement with the Scoutmaster of the Boy Scout troop to never speak to a soul about what he had done to me, or he would kill me. I had no intention of spilling the beans to my father, and certainly not to this asshole.

"Your guess is as good as mine." I said, finally, staring at him blankly. It was his move. He raised his eyebrows and eventually just shrugged.

"Well, I've got plenty to do. Call your dad and have him come get you then. When you're ready to come back you can set another appointment." With that, he excused himself, offered a forced closed-lipped smile, pointed at the phone on his desk, and left me alone in the room. I watched the door close behind him. I was somewhat in shock. That was the last time I recall ever seeing him.

We would become members of St. Mark's in Manchaug until my

father bought his big house across town years later, but our attendance became sporadic. The shine had already come off the apple for me regarding Catholicism, and I didn't really want to go. My father seemed to lose his resolve and decided it was up to me whether I went or not. He did not want to force me to be there against my will, but he wanted me to at least complete my Confirmation, and strongly urged me to do so. I did it to please him, but it was half-hearted, and it meant virtually nothing to me when I completed it. I felt bad when the instructor handed me a book and a welcome packet of sorts when I completed the program. I felt dishonest, like I had cheated. I scanned the book, which for a brief minute or two made me wonder if I should look a little deeper into the tradition. I kept the book on my bedstand for a couple of years, near the Living Bible which my father had bought me for the occasion. I rarely attempted to read them. Occasionally, I would open one or the other at bedtime and scan a bit here and there, but it wasn't enough to pull me in beyond a cursory glance.

A few years later, when I was a Senior in High School, my friend Gary, who lived across the street from the church, was hosting a party, and myself and about fifteen other people were there. I sat in the dark living room of the rustic home watching, reluctantly, "Faces of Death", a graphic celebration of the end of the existence of many humans perishing in disturbing and stomach-churning fashion. In the back of the room, I noticed a large, frumpy adult mostly hidden in shadow drinking whiskey from a glass in a rocking chair. I knew it was whiskey because the half-empty bottle was on the floor near the chair. Curious, and looking for any excuse to step away from the movie, I walked over and sat in an empty chair next to him and tried to start conversation. After a few minutes of garbled dialog, I learned that he was the priest of St. Mark's. He was already quite drunk and could hardly talk intelligibly. My father, when I told him about this, was not pleased. I don't think our family ever went back to church after that, except for a wedding or a funeral, to this day.

I have since read the entire Catechism of the Church and explored the many nuances of its doctrines. Whatever I may have missed back in my formative years I more than made up for, and still found the tradition lacking. But as a senior in High School, I was far more concerned with the Italian bombshell I brought with me to Gary's last party before graduation; the girl from the next town over that I had met at my college orientation. My classmates whispered to each other as she nibbled my ear, *that's who she is*, as they all had just assumed that I was either as gay as a three-dollar bill or else I had to be seeing some girl from out of town. How surprised and disappointed they would have been to learn that I was a virgin when I entered college. But I was a rock star on that night, in their eyes. After graduation, I didn't see any of them again.

According to an April 2019 report released by CNN, there were over 12,250 victims of sexual abuse perpetrated by over 7,800 Boy Scouts of America leaders from the period between 1944 and 2016. The number is likely far higher, since, like many others, I never went forward with my own experience, but attempted to process it quietly, silently, shamefully, and ultimately, only partly successfully.

The Boy Scouts began in Great Britain in 1908 under the vision and leadership of Robert Baden-Powell, a decorated British Army officer, with a noble set of values, and was intentioned as a training ground for young men to toughen up, get morally straight, and learn important skills which would benefit them through life. For the most part, the vision was realized, and many high achievers in a variety of professions have Eagle Scout as part of their early resume. Sexual exploitation by volunteer leaders does not appear to be something on the radar of the early participants and founders. However, just like Roman Catholic priests, any male authority role in which young boys are in intimate contact for long, unsupervised stretches of time will provide a conducive environment for abuse, and many perverted and sick men have recognized this and taken advantage of the situation. Perhaps this factor alone is why so much sexual abuse has been reported among so many Catholic priests and Boy Scout leaders.

As a friendless ten-year-old living in a new community, my parents thought it a good idea to enroll me in the local Scout troop. It seemed logical. Like I mentioned previously, this troop was active in the outdoors, leading extensive and aggressive wilderness trips into such remote places as Baxter State Park and Mt. Katahdin in Maine and the Mid-State Trail in Massachusetts, on which we practiced winter camping, as well as other adventures in the Green and White Mountains of Vermont and New Hampshire. I was excited to be a part of it.

I was a very self-conscious kid, and emotionally open and sensitive. Most of all, I was extremely trusting. There was one Scout, a few years older than me, who happened to be my Patrol Leader and who also lived next door to the Scoutmaster, who eyed me suspiciously when I was selected for the big trip to Baxter State Park in Maine one year. I was only eleven, and all the other boys on the trip were at least fifteen. He pulled me aside privately, and his blond hair partially covered his eyes as he spoke to me in a hushed tone.

"I see how Mr. Beck acts around you. If he tells you he wants you to be *nice* to him, be careful. Trust me." I nodded, not understanding. *Why shouldn't I be nice to the Scoutmaster*, I thought?

One day, I was at the Scoutmaster's house helping him pack supplies for a different trip. Mr. Beck asked me to come with him to piss in the woods near a structure behind his house in the trees. I had no urge to go, but he insisted. Once behind the cabin, out of sight from the house, he unzipped his fly, but rather than taking a piss, he grabbed me and pressed my face against his chest, grabbing my hand and sliding it into his pants. He forced me to touch him, telling me the whole time, *you're a special boy…just relax…easy now…you're a special boy.* I tolerated it for a minute or so until I mustered the courage to pull away and protest. After a threatening glare, I backed away from him further, and he forced a weak smile. This was exactly what my Patrol Leader had warned me about, I realized. But I was afraid of this man. He was large and powerful, even obese. I looked around to make sure no one could see us. He tromped off, zipping up his fly awkwardly as he walked, with his erection compromising his gait.

THERE'S NO SUCH THING AS MAGIC BLOOD

My Patrol Leader, Danny, approached me one day, sometime later, while we worked in tandem collecting firewood on one of our campouts.

"He got to you, didn't he?" I felt myself tense up.

"What do you mean?"

"You don't have to hide it from me. I know how he is."

"How do you know?"

"Because he did it to me, too." I looked at him in shock. I believed him.

"How did you stop it?"

"I didn't. *You* showed up. He stopped bothering me. Don't worry, I'm going to do something about it soon. I fucking *hate* him," he said.

"What are you going to do?"

"I'm going to report him." With that, he walked off to collect wood. I followed him, frantic.

"He told me he'd kill me if I told anyone." He looked at me, and I could tell he was angry. Danny was fair-skinned and thin but more rugged than he looked. He was a good leader and always calmed my nerves when we had roll call.

"I know it," he said. His mouth was tight. "Said the same. But it aint just me anymore. This has to fucking stop." He put his hand on my shoulder. "Don't worry, you don't need to do nuthin'. You'll know when I do what I'm gonna do." I nodded. I was thankful for him. For his courage.

Not long after this, I told my parents I didn't want to be part of Scouts anymore. They were surprised and wanted to know why. I told them I just outgrew it and had other interests. I was not yet thirteen and had achieved the level of Star. My father was disappointed I didn't go for Eagle first, but they allowed me to withdraw without too much protest.

My father came into my room at home one night. He said the Scoutmaster's neighbors had reported Mr. Beck to the police based on the testimony of their son, who had been a member of the Troop for over six years. He wanted to know if I knew anything about it. It was Danny. He had gone forward. I looked at my father carefully and saw the fire in his eyes, and I didn't know if I could trust him. I remembered him prowling our property with a baseball bat looking for the man who climbed onto our porch roof to watch my mother undress from the window. I remembered Mr. Beck threatening me repeatedly. I thought of my reputation at school.

"I have no idea about it," I said. My father stared at me, unconvinced. He reinforced the importance of telling the truth. I quickly rehearsed in my mind how on earth I could possibly share something with my dad which had gone on for just over two years off and on without me telling him. "I really don't know, Dad. Danny hates him, I know that. I know that."

Eventually, my father relented and left the room. I felt smaller than I had been after he closed my door; more insignificant. I had chosen to lie, because I didn't want my father to know about my shame and have him hate me for the rest of my life. I also let Danny down, who had shown courage. It is because of this that I am at times unreasonable in my desire to find and proclaim the truth about things.

Moving forward, I tried to shut it out of my mind. On the rare occasions that I would think of it, usually unexpectedly in random scenes which would flash through my thoughts darkly, I would become nauseous. I also never developed any sexual attraction to men or to boys, which is a false narrative often assumed by people who don't know how pedophilia works. It's not a contagious disease. I was decidedly heterosexual. The damage came in other ways. I had numerous attractive girls show interest in me in High School, but I pushed them all away, because I felt dirty, and sex was something I was mortally afraid of. Once a couple of attractive girls had been rebuffed by me, girls that most of my friends in our small school would have loved to date, there developed some chatter among my classmates that I might be gay. Back in the early 80's, the "coming-out" movement had not begun, and there was no one in my school, male or female, who would openly admit to being gay. Times have changed, for sure. But despite some of my classmates' gossip, this was not my issue. When I look at pictures of myself from my High School years, I can often see the fear and tension in my face and body posture in the photographs. I was not at ease with myself. I entered college as a good looking but frail-minded kid, younger than most of my peers, somewhat paranoid and susceptible to influence. I felt adrift, like a small boat lost at sea. I often thought that there was something that everyone else knew about and I was looking for hints and clues as to what it was, like a joke for which everyone knew the punchline except me.

There was a class hottie, a blonde whom all the boys of my class were in awe of, who called out to me one day during gym. She was intelligent, beautiful, and quick-witted and I had a bit of a crush on her, though I never told her. She ended up dating the starting center of the school basketball team, but I don't think they made it together.

"Nice legs," she said loudly, causing the students around her to spin their heads in my direction. I looked up and was surprised that she had aimed her words directly at me. Her eyes pierced mine, and I felt myself become flushed. After all, she couldn't have known that a large German man had gotten to me before she did and swiped away clean with my confidence. I lowered my head and waved weakly. The moment passed.

Chapter 3

———~~———

RIDING THE MAGIC BUS

THE CRYSTAL-CLEAR SOUNDS of Phil Collins's "In the Air Tonight" were blaring through the open third-story window of my new friend Steve's dorm room. Digital CD's had just come onto the market, and they had captured the imagination of nearly everyone. Few songs displayed this better than Collins's massive 80's hit. We hollered to the pretty freshmen women on the pathway far below our window, and cat-called them. Two dorks getting the attention of women who played in a different league made the digital investment worth every penny. Steve was on the same floor of my dorm, about five doors down, on the corner. He was a musician. He also had a friend in the room next to his, a Senior, who was a Deadhead (devotee of the Grateful Dead), named John, who had inside connections with the band. John had about four hundred Maxell cassettes of soundboard recordings of live shows, most of which had never been released commercially to that point, sitting on shelving along his wall. Over the course of first semester, they would succeed in converting me from metalhead to Deadhead.

Early in my freshman year, I met a woman, a graduate student. She seduced me one night and we became a couple for nearly four months. In fact, I moved in with her, as she was what they called a Resident Assistant, meaning she got greatly reduced room and board to oversee her floor in the Towers Dorm next to our own. She was privileged to have a private room with its own bath as part of this arrangement, basically a studio apartment. She was my Blue-Eyed Angel; a petite woman with fair skin, night-black hair, cut close-cropped to her neckline, a smashing figure, electric blue eyes and a smile that melted my heart. She was a bit of a punk rocker and was heavily involved in the college radio station and its events.

My lack of confidence left me on the margins of the social order. I never had a girlfriend in High School to speak of. My first was my Blue-Eyed Angel and she was twenty-two, soon to be twenty-three. I was seventeen, soon to be eighteen.

Once I arrived at college, away from the insulating cocoon of my parents' home, the full weight of the unresolved emotional trauma I had been carrying for nearly seven years came due. My emotional, sexual and psychological issues were not being addressed, but rather suppressed. At college, drugs, alcohol and a lack of personal discipline in my studies exacerbated all of it. Nor had I yet learned the skills to maintain healthy relationships. Adding additional stress, I was also stuck rooming with three members of the football team, including the starting quarterback. One of the three was a defensive lineman who was illegally sleeping on our floor every night. I was the odd man out, as I wasn't involved in sports. When the Blue-Eyed Angel came into my life, moving in with her was a no-brainer.

My father had instilled a Catholic ethic of chastity into my head and expected abstinence before marriage, reminding me frequently that he and my mother were virgins before their honeymoon. However, I was not a religious person at this point and quite honestly didn't care. My lack of girlfriends through High School was not because I was uninterested or due to any religious constraints. No, I just had no clue how to go about getting one. But I managed it this time.

Heavy-laden and depressed, I had developed the habit of going to the campus recreation center by myself a couple evenings a week. My Angel worked there at the desk part-time, and I would go when she was there, because she was far more exciting than the fat, pimple-faced young man who was there at other times. She would talk to me while I tried to play pool alone. After a while, she asked me to help her behind the desk. She would do playful things like poke my nose while I talked to her, or she'd put her hand on my thigh while she registered a student at the sign-in desk or answered their questions. One night, she invited me to a party. When I arrived with her, it was an older group with other graduate students and some faculty. She sat pressed against me on a couch with her hand on my inner thigh, dangerously. We shared gin and tonic. She got looks from her girlfriends, who said things like "Robbing the cradle, girl!" and then they'd wink at me before walking away. I'm sure I turned as red as an August sunset. She wanted to leave the party and take me to her room. When we got there, she put on some music. She liked alternative. I think we were listening to The Violent Femmes. There was a song about someone throwing their daughter into a well. I admired her body as she bent in front of me to adjust the stereo. Then, she offered to give me a massage.

"You've done this before, right?" She asked. I swallowed hard.

"No," I answered. Her mouth twisted up in a devious smile.

"Oh!" Her face was flushed. She was very aroused. But I had started shaking uncontrollably. It got so bad she stopped and became still.

"What's wrong?"

I told her my mind. I told her everything. I hadn't ever shared it with anyone. The Scoutmaster, the counseling that I rejected, all of it. She listened patiently while stroking my face, her eyes darting back and forth in my eyes. As much as I didn't want to lose my machismo, it was too late. I was emotional and embarrassed about what I was telling her. She held me for a long time. Then, without warning, we giggled. I don't know why, but something had shifted inside me. It was okay, now. The demon was gone. We made love as if we had snuck behind the circus tent during the final act.

After a month or so together, the Angel began intimating that she was thinking of getting an apartment with me near the campus after she graduated. She envisioned a long-term relationship.   By mid-semester, she had landed a three-hour weekly show on the college radio station for me, which I subsequently called the Graveyard Shift (it was from 11pm-2am on Sunday nights) and it was devoted to heavy metal. My minor was Journalism and I wanted to get something going in radio, so I was thrilled with this opportunity. I quickly called my High School friend Micah and got him involved. He was an avid collector and owned many hundreds of rare or obscure albums by unknown metal bands, and he immediately agreed to do the show with me. As bad as I was doing in my classes (which was quite bad) my social life was propping up. My radio show opened an opportunity for me to get exposed to the music industry. At one point, I had the chance to interview Ronnie James Dio, and I was even approached by Elektra Records as a potential northeast tour promoter for a New Jersey-based band called Fates Warning, although I turned them down. At the same time, my musical tastes were changing. I had been smoking weed and doing mushrooms and acid periodically as I got more and more into the Grateful Dead scene. I was finding some kinship with John and Steve and a few others from that crowd on campus. I was also meeting many of my girlfriend's crowd, many of whom were faculty or queer or post-graduates living off campus. Not a few raised their eyebrows at me. A couple of her queer friends hit on me. One of them handed me a hand-written note at a party which stated, simply, "I love hard penis". I almost vomited. But the Angel and I had become a couple and were treated as such, for the most part. A good percentage of her male friends were gay and were no competition for me. A few months went by. But one night, in a very unwise move, I accepted an invitation to drink whiskey with another friend down the hall from my assigned room in Larned Hall. This friend was a metalhead and got funnier the drunker we both became. We listened to bad bands playing gutter music all night, doing shots of cheap whiskey and laughing. At one point, long after I had become quite drunk, one of my roommates, Trent, the quarterback of the football team, showed up in my friend's room, with his older brother by his side. Trent's brother was an intern at a prestigious law firm in Boston and was feeling himself a bit. I stuck out my hand to him, and he reluctantly took it for a brief second only to slap it away from himself rudely. Trent laughed at me. They didn't look me in the eyes after this but talked about me derisively for another minute or two.

"I just wanted you to meet some of the losers I have to deal with." Said Trent. My metalhead friend turned red and looked at me apologetically. They left my friend's room.

"I'm sorry man. I thought you were Trent's buddy. I didn't know… I wouldn't have invited him in."

"It's alright. He's trying to impress his asshole brother, I guess."

I had a few too many shots and passed out on the lower bunk. I woke up early and stumbled down the hall to splash water on my face and hydrate at the water fountain. Then I threw up violently. I thought that I needed to eat, which I surely did, since I never had dinner the previous evening. *Just need breakfast*, I told myself. Grabbing my jacket, I groggily shuffled down the hill to the cafeteria a few minutes after they opened. I grabbed a bowl with the intention of getting some Cap'n Crunch, but something snapped in me when I was near the milk and coffee. I'm not sure exactly what went through my mind at the time, but whatever it was brought with it a tsunami of rage and pain which came from some unknown region, and I *screamed*, and then pushed several trays of porcelain coffee cups onto the floor, smashing many of them. I felt terrible immediately afterwards, and apologized profusely to the manager, to no avail. He called the campus security and they hauled me off. I faced fines to reimburse the catering company for the damages plus a one-week suspension from the campus. But my parents couldn't know about it, or my dad would pull me out of school, so I found a way to shield them from knowing.

My Blue-Eyed Angel owned an AMC Pacer, which had fold-down back seats and plenty of room. She offered to allow me to sleep in her car for the week. She provided blankets and snacks and taped dark paper over the back window. Being mid-winter, I shivered and slept fitfully the first night. She came to see me in the morning, a little past dawn. When she saw me, she laughed.

"This isn't going to work is it? It's really cold," she said. I nodded, laughing with her, and shrugged, sitting up. I couldn't quite sit up straight so I leaned on one elbow. "I have a plan," she continued, "But it's very risky and if you get caught I'll be in big trouble, so don't get caught." She said, still laughing. Okay, I said. She hopped into the driver's seat, and I crawled forward and sat in the passenger seat. I was frozen to the core and could hardly talk. My chest felt like a popsicle. She drove around the lot and up the hill towards the back of the Towers dorm, to the vendor service entrance. Using her RA passport, she got us through the security lock on the door and we hustled through the dock and then the supply room and made our way through to the student lounge and to the elevators. This stunt bypassed the front desk where I would have had to present my campus pass to gain entrance, which would have alerted the campus police. No one noticed or cared, and before we knew it, I was in her apartment. We took a hot shower together. I spent the remainder of the week there in hiding from the campus authorities. We enjoyed a terrific romp, but near the end of the week she became disturbingly quiet. On the next-to-last day of my suspension, she had been gone all morning for classes and had done some shopping. She showed up in the early afternoon with grinders which we ate on the floor, silently. She had stopped talking to me for the most part the previous day and wasn't laughing at my jokes anymore. I knew something was up.

"What's wrong?" I asked directly, finally. She stared at me, and I did not like the look I was getting. She turned her gaze sidelong into nowhere for a bit, then turned back to me to speak.

"This shit with the cafeteria…I've been thinking about it a lot. I'm not mad at you, but…"

"But what."

"I've been planning on getting a place after I graduate, right?" I just stared at her dumbly. "I really like you. But…" She began shaking her head, "We can't do that together. You know that, right?" My heart sank. I *didn't* know that.

"I really like you, too. Why don't you think it will work?" I asked. She nodded and then her face crimsoned, and she looked down, hiding it from me. When she looked up her lips were pressed together and her eyes had filled up. She sighed deeply and pulled herself together. She was steady when she spoke at last.

"You're special you know," a tear cascaded down her cheek as she spoke. "I want to wait for you to figure it out but…I don't know how else to say this…*this*", she waved her hand at the invisible ether, "You need to find a way to get yourself together, *okay?* I don't know what else to say about it." She wiped her tears with her wrist and waited for my response. I just stared back at her, dumbfounded. Awkwardly, I tried to lean forward and kiss her, but she shook it off and stood up.

"You just need some time to figure it out, that's all. That's what you need. You'll just…I don't know what the fuck you'll do, but it just won't work out. It doesn't mean I don't care about you and I love sleeping with you and all but, *this is it.* We can't see each other anymore after this week. I'm sorry." With that, she abruptly got up, gathered her purse, her coat and hat, and with keys in hand, headed for the door. She turned briefly, looked at me tenderly, her eyes still wet, before shutting the door gently and leaving me behind. I was still exiled from campus and had nowhere to go for another night. Rather, I just sat there, stunned, for hours. I don't think I moved for a long time. In a very brief period, she had become my identity, after a fashion. But it was obvious that she was very independent, and I was an appendage; an underage freshman with so much to learn, and she would be twenty-three when she graduated in less than three months. I was just now entering the adult world. I was naïve and relationally stupid. I felt like Rod Stewart in his song "Maggie Mae".

I wasn't sure if she was ever coming back that evening. I finally curled up on her couch with one of her blankets and went to sleep. Late that night, she woke me up unexpectedly and took me by the hand, leading me to her bed one last time. I thought, maybe, she had reconsidered. Maybe she thought so, too. In the morning, though, she reaffirmed her conviction. She bought me a sad and awkward breakfast at the Pewter Pot down the road, and then brought me to the campus police so I could fill out the paperwork I needed to sign for reinstatement. She waved at me from inside her car, offering what seemed to me to be a forced smile, and drove off. I figured at the time that after a couple of days apart we'd be back at it. But no, she was serious about making an end to the relationship. Maybe a member of the faculty had gotten wind of my antics and scolded her about her relationship with me. Or maybe she truly was turned off so badly that she didn't see me the same way anymore. I don't know. But much to my surprise and sadness I only saw her once more after this, and it was during a public event held by the radio station a month or so later. She was friendly and cordial but not intimate and when I hugged her, she responded gingerly without a true embrace. I tried to kiss her, but she deftly turned her head, so I only got her cheek. Then she smiled warmly, oh-so-tenderly, and briefly stroked my face with her hand as she stared in my eyes, with hers darting back and forth studying my face, as she would do, and just as quickly turned and disappeared into the milling sea of students. I thought to follow her, but then thought better of it. I never saw her again.

My relationship with, and loss of, the Blue-Eyed Angel was a major turning point for me, and I believe it led to my spiritual "awakening". I had been sexually frozen by trauma, perilously near to a psychic breakdown, and she largely fixed this problem in her unique way. But I wasn't ready for the relationship she desired, as she correctly said. When she broke up with me, I began thinking, for the first time in a long time, about the ten-year-old boy who lay in my father's field near the rusted shell of the broken airplane and who dreamt of the kind of life he wanted; a life committed to altruistic values and meaningful activities. *Where was that kid? Was he still here, somewhere? Was my life going to end up like this relationship with my girlfriend? Where was I headed now and what was my plan?* I was beginning to have conversations with my friends about God; conversations which most of them found a tad amusing if not irritating. I remember trying to have them with the Angel, but she merely tolerated it with disinterest, at one point telling me,

"We probably won't be together anymore if you end up following that path." Maybe that's the *real* reason she broke up with me.

I had also discovered, through this ordeal, that despite my friendly and agreeable personality, that I was still seething with rage and pain just a thin line below the surface. I felt I really needed to figure out the God thing. It had become, by the time I was back in my assigned room in Larned Hall, a priority. Interestingly, around this time, two campus Christian missionaries had knocked on my door and invited me to a small Bible study group. I almost accepted. They came back a couple times before finally giving up. I never attended. But I wondered about it and told them, in front of my Deadhead friends, to come back again and maybe then I'd be ready. They smiled and agreed, and my friends mocked me for leaving the door open to them. They started calling me Jesus.

Throughout this time, my drug use was escalating. But my use of drugs was strategic, and not entirely recreational. I was experimenting with altered stated of consciousness to see if I could expand my mind. That was my motivation. When I quit using them, I did so cold turkey, with no struggle. Once I saw what they were about, I was done. I did find some of them enjoyable, and my favorite was hashish, but after college I was done with all of it.

My hair had grown down to my shoulder blades and I was becoming a hippie. After the breakup with the Angel, I started going to Lawrenceville, a rough mill town northwest of Boston, with my friend Steve on the weekends. He worked in a music store that a friend of his

THERE'S NO SUCH THING AS MAGIC BLOOD

owned and he was trying to help me become the singer for his fledgling band, called "Backside". His drummer had a studio in his parent's basement where we would practice. His drum kit was huge, and used to belong to Vinnie Appice, former drummer for Black Sabbath. Our band didn't go far, but we had fun. Steve was the one friend who enjoyed my discussions about God. His parents were going through a difficult divorce, and Steve was thinking about some of the same issues. We would go to Denny's and drink coffee until three am discussing the meaning of life.

Back in Larned Hall, I was partying with the Grateful Dead crowd again, and no longer had contact with the Angel's alternative, punk, queer crowd. I put the lessons I should have learned behind me and forged new, uncharted directions of foolishness. Second semester was in full swing and so was the Grateful Dead's annual late-winter and spring tour. They would make stops in Philadelphia, Maine and then Providence. The Providence shows would occur at the end of Easter weekend. This was a big weekend for my family, traditionally, and one of the few times a year they prioritized us being in church. I had made my decision, though. I was going to stay at school instead of coming home and would be attending the Providence shows. I had earned enough money from my part-time job to pay for the tickets. It was all arranged in advance with the party crew. I would ride with John and whoever else could fit in his car. Steve would meet us there from Lawrenceville with a couple of his friends, including our drummer. But things were about to change drastically for me in my tenuous and suspect social life.

Thursday night was party night in John's room. We would smoke weed with him frequently, but on Thursdays, he would break out the heavy drugs, such as mescaline, speed, opium, hashish and sometimes, LSD. We would get high, listen to jam music, play cards and talk loud and well into the night. When girls showed up the party would take on a subcurrent of sexual tension, but on average it was always the same crowd. John, who was the oldest in the group and the most influential, had really welcomed me in. I was an 'insider' now. He knew Bill Kreutzmann, one of the Dead's drummers, personally, and had promised to introduce me. Kreutzmann's daughter also attended Framingham State College during the time I was there, and John told me I'd meet her soon. Then, a beautiful blonde with a bubbly personality began frequenting John's Thursday night parties and it was clear that John had a thing for her. The problem for him was that she kept hanging all over *me*. This was particularly galling for him, it seemed. One night, with too many of us on the couch, she decided to sit in my lap, with John right next to us. A short time later, she took me by the hand while the party was still raging, led me out of the room and brought me to her room across campus for the night. John turned on me after this. He told me, in matter-of-fact style, the next time I saw him, that I would have to find my own ride to the shows, since his car was now full. He suggested I ride with *her*. I got the point. Of course, she was not on campus at the time. Steve was able to squeeze me in with his group for the Sunday night show, but I would have to ride back to campus with someone else, which he was arranging for me, since he wasn't going to the Monday or Tuesday night shows. I rode back to Framingham, MA with strangers. And they weren't friendly.

My spiritual odyssey was about to pick up steam, and I was quickly running out of friends. There were some things, as it turned out, that my Blue-Eyed Angel could not have helped me with.

Chapter 4

───── ∿ ─────

Playing In the Band

THE CULTURAL PHENOMENON of the Grateful Dead, when they were on tour, was fascinating. Their concerts were like attending a secret performance at the nightclub in the basement off the back alley past the Chinese laundry. The mystery surrounding the devotion of their following drew me in as much as their music, initially. It was just a rock band, but the community which had formed around them suggested a cultic experience as much as a musical one. The tour community boasted an eclectic kaleidoscope of characters, many of which were permanent adornments of the scene, and which created a sort of garment draped over the music. The people dancing in the concourse by themselves, the history, the folklore, and the possibility that *this could be the night we experience something special that will go down in history*, all conspired to create the mystique of the "Deadheads" and their world. The band itself, for their part, openly admitted to their attempt to use music to create a form of transcendental consciousness. It was why they allowed many fans to tape the shows from the floor of the arena for their own pirated distribution. In the words of Jerry Garcia,

"Once we're done with it, they can have it." Fans had a term: *tour magic*, an ambiguous phrase which could refer to just about anything, but usually it meant serendipitous circumstances surrounding the tour community, or the experiences fans had getting to, getting home from, or getting to enjoy the show. A dedicated core followed the band from stop to stop and lived on the road, shadowing the band. Many sold tie-dye shirts, or were food vendors, or hooked people up with illegal drugs. In some cases, they did all three.

Once my ride arrived back at my dorm after that first night, the driver looked at me as I stepped out of the car and told me when he would be picking me up the next afternoon for the Monday show. I passed him a ten for gas and waved as he drove off. I could hardly wait until the following night.

Monday night's show was what fans of the band would call a *hot show*. My own experience was unique, though. I was not there to be entertained, really. I was on spiritual hyperdrive and was *studying* the show more than I was enjoying it. I was looking for something beyond the music. At one point I extracted myself from my group and wandered until I found myself in the nosebleed section high up on stage left, where there were hardly any fans. I could think there. Something big was on its way, and it was going to change everything. I could feel it in my gut, but I couldn't identify why or how.

The show, as it turned out, ended in bizarre and unprecedented fashion. Some idiot launched an empty beer bottle towards the stage during the end of the 2nd set, narrowly missing hitting drummer Bill Kreutzmann in the head. Bob Weir came to the stage shortly afterwards to announce, apologetically, that there were issues backstage and that there would not be an encore, saying goodnight. A moment later, after Weir waved goodbye and left the stage, Kreutzmann ran onto the stage and threw his middle finger to the section of the auditorium that the bottle was perceived to have come from. Many fans started booing. It was a most unbecoming scene for the community. This proved the only such time this ever happened in the band's decades-long history.

And I was there. Was that *tour magic?* I didn't think so. I was quiet and disengaged on the ride home, after considerable effort reconnecting with my travel crew. The show had been great, but I was deeply unsettled by it. The lyrics, the disoriented guy in the men's room who was tripping so badly he couldn't form coherent sentences or figure out how to unzip his fly, and what I perceived to be the dark overall message of the music. I was hearing and seeing something I hadn't noticed before. But I suppressed these thoughts and tried to focus on the opportunity to see the band live three nights in a row.

I was really stoked for the show on Tuesday and had a plan. The previous two nights, I attended the concerts "straight". Sure, I may have enjoyed a shared toke or two from a joint during the show, but for the final show, I had decided to use my secret stash of Berkeley-Stanford LSD, since I wasn't driving.

I had "dropped acid" numerous times over the previous six months, but each time I had been in the company of friends who knew what I was doing and could smooth the experience for me if things got hairy. I had also been warned of the dangers of the drug. For one thing, its effects were long-lasting, as a single dose could affect you significantly for as much as twenty-four hours (in extreme cases) and would stay in your system far longer than that. Many habitual users experienced "flashbacks" in which they would suddenly, and unpredictably, find themselves in the full throes of the drug's effects even if they had not taken it recently. Also, not every "trip" was enjoyable. Sometimes, based on your mental state, or your circumstance, the drug could induce a living nightmare of fright, time-warp, and hallucinations. According to the band's biographers, Jerry Garcia had used LSD so much in the beginning of their career that he earned the nickname "Captain Trips". There is a popular rumor that if you ingest LSD any more than seven times, you may be declared legally insane. It turns out that this is an urban legend, but if it were true, I'd be certifiable.

Now, on this final night of the Providence leg of their tour, I wanted the experience that folks like Ken Kesey had enjoyed with the "Gang of

Merry Pranksters" on The Magic Bus, during their grand nationwide tour in the mid-sixties, which was immortalized in the "Electric Kool-Aid Acid Test" by Tom Wolfe. I wanted to know, also, if it was true that the Grateful Dead was a spiritual experience at its height, or if this was overblown. According to the band themselves, their music was born out of the government-sponsored LSD tests near Berkeley, California. I reasoned, therefore, that I could not consider myself to have truly experienced the Grateful Dead and their music unless I also endured LSD while listening to them.

I took an enormous amount of LSD; more than twice, and probably three times as much, as I had taken before on any other occasion. I took all I had. The blots went on my tongue at around five, about a half hour before my ride was supposed to arrive. Except, my ride *didn't arrive*. At first, I was relaxed and unconcerned. People run late sometimes, and there was plenty of time still. After a while, though, I felt stupid standing on the sidewalk by myself. I went inside and sat on one of the benches along the wall in the foyer. I looked at the large clock over the lobby security desk. It read 6:10. The desk attendant asked me what I was waiting for. I told him. He said, "You got stood up dude, sorry." I didn't want to believe this. The slate tiles in the floor started leapfrogging each other in strange rhythmic patterns. This was far sooner than I expected. *I took too much*, I thought. I continued to wait inside for some time, staring out the front windows, but it seemed more and more likely that the front desk attendant was right. What was I to do? There were no cell phones in those days. The dorm was mostly empty. I had no idea who I could even reach out to. This was not something I had anticipated.

I went back outside, against hope. The wind in the leave-less trees was like a strange language that I could almost understand. The cement felt compliant under my feet, as though I could spin the world by the thrust of each step, simply by pressing them forcefully into the ground. Feelings of rejection and abandonment started flooding my thoughts, turning my mind down a dark alley, which is certainly not what one wants when under the influence of LSD. It was still light outside, but the sun was arcing near the horizon, and the rays were shooting prismatically in all directions. The concert would start in less than forty-five minutes and *my ride was not coming*. I was stuck on a hill in Framingham, near an austere concrete shell which formed my temporary home, and the drug was starting to hit strong. This was not a gentle, warm climb to bliss and mind-expansion, as had happened before. This was a freight train careening in record speed towards thornbushes and electric, purple tunnels filled with razor wire. I was alone at the base of the on-ramp of what folks called a "bad trip". We all have a mind within our minds; that secret place we rarely access consciously, yet which we know is there. On LSD, this became inverted for me, and my inner mind, long concealed by observable reality, was now ascendant, and everything else became subjugated to it. I had been told by someone some time previously that *I would feel as though I had solved all the world's problems, but I hadn't; it was just the drug.*

I had gone back to my empty dorm room, and, after hours of literal insanity and a complete breakdown of my ability to function normally, I tried to crawl into my bunk and go to sleep. This would prove impossible. The gloominess had overcome me and colored all my thoughts, which were raging out of control. It was as if every idea was on a pinwheel. The more I thought a thought (whatever thought it might be) the more it would spin in my head. I felt like the kid that tries to slow down the turnstile at the playground after the muscle-bound father has spun it much faster than he should have. My only option was to ride it out. This went on for a tortuously long time. I remember, at one point, squeezing my eyes shut so I could utter a prayer. I said,

"Dear God, I don't know if you're real or not, but I can't survive this. If you're real, please make this stop!"

Miraculously, it did. Right then and there. Like an ice-skater stopping on a dime from a racing sprint, spraying a riot of frozen water, the wheel came to a halt and I felt a cooling sensation flow over my skin as the noise inside my mind stopped. In its place, I saw, in my mind's eye, a vision of a janitorial closet. I could smell the stale dampness of a mop that needed to be sanitized. Somehow, I intuited that this would be my future if I didn't change course immediately. I would experience utter loneliness and abandonment. And silence. It was dark, lonely and hopeless. *I wanted out!*

After this gloomy vision crested and waned, it was displaced by a great calm. The spinning wheel had stopped. I sat up feeling clammy, but not as in sweat. Rather, it was more like morning dew. *It's okay now*, I remember thinking. I envisioned a reprieve; that God must be real, and that he had answered my prayer. I knew what to do, with sharp clarity. I grabbed change from my desk drawer, walked down the hall to the payphone near the elevators and called home.

"Hey dad, it's me." A pause. My voice echoed in the vacated lobby.

"What did you do? It's one-thirty in the morning. Are you in jail?"

"No. I just need to come home."

"What do you mean, *"I just need to come home"*? Why?"

"I need to come home right now. Tonight." Another long pause.

"You need me to come for you right now??" He sounded incredulous.

"Yes." I clenched the word tightly in my throat, choking back tears. I didn't know how it was possible I was having a coherent phone conversation on 450 micrograms of Berkeley LSD, but I didn't want to push my luck. Our exchange continued for another minute, until he tired of questioning me and getting one-word replies in return. Eventually, he sighed.

"I'll be there in an hour. Be ready. Don't make me come inside to get you." I managed to say thank you and hung up. When I turned from the payphone, a young woman was standing there, who seemed to appear from nowhere. She was an extremely pretty girl, heavyset, with long black hair, kind green eyes and a fair complexion. She cocked her head a bit and said in an understated half-whisper,

"That took a lot of courage." She approached me and wrapped her arms around me and allowed me to bury my head in her neck.

I wondered how long she had been standing behind me. It seemed a miracle in and of itself.

Abrupt stop. I need to pause the video here. This entire episode was always a big part of my "salvation story" which I would tell anyone who wanted to know. It was my *born-again testimony*. It was repeated on countless occasions over many years. But memories are different when one removes the hyper-spiritualized and over-emotionalized layers from them. For a long time, I remembered all these details quite differently. In my "salvation story", the sudden reprieve from mental torture after crying out to God, the feeling that I had just stepped out of a pool of water, was God removing the effects of the drug and saving me. However, the truth is that I continued to experience hallucinations and sensory distortion well into the following day. I had ingested a huge dose of LSD and I was not out of the woods at the time I made that phone call to my dad. In fact, I was still peaking on the drug and had not even begun to come down the other side of the mountain yet. In my "salvation story", the vision of the janitorial closet was always equated with a vision of hell and of isolation from God. In truth, it was just another wildly vivid drug-induced vision and was consistent with my mental condition at the time. I had been fighting off feelings of isolation and rejection all that night. Finally, in my "salvation story", the attractive woman with the black hair who appeared to me after my emotional phone call to my dad was the Virgin Mary, who of course had appeared to me because I was meeting her Divine Son for the first time (this is what I told people for many years). The truth, once I reconstructed events rationally, was freeing. She was, in fact, a female friend that I used to hang out with occasionally, and more frequently in the time leading up to this moment. More than that, her and I nearly became an item, but I had largely resisted that, except for one long and rather passionate kiss one night outside her room. And she didn't just appear out of nowhere, either, as I had imagined. In fact, her room was right near the payphone by the center foyer near the elevators. She no doubt heard my phone conversation, recognized my voice, and came out of her room while I was talking on the phone. I had no expectation that she was even in the dorm, yet there she was. Had I known, I would have sought her companionship much earlier in the night and saved myself considerable suffering. By the time I saw her, I was completely out of my mind and just wanted to go home and regroup. But at 7pm? I was still cognitive then.

As I packed up my things to leave, she came to my room and put her hand on my arm and turned me towards her. I imagine she sensed I was leaving school for good. Or maybe she felt lonely since she was also one of the few people on campus. I told her that I would come and see her if I came back. She teared up. I remember her telling me that I didn't need to leave. I told her I did because my dad was already on his way. With that, she kissed me on the cheek, said goodbye and left the room. I can still see her long, shiny black hair glistening as she spun her head to glance at me before she turned to go down the hall. That was the last time I saw her, too. But this last encounter never made it into my salvation testimony because, for the longest time, I didn't remember it. Why? I think it's because my brain decided that remembering this would be inconsistent with what I told it to believe. The memory, like a file in the back of a long drawer, seemed to disappear.

The mind is a powerful thing. And if you chemically alter it through a psychedelic drug and add the ingredient of intense emotion and feelings of insecurity and desperate longing, it can make many things that aren't real *appear* real. But our minds are capable of this trick even without the use of drugs. I didn't invent the Virgin Mary story because I wanted to impress people. I honestly believed it for a long time. My subconscious apparently transformed a traumatic and embarrassing situation into something that could be thought of as spiritually powerful which removed shame and restored dignity. Therefore, I convinced myself that it was true. Once I lost faith in Jesus, however, I opened this box of memories for the first time in decades and evaluated them fresh and with a new lens; a more rational, honest lens, and suddenly, I knew the truth. It was there the whole time, I just needed to be open

THERE'S NO SUCH THING AS MAGIC BLOOD

to the possibility of accepting it. When my perspective had changed, it was all waiting for me.

One thing cannot be denied about that night, however. I was a different person, mentally, after it was over. My intense LSD experience had changed me in cognitively measurable and profound ways. Over the months and years that passed, this became apparent, but as all of this was happening to me, I was not thinking of this. All I can say I knew with certainty at the time is that I made the intentional decision to rip myself away from my college environment, and I didn't go back to it. My perspective had been changed through shock, perhaps. My Christian friends would later describe this as "getting Jesus in me", and for a long time I agreed with them. Today, I think it was something else entirely. I also know this: If I had knocked on my woman-friend's door, rather than retreating to my room, alone, earlier that evening, I would probably have spent the night in her room rather than alone in my own, and I may have even greeted the morning with my arms around her. Her behavior, as it was, tells me that this is exactly what would have happened, and I would have thus ridden out the drug's effects with a supportive, stable person, who would have calmed and reassured me considerably, and I would not have called my dad, and would not have thought she was the Virgin Mary and would likely have remained at college for the rest of my freshman year. *Why didn't I?* Is it because God prevented me? Had I "fulfilled" God's purpose for my attendance at college by "meeting Jesus", as many later church friends would suggest? Maybe, and far more likely, "Jesus" became the *concept* that rescued me from the embarrassment of being a messed-up and undisciplined young man who was flunking out of school for no other reason than his own immaturity. Jesus became my scapegoat, just like the Christians claim. Except, for me, it was psychological, not theological.

The ride home in my father's van was surreal. He didn't talk much, but what he did say was measured, precise and stern. His words had a certain finality to them. I knew better than to say anything at all.

"You're done with school now, you understand?" I felt him staring at me, threateningly, waiting for a reaction, but I didn't have one. "You're going to get a job and you're going to pay rent, and that's it. I'm not supporting this anymore. If you want an education, you can pay for it yourself. You're going to learn to pay the price and stop making me pay the price for you." He continued. I didn't protest at all, and I dared not argue. For the first time, I felt that I had experienced God. I didn't consider the implications of what my father was telling me, such as the idea of giving up on my education. *It was going to be okay, now*. Yes, it was my dad talking. But my mind told me it was *God* talking, and my mind added to his words to match my expectations and this formed a spiritual baseline from which I would approach the next decade of my life.

THERE'S NO SUCH THING AS MAGIC BLOOD

Chapter 5

———∽∽———

SAVED!

MY ADOLESCENT BED seemed so small now. But my room was just as I had left it at Thanksgiving break: Grateful Dead, Led Zeppelin and Doors posters hung on every wall. On the headboard book casing behind my pillow sat the Living Bible that my father had bought me for my Catholic Confirmation. Still unable to sleep, I sat up in my bed and opened the Bible to the beginning of the New Testament book of Matthew and began reading. It was 3:45am. The words of the New Testament seemed to leap off the page at me, and I felt a great sense of assurance as I read them. However, I remind myself of the words of that tall, skinny Deadhead who warned me:

You'll think you've figured out all of these neat things; mysteries of the universe, of God and all that. Everything will seem to make perfect sense to you...but it's just the drug. Then he shook his head and walked off.

I read the entire book of Matthew before I stopped for a break. I felt calm, and clear-headed. Except, I wasn't. I had a large poster over my desk showing Led Zeppelin's lead singer Robert Plant, on stage, smiling, with a white dove perched on his hand. I looked up from the

Bible and it appeared that the dove took off and flew across the room towards me. I remember quickly ducking because it seemed to be so real. But when I looked up again, nothing of the sort had happened. I was still hallucinating. Again, for years, I had forgotten this. It was only after I allowed my suppressed memories to surface that I rediscovered this and other images from that night. My bedroom window faced east, and the sun was beginning to come up. The pond at the end of my father's field was releasing heavy, lazy vapor into the early spring air, and the treetops behind it were receiving the first light of dawn. I went over to the window and thrust it open. I heard what sounded like a thousand birds singing at once. The trees seemed to sway with the breeze, magically, their leaves rustling to their own music. The trees, the birds, the morning light…everything was brighter, livelier and cheerier than I remembered them ever being before. Except, there were, in truth, no leaves on the trees yet. They had only begun to bud. It was an illusion. But the dark clouds had seemed to lift from my mind for the first time in years. I felt so happy I began to cry tears of joy. All was new. One of the aspects of LSD was the propensity to exaggerate the intensity of sensory details and it was also common for the user to experience drastic swings of emotion. Both were in play here. As I stared through the mesh screen of my bedroom window, taking in this lush sensory experience, I suddenly lurched and had to rush to the bathroom, where I threw up bile. There was no food in my stomach to throw up. I saw some blood swirling in the bowl as well, and my stomach and esophagus burned. This is probably what woke up my mother, because when I went downstairs to make myself a toast and drink some apple juice a certain time later, she was sitting at the table, looking haggard and worn out in her fluffy white bathrobe and large coffee. It steamed little wisps while she stared at me, perplexed.

"What's going on?" She asked. "You can tell me. We don't keep secrets, remember?"

I looked at my mother with sympathy. *She didn't understand*, I thought. I was smiling, and this confused her, as it should have. But I could not help it. I felt so happy. Everything made so much sense to me now. Everything in my life to that point had simply led up to *this day*. It was divinely orchestrated. I felt free with this new knowledge, even empowered, no longer under the weight and pressure of failure and sadness.

"I'm really happy, mom. It's going to be okay now." I said to her. She just looked at me. She tried to smile but couldn't force her mouth to hold it. She raised her mug instead, taking a long swig of coffee.

"Have you slept?" She asked. I shook my head.

"It's going to be okay." I repeated. I explained the previous few days, about the concerts, the epiphany I had the previous night, my reading of Matthew earlier that morning. I was trying to tell her that I understood things I did not understand before and it would be different now. She needn't worry, I told her. She was nonplussed.

"If you have found God through this, well, that's good. But your father made it clear to me that college is *over*. You have a tough road ahead of you, kiddo." As she said this, she began to cry. Yes, I thought, I knew his feelings on this. But I had never considered the possibility that my mother did not agree with him. And she seemed heartbroken at what she felt was going on. I was too self-absorbed in my own thoughts to even ask her.

I learned to pay the price alright, as my father told me I would. Yes, I botched my first attempt at college. But I had plenty of time to regroup, get myself together and try again. I was not married, had no children and was not even dating anyone. I had no debt. Why the hard line? Didn't it matter if I got a good education? Apparently not. In fairness, he would ask in response if it even mattered to *me*. It was highly questionable, to anyone who knew me at that time, if it did. And my father is part of a different generation, as I mentioned earlier, in which college was not considered necessary for success, something which he reiterated to me often. However, I was an intelligent person with talents that needed to be honed with a professional education, rather than just the "hard knocks" of life. It was true that I needed to grow up and my father had reason to be upset with me. However, the better alternative to re-enrollment in college was to see me take a minimum wage job in a meat-packing plant? Apparently, because that is exactly what I did, and he seemed more than okay with that. This is mystifying to me today, but back then I rolled with it and didn't think to complain. I suppose, from his vantage-point, he was applying tough love. I'm not sure, of course, because he never explained his thinking to me beyond his words in the van after picking me up that night at school, and one could make a strong argument that his tactic was justified, at least in the short run. Had I not been caught up in a burgeoning religious fantasy in the months immediately after leaving school, I probably would have deduced all this independently on my own and paid my way through college after all. This is perhaps what my dad thought I might do. But that is not where I was at. I believed, then, that God had given me marching orders through my father that fateful night, and I intended on walking them out.

One of the stimulating jobs I had at the meat-packing plant was rolling the fresh, steaming gut barrels from the slaughterhouse to the cooler and preparing them for rail shipment. Cattle would be marched single file into a narrow chute, where an operator on a raised platform would shoot them in the side of the head with a metal rod attached to compressed air. The animal was then hoisted on an oversized meat hook attached to a conveyor, and while slowly traveling on the motorized rail, was sliced open from neck to groin and its guts raked out of its carcass and plopped into 55-gallon metal drums. Eventually, chemically treated, these bubbling barrels of cattle entrails would be moved into the waste cooler before being covered, sealed and brought on pallets to the loading dock behind the plant, where they would be loaded onto a train and hauled to some destination unknown. Perhaps, they were put in breakfast sausages so that you could enjoy a wholesome start to your day.

I tried to read my Bible every day after leaving college. There was a good deal in it that did not make sense to me and a good deal more that seemed incredulous, but it was all going into my mind. I was like a sponge. There were some bizarre teachings in the gospels, such as the scary apocalyptic visions at the end of Matthew, and the Gentile woman crawling like a dog at Jesus's table, begging for his "crumbs". Also, for a Jewish guy, Jesus sure didn't seem to like his own people very much. He seemed much more positive about the Romans. That was strange. Paul seemed to make more sense to me than Jesus did, although Paul shared the same odd animosity towards his fellow Jews that Jesus had expressed and also enjoyed good relations with the Romans, which, again, seemed somewhat unexpected, but I didn't do much more than cock my intellectual eyebrow at the anomaly. In fact, whenever Paul got in hot water, it was the Romans that bailed him out and plucked him from harm. This was very odd, indeed.

When I began reading Paul's letters, I saw some practical teachings that I could connect to modern life. Regarding Jesus, the Sermon on the Mount was a wonderfully rich bit of existential philosophy, but Paul seemed to put feet to it in practical ways, or so I imagined. Paul also talked about such concepts as conquering sin and his *body of death*, through Jesus, who was, as Paul explained, *in him*. It was a psychological gymnasium which sort of made sense to me and sort of didn't. At least, it was a long way off from my simple cry out to God for help while in the throes of LSD in my college dorm room. In hindsight, it seems as though the New Testament had simply become my mental landing pad from the transformative experience that the drug created, and that any spiritual texts could have conceivably filled the role just as adequately.

Reading about the heroic deeds of Paul in his missionary journeys as well as the steely-eyed determinism of Jesus to allow himself to be crucified left me with a sense of personal insignificance and unfulfilled purpose. Rather than inspire me with awe, it made me feel small. I was nothing. I was neither a success in the world, as a college dropout, nor a success as a person of God since I had sinned sexually in so many ways. I had failed at college, at radio, at the rock band and I had failed the Blue-Eyed Angel. I can see now why so many people who convert to Christianity ultimately conclude that the only way to make proper use of their life, and to amend for their past, is to strive to enter full-time church work, or at least to devote all their spare time to it. They feel that nothing else matters, especially after comparing their pitiful, "fleshly" life to the colossal champion of faith, Paul. More important, though, than all these things, is that I felt I had disappointed my father. It weighed heavily on me. How could I impress him and make things right?

While I was ruining my educational opportunities by chasing the Grateful Dead up the east coast, my father had started an Amway business, through the parents of one of my few High School friends. They were a non-observant Jewish family. I tagged along with my dad to their house for an "opportunity meeting", in which prospective distributors get exposed to "The Plan" (as distributors called it), meaning the Amway distributor compensation plan. I thought I might join my father in his new business venture so that he could see I was serious about life and could potentially be successful like him.

After the presentation, as I poured myself a coffee in the kitchen, I met a tall young man named Jon. Like me, I would learn, he was going through a spiritual transformation of some type and, in his case, was participating in the Amway business primarily to help with his mental outlook and to meet positive people, and perhaps, his future wife. We locked into animated conversation, and I told him my story of how I left college and what had brought me to the meeting.

"You became born again," he stated, matter-of-factly.

"What do you mean?" I asked. "Like that Nicodemus guy?"

"Yeah, born again. You are alive now. Spiritually alive."

This was the first I had heard of such a thing. Having been raised Roman Catholic, it was not territory I knew about. But I was paying careful attention. *Spiritually alive.* Yes, that was it.

"To be saved, you must ask Jesus into your heart. As soon as you do this, you are born again and have eternal life," he said, smiling. Hmm, I thought. I saw a problem with this formula. I felt my eyebrows clench together.

"Maybe I missed that part. You'll have to show me where it says that. Besides, that's not what I did. I never asked Jesus into my heart. I prayed to God directly." At this, a look of concern flashed across Jon's face, but he recovered quickly.

"I understand, Dave, but that's no problem. You see, Jesus *is* God." His grin, wider now, returned.

Both of us were being insensitive to the fact that we were in the kitchen of a Jewish home. I have no idea what they, or others, were thinking as we carried on this intense religious conversation at the end of their business meeting. Suddenly conscious of this myself (since I knew the family), I decided just to nod and end the conversation. I did not understand how Jesus could be God. Does this mean that God died on the cross? Who was running the universe while God lay dead in the tomb for three days? What if planets accidently collided while he was dead? I felt I needed to leave it be. We were in mixed company. Perhaps he knew more than me and could explain it at a more appropriate time.

"You should join me for church this week. I'll introduce you to my pastor, and we can study together," he offered. *Great!* I agreed.

His church was Southern Baptist and was about forty-five minutes from me in another town near the New England Patriots stadium, and several of the Patriots players attended there, which was a nice feature for me, being a huge football fan. There was All-Pro linebacker Steve Nelson, placekicker Jon Smith and tight end Don Hasselbeck (whose sons would both go on to become NFL quarterbacks, one of whom led the Seattle Seahawks to a Super Bowl). The services were interesting and inspiring. There was choir music. But I mostly enjoyed the preaching. The pastor was a middle-aged, slender man with a shock of blonde, curly hair and goatee. At the end of every sermon, he made an emotional plea, accompanied by gentle piano music, for people to come forward and have the elders pray over them for salvation or at least rededication and for special prayer needs. I went forward every single time. I needed to be sure that God knew I was serious about this stuff. *I was in it to win it.*

One such week, when I had decided, as I always did, to go forward, I was thinking hard about what I should pray for as I marched dutifully up the aisle to the kneeler benches up front. The message had been about hidden sin. *Heaven forbid*, I thought, that I would leave sin in my proverbial spiritual bank account without dealing with it. That sounded bad, for sure. I agonized over what to confess. When I had been Catholic, the confession process was so intimidating. You went into a wooden phone booth and the priest would be shielded from view behind a screen. You'd talk to the screen. The priest, if he wasn't sleeping or hadn't stepped out for a smoke while you were mumbling incoherently, would prescribe something for you to do, such as pray the Rosary every day for a week and stop masturbating. That was it. I only did it a few times, confession I mean, because it felt like Holy Interrogation. But now that I was, as Jon told me, "born again", I was all about this *confession* thing and wanted to do it right. There had to be something I could or at least should confess. As I thought about this, an elder came forward and placed his hand on my shoulder and knelt beside me. I felt his breath in my ear as he spoke to me in a hushed tone.

"What can we pray for together, brother?" he whispered. "What is on your heart?"

"I am struggling with masturbation, and I think I'm making God angry," I said. The elder, an aging, silver-haired man in a polyester blue suit with matching tie and bloodshot, glossy eyes, asked if we could pray in a side room instead, the ones usually reserved for serious issues that needed the ultimate privacy. When people went into one of those rooms, you could see wives in the congregation leaning towards their husbands and gossiping about what it is they were praying about. He had me kneel on the carpet next to him after closing the door, and he placed his open hand on the back of my neck and started weeping. I heard him sniffling and his voice was sputtering. He uttered a short prayer and then began to sob in deep, elongated, choking convulsions, all while grasping my neck and slowly shaking me from side to side. I tolerated it, for his sake. I don't think he knew he was doing this to me. He was a wreck. I tried not to stare at him from the corner of my eye, but it was hard not to. He prayed about sexual sin, but I prayed that he would let go of me. I never wanted to find myself in this position again. When we were finally done, or I should say when *he* was finally done, he hugged me and thanked me for my humility and for being willing to be "led by the Spirit". I felt better after that. God was pleased with me, I surmised.

My early Christian education was an exercise in rampant confirmation bias. There was no intellectual discussion of the text, the historical context of the documents, the state of Israel during the Roman War leading up to the writing of the gospels, the Jewish understanding of an anticipated Messiah, nor any number of other relevant issues. Of course not. Nor did I expect any of that, as such topics were out of mind. But they should have been part of it, if my teachers were intellectually honest, or at least not brainwashed themselves. Never, in all my early years within Christianity, was I ever exposed to the many controversies in the early centuries of the Church concerning doctrines, dogmas and practice, but I should have been. Doctrines, for example, such as the Trinity. I was never exposed to the development of the Trinity doctrine, which occurred over hundreds of years and was never an official doctrine of the Church confession until the Fifth Century. Instead, I was expected to believe in the Trinity as a condition of my salvation, even though neither the word nor the concept is found anywhere in the Bible. But I was expected to believe in such things, not to question them. And I didn't question them openly, because, generally, things were going okay for me. Jon was a good guy. We were memorizing scriptures together, eating at fast food restaurants, talking about the wives we would marry someday with whom we would build our beautiful Christian families, and commiserating about our lack of success in Amway. Regarding all the other stuff, I was told that Jesus was God and that faith in him was the answer to any question I might have. And that should, after all, have been enough. Because Jesus, you see, had enabled me to become "saved". Jon had assured me of this.

Chapter 6

———— ❧ ————

I CAN TELL YOUR FUTURE

I LEFT THE meat-processing plant and took a job as a dishwasher and then as a dietary clerk and short-order breakfast cook for a nursing home. It didn't pay very well but it beat rolling barrels of cattle intestines around.

It was an enriching but somber experience to deal intimately with the elderly in their last phase of life. In my role of dietary clerk, I often had time to sit and chat with the residents, many of whom would perk up when I came around. Mostly, it was the old ladies that would want me to visit. The men generally were ornery, but the women were different. There were shadows in their eyes as they shared parts of their life. They were talking to me and looking at me, but their gaze was elsewhere. Typically, they would ask me about my family and if I had a girlfriend. I would, in turn, ask them about their family and their life. Many, if not most of them, had outlived their friends and, in most cases, their spouse, some of their children and even some of their grandchildren. This seemed particularly painful to them and I don't recall a resident who shared these things with me who had really gotten over the loss of their loved ones. The pictures of their departed were the most cherished remaining possessions that they owned. They carried trainloads of mental relics and thoughts about the life they had lived and the world in which they had lived it, but they found themselves pining away their final years, months and days cooped up in this little room with nothing to see out the window but sky and a few tree branches, watching the television, eating their meals (many at least got to come to the dining room for that), playing bingo in the lounge and staring blankly at the wall. You could tell when they were losing their will to continue. When they died, I felt it was as much from heartbreak and loneliness as from health problems. As I conversed with them, with rare exceptions, the question at the tip of their tongue was, *What did it all mean, after all?* I had no answer for them. I would just hold their hand, which they appreciated. They were always cold, as their body core couldn't keep them warm anymore. The flame was slowly dimming within.

My newly found faith was exuberant, and as a result I'm afraid I was somewhat shielded emotionally from the sorrow in the stark grey countenances of these precious people who found themselves in circumstances they wouldn't have chosen voluntarily many years prior when they had the chance to have a say in the matter. I had been taught to be ready and quick to share the gospel, and to believe that God only placed me in the path of other people to do that very thing, and so many times, in those days, I tried. But not in the nursing home. That was different, as there was a certain finality to their situations. Their life was nearly over, they could never reel back the clock and live it over again, and they were more aware of this than I was. Whatever their life had been is what it would remain forever. It was over for them. There was no "brighter future in Jesus."

Of course, this was true for everyone, I eventually realized, on a grander scale. The only way to change the life you have already lived is to recontextualize it in your mind through new understanding. There is no changing the deeds and events of the past, but what you could do was manipulate your imagination and convince yourself that it was *something else*. And, in fact, we do this all the time. This is what my "spiritual awakening" at college, and immediately afterwards, had done for me. More than anything, it enabled me to color the way I viewed the events and circumstances of my life through the opaque filter of the conceptual idea that people call *Jesus*. And that is what Jesus is, really. More than a person, Jesus is a *concept*. Everything about my life, and about reality itself, was now to be apprehended through this conceptual idea called *Jesus*. He was supposed to be *in me*, after all, and this should, and most certainly would, reflect itself in my experiences in this world from that point on. The proof that Jesus is a concept more than a person is the fact that there are so many different versions of Jesus which people hold up before the world. There is Social Worker Jesus, Miracle Worker Jesus, Communist Jesus and Capitalist Jesus, Democrat Jesus and Republican Jesus, Jewish Jesus and even Antisemitic Jesus. But most prevalent of all was the Pauline concept of *Jesus in me*, which could only exist in my mind. It was an idea which had been suggested to me, but which I had chosen to adopt. It did not actually have any tangible manifestation in the physical reality of the real world or in my experiences within it. It only altered my personal perspectives on them.

As I listened to these elderly residents share their stories, I was acutely aware that my personal faith in Jesus could not in any way impact or even offer context to their own journey through life. It had been *their* journey, not mine. What mattered, truly, was the reality of our time shared together; something which existed uniquely in that moment, and which survived only through memory, would exist forever in that context alone, and not in the context of any existential concept of Jesus which could not be seen, heard, felt and touched. Such mystical concepts could be dwelt upon and wondered at, but they had nothing to do with the sense of shared community I experienced with these residents, which transcended any dogma or belief I may have ascribed to.

The imperative within evangelicalism of "witnessing" to people (sharing the gospel person to person) became something that I began to loathe during this time, and this loathing never left me after it settled in. The privilege I enjoyed of being a listening ear and a friend to these people in such sensitive and vulnerable circumstances I dared not sully by shifting into "pastor visitation night", during which you are expected to facilitate a conversational transition from the mundane topic at hand into "more important" issues, such as "sharing Jesus that you might save their soul." I don't recall ever doing so with any of these residents. How could I? How could a nineteen-year-old kid have the audacity to share dogma and doctrine with a ninety-six-year-old woman who could not think about the future, but only the past? What exactly would these precepts be assisting her with, anyway, her *recollections*? These people had lived nearly a century, in some cases. They were aware of Christianity. They didn't want that from me, or frankly, from anyone else. They just needed someone to talk to. I found that this was also the case with everyone else I encountered in life, regardless of age. People need to be listened to and genuinely heard far more than they need to be preached to about what they are supposed to believe.

This was an acute problem for me that created a vacuum of cognitive dissonance. The guilt began to pile up like a compost pile, becoming an imaginary eyesore in the landscape of my conscience. *I was failing at my most important job*, I thought to myself. My Christian teachers had taught me that wherever I found myself in life, that the only reason I was there was to share Jesus with the people I encountered; somehow, some way, preferably through my "testimony". But I couldn't bring myself to do it. The time spent in the nursing home brought me back to my memories of wandering the woods and fields of my father's property, contemplating my place in the universe. I shuddered to think that I might be getting a glimpse into my future as an old man, should I live that long. Even the Bible itself, in Ecclesiastes, warned of this. You took nothing with you from this world when you died. Could there be a way to leave behind value in your wake? What would that look like, I wondered? What was there beyond the grave,

THERE'S NO SUCH THING AS MAGIC BLOOD

ultimately? Most of these residents, I imagined, like most people in Christianized America, believed in God and in going to heaven. The idea that such people could be denied their hope of such an imagined rite of passage, merely for the lack of an assent to some dogmatic creed of belief made no sense to me, and in fact was offensive to my sensibilities and my humanity. I, for one, don't believe in the idea of my soul "going to heaven", today. At that time, I did, but I was not going to debate the subject with a person on their deathbed. How could their eternal destiny possibly hinge on a dietary clerk's evangelistic efforts as they lay dying in a nursing home? *Was their soul possibly that cheap?*

There were two nurses at the facility who took an interest in me and invited me to attend their church's Easter play. I agreed to go. They belonged to a large Assemblies of God church, which is a Charismatic Christian Protestant denomination that is very outreach oriented and demonstrative in their faith expression. We watched the play together from the balcony, because we arrived late, but this provided an interesting view of both the play and the audience. It was a professional and, it appeared, costly production, yet admission was free. I remember the penultimate scene in which the great stone was rolled away, and Jesus emerged from the tomb alive. The house lights were dimmed, and a great flash of hot white light combined with the artificial smoke of the dry ice machine emanating from within the tomb to silhouette the white-robed Jesus from behind as he stepped forward. Loud, triumphant music thundered through the auditorium. The audience, unprompted, rose to their feet in unison. I joined them, of course, since it seemed the thing to do. But something strange happened. The people were not just clapping and cheering. Some burst into tears, some hopped up and down in place, screaming *Jeeesssus!!* at the top of their lungs until their voices cracked, they turned purple, and they almost passed out. Others fell to the floor, writhing like they had been shot in their side with a stray bullet, while still others closed their eyes and began chanting in some sort of Pig-Latin, which I later was told was "speaking in tongues." This went on for several minutes while the white-robed, now-untombed actor playing Jesus stood patiently, waiting for the tumult to die down before moving on to the next part of the performance, as though the cast expected such a display and were prepared to accommodate it. I was considerably unimpressed. I wasn't looking for a dramatic cinematic presentation which manipulated my emotions to reaffirm my experience of and belief in God, and I was at a loss as to why everyone found this Broadway-style production so enthralling. Today, however, rather than understanding it *less*, I understand it *more*. You see, this is the true *original* expression of Christianity to the masses. People talk about the "Hebrew roots" of the faith, but the charismatic movement is much more likely the true template of the earliest believers, and not anything close to Judaism. Today, serious Christians study the gospels and the epistles with keen interest; they read commentators who pick apart the Greek syntax and try to read between the lines to discern the tiniest nuance of doctrinal application and theological significance from the text, twisting it at times into monstrous contortions to support this or that hypothesis. But during most of the early period of the church there were no such opportunities, because people weren't studying the texts in that way. The message was proclaimed in theatres, in the *passion play*, just like what this Assemblies of God church was presenting. It was "Christ crucified" which was preached, and it was acted out much like this, in amphitheaters across the Roman Empire. As the centuries wore on, it was mostly the elite scribes and rulers of the church who read the texts. Many of the participants in the religion through the centuries were illiterate and needed the religion *acted out before them* to understand it. This is no doubt a major reason the Catholic Mass has so much theatre to it. The message of Christianity is about the Hero Story, and the *magic blood* of Jesus, not about four-hundred-page commentaries on the book of Romans. People *feel* the story more than they intellectually comprehend it.

My first exposure to *Jesus theatre* fell flat. It always fell flat for me. I am not a movie lover. If you ask my family, they will confirm this. I watch movies as a vehicle to spending time with my family. I almost never desire to sit and watch one, though I force myself to do so, for them. I find most of these productions contrived, manipulative and boring. Once I figure out where the plot is headed, only the best screenwriters and actors can hold my attention. I just don't enjoy the emotional ride. I especially detest superhero movies. They are the absolute worst. Maybe that's why I was so unmoved by the Easter play. Rather than inspiring, I found it hokey, juvenile. If Jesus and Christianity were real, as I felt and believed at the time that they were, the faith presented should be serious and able to withstand intellectual scrutiny and vetting. This Easter theatrical play was certainly not any of that. Additionally, and adding to my irritation, was that I had questions about the resurrection story which I felt couldn't be asked in mixed company, and which, even at this early stage of my Christian experience, I found disconcerting. I even had ordered a paperback book by a writer named Josh McDowell called "The Resurrection Factor", which had been promoted to me through the Trinity Broadcasting Network, to help me with my concerns about the issue.

I had taken note over the course of the previous year that none of the resurrection accounts in any of the four gospels agreed with each other in terms of sequence, characters or dialogue. The Gospel of Mark, which I was told was the first gospel written (though it wasn't the first presented, which was strange) had literally nothing to say about it compared to the other three, especially if you paid attention to the margin notes and learned that the last fifteen or so verses of Mark were added by scribes perhaps centuries after the original version. This meant that the original gospel which was circulated to the sect's followers had no resurrection narrative recorded. The gospel of Mark originally ended with the women at the tomb running in fear for their lives after a stranger, *who wasn't Jesus*, met them inside the tomb. In fact, the original ending of Mark supports the Jewish claim that the body of Jesus was *stolen*. This was astounding to me. What did it mean that the single most important claim of Christianity, that Jesus rose from the dead, did not enjoy a consistent and detailed testimony by his earliest followers? How could they have botched this? Maybe, just maybe, it was all made up and never even happened. Perish the thought! For certain, that is the story the Jews told, or at least that's what the New Testament tells us they said. Christians laugh at the "stupid Jews" who were forced to make up "conspiracy theories" about the empty tomb, but what if these conspiracy theories were true? The resurrection of Jesus is something which has no corroboration anywhere outside the pages of the New Testament, and the gospels were all written some forty to a hundred years after the events they describe, according to most scholars. Surely, someone outside of the disciples of Jesus could have verified this incredible miracle, if it actually happened. It turns out that no one could, or ever has. Perhaps more important even than this is that the very disciples of Jesus themselves cannot provide such corroboration, as their accounts are contradictory, meaning that we cannot even confidently rely upon the single testimony we have had handed down to us. Didn't anyone bother to mention to the writers of the four gospels that getting this part of the story straight was somewhat important to the credibility of their testimony? Apparently not, but neither did it matter for most of history since most people never question such things. Of course, as I said above, the earliest Christians had no way to compare notes concerning the texts. There were dozens of variations of gospel narratives in circulation before the Canon was formalized. This developmental period covers a vast amount of time, too. Ultimately, these questions would chip away at my spiritual confidence until they erupted, through life circumstances, into a crisis. I was not having a crisis yet on this night at the Assemblies of God church, but I had some suspicions that all was not well with what I was seeing. I couldn't put my finger on it exactly, but many years later I realized the problem. You see, once you put the gospel story into action in a life-like portrayal, as in a movie or in a production such as that Easter play, you suddenly realize how incredibly insane the whole thing is. It defies all rational thought. This is perhaps what perplexed the creators of Jesus Christ Superstar, the hit play, movie and soundtrack from the 1970's which was widely panned by church-goers for its cynical treatment of the resurrection narrative. For example, the entire sequence of Jesus's "trial", or should I say "trials", is beyond the point of being childishly ludicrous. No collection of Jewish leaders, Sanhedrin or otherwise, would ever hold any sort of legal proceedings, *for any reason whatsoever*, on Passover. That simply is religiously and historically impossible. It just quite plainly could not have happened. The gospels were, therefore, blatantly lying about this. Which begged the question: *What else were they lying about?* Once I began learning about Jewish law and practice and the history of such things in the Second Temple period, this was a huge problem. Not to mention the antisemitic claim in the gospels that portray a mob of Jews (who just days earlier were praising Jesus as a King as he rode into Jerusalem on a donkey), demanding he be crucified and that the guilt of his blood be *"upon us and our children"* (Matthew 27:25). This statement, alone, is probably responsible for more death, suffering and persecution of Jews through the centuries than any other. It truly makes one wonder what the actual perspective of the author of Matthew was.

What bothered me even more than the play, though, was the unhinged reaction of its audience. This projected fantasy invoked such a cathartic psychological release from them that it reminded me of an orgasm. Today, I believe that this is an accurate way to describe the "born-again" experience, *a psychological orgasm*. Christians, at least evangelical Christians, once they have experienced such a psychic release from shame and guilt and feelings of insignificance, seem to spend the rest of their lives trying to recreate the feeling. And that attempt, in my estimation, is what most church services, sermons, worship music performances and revival meetings are all about. It is what literally drives the whole experience for many committed evangelicals; reinforcing belief and recreating the psychic innocence of virgin faith. *Do you remember your first time?* Evangelicals surely do, and they attempt to relive it every week. More than that, they are willing to invest millions towards breaking you in and loosening you up. They'll even pray with you while you wash the bedsheets. But first, you must spread your spiritual legs. The daily devotional they hand you afterwards is just the cigarette you inhale after the climax. Forgive my crude analogy, but I use it because I believe it's apt.

I also noticed that Paul never discusses the resurrection event in his letters. Oh yes, Paul certainly claimed to preach "Christ crucified", but there are no points in Paul's letters in which he even hints at details of the crucifixion of Jesus as we find in any of the existing resurrection accounts, other than to add the strange comment that Jesus appeared to him as "one born out of time" and that Jesus "appeared" to James and Peter and "five hundred disciples at one time". Yet, we have no mention of any of this by any of the gospel writers. How could it be that only Paul, who was not an original follower of Jesus, can tell us that "five hundred at one time" witnessed the risen Jesus, yet decades later, Jesus's spiritual biographers, who cannot, or do not, corroborate Paul's claims? None of the gospel writers even hint at Paul's claim of the witnesses. In fact, none of the gospel accounts acknowledge that a person named Paul even existed at all. Weren't Paul's letters written first? How can this be possible? And while we are stripping the topic naked, what about Matthew's incredulous account of the righteous dead rising from their graves and walking through the city of Jerusalem after the crucifixion of the Christ? There is not a single historical verification of such an incredible miracle. Imagine experiencing this, or even hearing about it, and not remembering it or mentioning it in your writings. *I can't, can you?* Yet Paul, Mark, Luke, John, Peter, and Jude and the author of Hebrews all have amnesia about it. How unfortunate for the faith's credibility. The Pharisaic Jews, who proclaimed the resurrection of the dead and argued vehemently for it with the Sadducees, would surely have catalogued this miracle to substantiate their own claims on the issue, irrespective of Christian claims, but there is not a single Jewish

THERE'S NO SUCH THING AS MAGIC BLOOD

source which can verify it ever happened. Do you know why? *Because it never did.*

Likewise, John's account of the raising of Lazarus from the grave by Jesus is perhaps the most dramatic scene in his gospel. And it is credited with causing the Sanhedrin to plot Jesus's death. This was an incredible miracle, and yet neither Paul, Peter, James, Jude nor any of the other gospel writers saw fit to so much as *mention* it, even in passing. Do you know why? *Because it didn't happen.* It is fiction. To think otherwise is to denigrate one's own cognitive ability. There is no plausible explanation for the story's omission from the other New Testament authors' writings than that it simply isn't true. It apparently is just part of John's fanciful storytelling, and reflects the century or so which separates John's account and the events they supposedly describe.

Another curious fact about the resurrection: Why is it when Thomas had doubts about the resurrection, Jesus saw fit to appear *physically* before him, amidst his other followers, and encourages Thomas to place his fingers into the gash in his side (gross!), but extended no such opportunity to Paul? No such physical appearance ever happens for *him*, and yet we are told that Paul is the steward of the most important revelation ever given to mankind, *the revelation of the church and its practices.* Who was Thomas in comparison to Paul? Why would Jesus appear physically in his resurrected state to the original disciples but not to Paul? Wasn't Paul the most important teacher of doctrine in Christian history? Did Jesus lose the power to physically appear to people? This is no small matter to consider. Paul portrays his revelation as so important that he was willing to put in writing his utter disdain for the core disciples of Jesus and their presumed authority *("these supposed pillars…who added nothing to me")* in his letter to the Galatians.

How could Paul's visions of a risen Christ, apprehended in his imagination alone, be considered more authoritative than the personal testimony and witness of the men who walked with Jesus? Further, why would Jesus tell Paul things via mystical utterance and ecstatic visions that he failed to reveal to James, his brother, whom he left in charge of the church in his absence, while he was still in person?

None of it made sense to me, either then or now. But I tried not to think too hard about it. I tried, instead, to increase my faith. *Help me, o Lord, with my unbelief.*

Chapter 7

Jesus Wants You to be Rich

SOMETIMES, WE MAKE decisions by default by avoiding making decisions. I slowly allowed the idea of college to drift from my mind. I think I may have been afraid to go back. It was therefore an emotional decision, not a logical or strategic one, when I chose to join my parents in the Amway business. My father should probably have prevented me from doing so, as I was not a good prospect for it, and told me to go back to school, but this was not his *modus operandi*. I am not wired, in any case, to be part of the slick, shiny world of business. It holds little allure for me. I get no thrill from financial achievement. I am a teacher, a philosopher, a thinker.

It was difficult for me to understand the mindset of the people I dealt with who were achieving notoriety in Amway or to understand how they managed to succeed. They were different than me, in some way, and I couldn't figure out why they made it while I and many others didn't. Oh, I heard all the reasons that they gave from stage during the rallies, about how they just "put in the work", but lots of people put in lots of work that also got nowhere and had little to show for it. I doubt many of these people who achieved success honestly had a clue as to why they had succeeded. They mostly just parroted the things they heard others say while they were ascending the ladder. The speakers were, in my estimation, grasping at straws to try to rationalize what had happened to them, and the more believable the rationalization, the more we frantically took notes. *That must be it!* We all chattered about the new insight amongst ourselves over our rubber chicken during the banquet. But I came to believe that success, or lack thereof, in such enterprises had much deeper roots of origin than anyone short of a clinical psychologist would normally be able to discern. The few successes I achieved, after all, only served to completely stress me out, rather than motivate me. Creating something like a business organization, complete with real people who looked to you for help, was nothing short of terrifying. I doesn't matter how much money was at stake. In fact, I think that this was a bit of an existential crises for many of my colleagues, also, whether they would admit it publicly or no. I remember a particular speaker who had come to share his wisdom at one of the functions, making headlines with his *avante-guard* management approach. During his speech, he said:

"I have a distributor who came to me and said, *"How do you deal with a prospect or distributor who has this problem?"* I said to him, "Go sponsor another one". They went on, *"What about someone with* that *problem"*. "Go sponsor another one", I said. "Not happy with your organization? Don't like the people you got? Go sponsor another one!" He declared all this nonsense triumphantly, as if he had discovered the very fount of business acumen. With each emphatic declaration, he pounded the podium for effect. We all clapped and cheered him on with deafening applause. I said to my dad, afterwards,

"That sucked. What a dumb ass. Basically, he just admitted he's a terrible leader. He can't help anyone with their problems, so he just replaces them. That's not a good strategy." My dad just looked at me and shrugged.

"Well, David, he's on stage because he has a big organization. What do *you* have?"

"People I care about."

You have so much more to think about and to worry about once you sponsored people into your network. And if you are not committed to being completely immersed in the enterprise and seeing it through to completion, you'd really be best served to not even start the process, because it will eat you alive if you try to play games with it haphazardly with only a passing level of interest. But some people, like my dad, were seemingly equipped for this sort of venture. They thrived upon it. I tried to be that person, but I always felt like I was dressing in someone else's outfit. It became even more awkward for me as my father began to succeed in it. And he didn't just succeed, he in fact became one of the most prominent Amway distributors in the United States. This put me in a spotlight that I handled well on the surface, but which created a non-stop crisis beneath it. People in the business, of course, simply assumed that I was a chip off the old block, and people I barely knew, or didn't know at all, would seek to get into my good graces since they figured I'd be taking over the enterprise one day. If my father had not become so successful so quickly, I probably would not have lasted more than a year in the business.

Nonetheless, my chief goal at this point in my life, which was to make my father proud of me, was not being achieved, and that's essentially, as I look back on it, the only reason I was sticking around and not moving along to other things. My father's mercurial arc of success only served to highlight the stark differences between us, unfortunately. The things he felt were important I generally couldn't be bothered with, and vice versa. Rather than sticking close to my wife (once I was married) and charting my own path, I insisted upon staying on this masochistic treadmill of multi-level-marketing and its wellspring of never-exhausted hope which it promised of attaining limitless financial increase. Put simply, *I couldn't find a way to quit.* After all, that would make me a "quitter". No, I kept convincing myself that I could find the motivation, the discipline and the drive to become successful, and then all would be well. I just needed to follow the advice on the tapes and *persevere*.

The world of Amway, at least for the organization we were a part of, was about God, America, and wealth-building. For most of the leaders in the business, these ideas were what amounted to a veritable statement of faith which would be articulated in a consistent and systematic manner of indoctrination. Belief in Jesus became inseparable from an equal commitment to Capitalism. I began ingesting a steady diet of books that the charismatic leaders of the organization wanted me to read, written by Dr. Robert Schuller, Dr. Norman Vincent Peale, Og Mandino, and the like, and tried to check out the Christian teachers that many of the leaders quoted, such as Kenneth Copeland, Pat Robertson, Chuck Swindoll and just about everyone on Trinity Broadcasting Network (TBN), such as Paul Crouch and his wife with the electric purple hair, as well as all manner of health and wealth doctrinaires; people who melded together the gospel of Jesus with prosperity theology, personal ambition and the good 'ole American Dream. Today, such luminaries as Creflo Dollar, Joseph Prince, T.D. Jakes, Joyce Meyer and Joel Osteen occupy those exalted thrones. There were also motivational giants such as Dr. Denis Waitley, Zig Ziglar, and others, all of whom were prominent figures, and many of whom I met in person.

Because of my father's success, I met many famous people and had numerous opportunities to do large-scale public speaking. I even spoke before fifteen thousand for ten minutes at a "Free Enterprise Rally" immediately before President Ronald Reagan took the stage. (I also met Johnny Cash that same weekend, which I think was a bigger thrill.) For the gurus who controlled the distributor network to which I belonged, the Amway business was not merely a vehicle for becoming gaudy, ostentatious fat cats, but was in fact the way that they conceived of spreading the gospel. They passionately believed that America was God's Nation of Promise, called to bring forth the kingdom of God, the Jews to Jesus and the Free Enterprise system to the world. It was part of their eschatological destiny. Amway, in this manner, was their *church*, their *denomination*. The old, rugged cross of the Baptist tradition had been given a modern facelift with Cadillacs, diamond rings and fur coats.

It was the mid-eighties, when an entire industry grew and expanded from nowhere; a self-help, motivational guru-culture from which Tony Robbins and others like him emerged. It marked the beginning of the profession called "life-coaching", a phenomenon no one had ever seen or heard of before. I read the Magic of Thinking Big, Think and Grow Rich, How to Win Friends and Influence People, The Seven Habits of Highly Effective People, The Power of Positive Thinking and many other books. Not once, mind you, and not twice. I read these books repeatedly, like a song list on constant shuffle. I don't regret doing so today, but I must say that the ultimate impact they had is debatable. This intensive approach to personal growth had some interesting aspects and some benefits, I suppose, but I believe they are greatly exaggerated by their proponents. One merely had to peer into the slums of India, the metal-barred windows in Mexican border towns like Juarez, or even more horrifying, the Holocaust, to understand that the concept of one's "limitless potential" was a fantasy which cold, hard reality was happy and even eager to destroy, and with extreme prejudice. Not everyone had the opportunity to change their life the way that the self-help champions proclaimed that you could. Sure, certain universal principles could be applied anywhere, at least internally. Victor Frankl's monumental work "Man's Search for Meaning", detailing how he was able to survive multiple Nazi death camps, was proof of that. However, the reality of the extreme cruelty that man was capable of when driven by his uncultivated nature, as well as the unyielding grind of the wheel of time, served to ruin the reverie of the meditations and visualization techniques I had learned in Think and Grow Rich. I also remembered the elderly in the nursing home. A week or two after they died, and their personal effects cleared out, a new resident would be setting up house, hanging pictures and decorations in the same room. The name on the door was changed, the new resident was registered in the system for my dietary clerk printouts, and the prior resident was removed from these lists. They were gone.

After years spent filling my head with every resource on personal motivation I could find, I have concluded that the great majority of these resources effectively only accomplish one basic thing: selling books, courses and lectures which directly benefit the producers of these books, courses and lectures. So, if this is your type of entertainment, *have fun*. I experienced enough of it to last three lifetimes, and I want nothing to do with it anymore.

I met my wife at an Amway opportunity meeting. She was deeply tanned, with streaks of blonde frosting in her dark brown hair which went down to her mid back in semi curls. Her warm, lovely brown eyes were electrified with full, voluptuous lashes. She wore a pink leather miniskirt which showed off well-toned, long, shapely legs. There was no way she would ever talk to me, I thought to myself. Surprisingly, she didn't object to me claiming the empty seat next to her, and I thought maybe that was my thrill for the night. Unbeknownst to me, in the row behind us, sat most of her family, including her parents. My future mother-in-law elbowed my future father-in-law and said, "Hey, that's the boy that Chana is going to marry."

"Shut up," he said. He was having none of it.

My mother-in-law was like this. She was fiercely Roman Catholic, prayed to the saints and to Mary and believed unwaveringly in the *magic blood* of Jesus. She would occasionally have these clairvoyant premonitions of something; some issue or event to come, and you couldn't convince her of anything other than what she felt was true when this happened. In this case, she saw me marrying her youngest daughter.

We started dating, eventually, and things became serious much sooner than either of us expected. This caused me to become conscious of a problem. Whereas I had become "born again" a couple of years before we met, she had not, and at the time we started seeing each other, she was agnostic. I was becoming concerned about being "unequally yoked with a non-believer", which is a deep and ever-present issue among evangelicals. This predicated my urgent need to have the "conversation" with her about Jesus. (The fact that I felt the need to lead her in the "sinner's prayer", even though she was a confirmed Catholic, should tell you a lot about evangelical perspectives.) She was amazingly pliable to the idea. I brought her into my bedroom in my father's house and kneeling with her at the foot of my bed, led her in the repetition. There was no emotional outpouring. No tissues were needed. She turned to me after the prayer was done.

"Is that it?"

"Uh…yeah."

"Really? I don't feel any different. Am I supposed to?"

"You won't in the beginning," I answered. This was bullshit, but it stopped the follow up questions, and that mattered since she had already scared me. I didn't expect her to feel *nothing*, after all. But here we were. Chana never "felt" it, it turned out, until we attended an Amway function as a couple for the first time. The wife of the most successful Amway distributor in history shared a story on Sunday morning in the hotel conference room of her struggle to deal with the death of her brother as a teenager. She shared how Jesus had healed her of her pain of loss. Chana had lost her oldest brother when she was thirteen to a freak and tragic accident and had never quite gotten over it. Weeping, she answered the altar call eagerly. She *felt it*, whatever "it" was, that morning.

I learned over the years that *feeling it* was a big deal for most evangelicals. A large percentage of people in the "born again culture" did not think that their faith was fully legitimate unless they *felt it*. And they were constantly chasing that feeling. Through music, mostly, and in some cases, through Pig Latin. The worship band would start to strum that rhythmic cadence that seemingly every top-forty, country-rock-Christian worship song had, their eyes would close, and they would start to sway and then, they would be *feeling it*. If I were to ask them what they were doing, they would tell me that they were experiencing worship. As far as I could tell, however, they were listening to melodic music and swaying, but what do I know?

A few years after Chana and I finally married, and had begun having children, we reached an important crossroad. We had decided, together, that the message being promoted to us at the Amway functions was not what we wanted. We desired a more conservative approach to life. We wanted a real church community and were no longer satisfied with "Christian Tape of the Week" through the business network. One week, upon visiting a local church, we felt we might have found a match. We were three years into a rocky marriage, and had just moved to Rhode Island, and were living next door to my grandparents, in the same duplex I had lived in as a toddler. With a lack of peace in our relationship, consistent failure in the business and mounting financial pressure on our young family, my wife was looking for hope. She had grown tired of the Amway lifestyle, and she particularly hated the large weekend functions. We both wanted meaningful friendships, a genuine sense of belonging and a vacation from the feeling that we were constantly obligated to sell the business to people. The church offered this. We wanted to attend mid-week services, maybe join a home group and even volunteer at the church in some capacity. I told my father what we were thinking, and he wasn't pleased. Everything I was telling him that we wanted directly conflicted with our ability to build the business. As far as he was concerned, we would be *quitting Amway* if we walked in what we were telling him we desired. He wasn't wrong.

There was no Zoom in the late eighties and early nineties. The concept of video calls over a personal computer was unheard of. There were no I-pads, Smartphones, or even flip-phones, either. My father had an early version of a cell phone: It was a large black box that sat between the front seats with a removable receiver. The set up weighed about seven pounds and cost a fortune to use. I know, because I used it to call in to a radio sports talk show once and my dad questioned me about the massive charge which showed up on his statement. I had been on hold for fifty-three minutes waiting to get on the air, I told him. Whoops.

You built the business (in those days) by physically driving to people's homes, explaining the opportunity in person, and then, if they wanted to join, you had a separate meeting to "pass the kit", help them build a prospect list, help them make calls, host a couple of meetings for them, then do the same process for their prospects and then so on down the line. It was called "building depth", and if you were serious about accomplishing anything, it was seven days a week. There were also motivational training meetings and weekend rallies designed for your new distributors to get a taste of what was possible and to learn about the enterprise. Many of these were all-day affairs, or all-weekend gigs, and cost a pretty penny to participate in. As it turned out, the "development system" of tapes, books, business building tools and functions were an industry unto themselves, and many of the most successful distributors made far more on all of that than they did selling Amway products through the organization. I earned about $8.00 an hour in my day job and my wife was a stay-at-home mom. I was racking up debt on my American Express card paying for plane tickets and function entrance fees for large weekend functions and I was not paying these charges off fast enough. It couldn't go on the way it was. Something needed to change. We did, in fact, want to step back and get off the treadmill. My father was correct; this would, if not immediately, eventually equate to a form of quitting the business. So, when I told him all of this, he, in his own way, *let me have it*. Honestly, I should not have been consulting him for advice on the matter. His advice had always amounted to the same thing: *Build the business, no matter what the cost. Work on your personal issues as you go. Pay the price now and your kids will thank you later.* After this lunch date, he took it a step further. He consulted with the Major Domo Guru of our upline since that man was a Christian and my father assumed he would better understand our dilemma. My father was not an evangelical or even a practicing Catholic and did not comprehend our perspective, nor did he appear particularly interested in trying. He returned from his meeting with the Guru with an air of confidence, and was eager to share the man's advice, which was, in summary, that building our Amway business was our *ministry for Jesus*. According to this guy, there was virtually nothing I could possibly do that would serve the kingdom of God more effectively than building a honking Amway empire. To my father, of course, this logic was empirically unassailable, and the topic was now closed for further discussion. I would either suck it up and get busy building again or I could be an average loser like most of my church friends. It was my choice.

Influential to our decision was my father convincing me that the small business group we had started was starting to grow rapidly in the part that *he* was working in, and if we were disciplined and kept working hard it would take off within the year. *Don't give up now*, was his exhortation. I really wanted my father to be proud of me. I didn't even fully understand at that point how deeply this drive ran inside me, or how it subverted logic. But what this meant, of course, was that the church community was *out*, and the business was back *in*. Eventually, since we could never make it to services, we stopped attending the church altogether, and the promising relationships we had begun to cultivate disappeared along with it. It was clearly the wrong decision, not because we needed more Jesus in our lives, but because we desperately needed the emotional and psychological support which would be provided by a healthy group of friends with whom our association was not profit-driven. This would *never* be provided in Amway. In the end, my decision to listen to the Guru's counsel led to us filing bankruptcy. And it was unnecessary. My parents did, indeed, push my business to the status it needed to reach for them to go Diamond, a very significant and financially auspicious level. They did so by using our family relationship to literally purchase the volume necessary to do so, under our name, with our consent, and they experienced a huge windfall in new income and opportunity as a result. Not so much for us. There were no such benefits for Chana and I and our family. As our reward for participating in this strategy, we enjoyed the opportunity of filing bankruptcy, having our phone service shut off and eating lots of spaghetti. We got literally nothing out of the arrangement except false status, stress and a sense of vaudeville existence based on mirrors. My parents ultimately quit Amway and moved to southern Florida. We were poor and couldn't travel much. I didn't see my father again in person for nearly nineteen years, although my mother traveled north on several occasions to visit, which was nice. I cannot know if my father is self-aware of his part in the breakdown of relationship between himself and my children, but he should be, if he isn't. Now that I'm older, however, and have had to move to another state for a fresh start myself, it's much easier for me to empathize with the situation he was in when he and my mother moved south. Sometimes, life is not convenient. But there is a tradeoff in everything we choose to do. Perhaps, in twenty years, my sons and their families will say similar things about me. I sure hope not.

As a result of this entire Amway experience, I do not, today, aggressively denounce Christian belief or church attendance. I respect it. I respect anyone who desires to participate in religious activities, because these types of people tend to also be family-centered and of good moral character. Generally, I mean. Okay…*more often than not*. Can we agree to that at least? It truly doesn't matter if their religion is true or false. What people gain from their involvement, in terms of relationships and cultural stability, far outweighs the theological veracity of their beliefs. I say this as someone who left the faith, because it's precisely the lack of these things that created so much instability in our own lives.

I am often asked why it is that some people question their faith and its teachings, and so many others don't. What is the trigger? I believe the main reason that most people don't question their beliefs is because their religious life is not centered around their beliefs, but around the emotions they associate with them due to the relationships which they establish in their community, and with their own family who indoctrinated them in those beliefs. I'm speaking in general terms, of course. Most people who outwardly identify as Christian are generally oblivious to what the Bible says. Just try telling them what it says, and you will recognize this rather quickly. They will not appreciate you pointing it out to them, even, *perhaps especially*, when you can prove that you're right. People believe what they are told to believe, and when they sit down and take the time to read their Bibles (and not many do this consistently), they tend to find what they expect to find. On those occasions when they come across passages that don't make sense to them or that seem inconsistent with what they expect to see or that contradict their assumed understanding, most don't question it, even then. Usually, they read right over it and fail to notice, or, if they do have a flash of cognition, once they question it, their spiritual leaders are quick with a sermon, pamphlet, blog post or some other explanation which recalibrates them away from their doubtful questions and back in line with the groupthink. The people who enjoy stable, fulfilling relationships in these religious environments are generally easily placated by shallow, even mindless apologetics. They are incentivized, emotionally, to agree. Thus ends their critical analysis. Later, even *years* later, when someone like you or me bring up that same objection or contradiction, they reach back into their memory banks and say to themselves, *I've already dealt with this*. It doesn't matter what denomination or even what religion is in question, either. The overwhelming majority of people will remain, for life, at least at some level, within the confines of the religious perspective of their upbringing. They may vary, at different points in their lives, in their outward observance of the tradition, but they will rarely stray that far from the nest of origin of their core beliefs. There will always be some emotional attachment to it, unless all emotions associated with it become negative.

Many people, consequently, who do leave their religious tradition behind tend to portray it in hindsight as abusive, controlling and something which they felt they needed to "escape". It's not enough for most to simply change their minds or walk away because the beliefs no longer resonate with them. The guilt associated with betraying their parents and their peers requires something more substantive. It's one reason why there are so many "angry atheists". *Why are they angry?* If they've freed themselves so successfully from the confines of religion, they should be relaxed and happy. But many aren't. They appear miserable. Just as miserable, it turns out, as they were when they were part of the religion that they blame for their current mental problems. This is because, in many cases, their misery is self-inflicted. And in other cases, they have no sense of satisfactory closure from the experience. The pain of broken relationships and mistreatment at the hands of religious leaders is associated directly with the religion that those relationships were framed within. Also, they have often not replaced their former religious belief system with another system of belief that provides practical moral guidance. They are adrift, mentally, and sometimes morally. The devotional energy once placed into that system they formerly belonged to is now dedicated to destroying it, and this creates a lot of *negative* energy, which no one needs. Many of these former religionists spend an unbalanced amount of time obsessing over religious ideas and religious origins, at a time when they probably should just move on with their lives and focus on more constructive, useful processes. Those who have found a workable value system that allows them to live at peace with the greatest variety of people seem the happiest and most well-adjusted of those who have left their former beliefs. Conversely, people that stay in a religious tradition happily without issue, and who refuse to entertain criticisms of their beliefs, are not always unintelligent or unthinking. They often just care more about other things and spend their mental energies on other problems. It doesn't make their religious beliefs *right*. They are just unconcerned about such questions. It doesn't cross their minds. Their religious life is not, in their view, a problem that they feel needs fixing. In most cases, it's the opposite. They feel it is the one area of stability which gives meaning and purpose to the struggle they experience everywhere else. Even more reason, therefore, that they are loathe to listen to people like me criticize it.

As for me, I was overly dependent upon my father's opinion of me for my sense of self-worth at this stage of my life, and my father, for his part, was partially blind to our needs for emotional stability because he was pressing hard to achieve Diamond, and he was counting on me towards that objective. He also viewed our longing for religious activity as impractical when we had financial needs that were urgent. He wasn't against our religious convictions, just confused by our desire to put aside something that could set us up financially in favor of having coffee and doughnuts with a bunch of average, unmotivated people who were not trying to accomplish anything. In fairness to my dad, this not only signified our personality differences, but also represented the mentality that was fostered in the business. The "outside" world (the people outside the business) consisted mainly of slow-moving, slow-brained, slack-jawed cows, content to go back and forth to their go-nowhere jobs and accomplish nothing and to be told what to do the rest of their lives. Only a *loser* would be satisfied with that. Such was the narrative from the leadership.

But there was another, more insidious problem. My understanding of the evangelical message presented in the New Testament, combined with my personal insecurities and maladjustments, along with my training in the Amway business, had made me a perfect candidate to become a religious extremist. I found myself overwhelmed with a desire to discover my *destiny*; my *calling*. Adding to this, most of the Christians I knew at that time were also fellow Amway distributors. They were typically just as invested in the Amway lifestyle, and ingesting the same diet of "prosperity teachers", who taught us that Jesus wanted us to be rich. These people were not unlike me: they were *mission oriented*.

The goal in evangelical Christianity was always the same; advance the kingdom of God, which meant *preach the gospel, save the lost and take territory from the "enemy"*. All else in life was secondary and even mundane to a committed evangelical. In the world of multi-level marketnig, this mentality went into hyper-drive. We must, like Jesus, set our eyes like flint upon Jerusalem, ignore the pain and inconvenience, the poverty, the heartbreak, and count it all as joy. This is the *call*, and your job is to figure out where in the army of Jesus you were supposed to be. But make no mistake, you were supposed to be *somewhere*, and once you figured out *where* and put yourself *there*, you'd be fulfilled. In many evangelical settings, in fact, you would never succeed in getting anyone to truly embrace your goals or visions for your life unless you could convince them that *the Lord had shown you something in the Word*, or that you felt it was your *calling*. It was, for all intents, the linguistic parlance of the committed Christian life. In Amway, this same idea was present, but it scaled to match the size of your network. The bigger the network, the bigger your calling must be. Those with the biggest networks were clearly the favored servants of the Most High.

My wife and I were being skewered on life's proverbial fire pit as a result of this dysfunctional mindset but escaping it would simply mean leaping out of the frying pan and into the fire, unless our *mindset* changed. I didn't yet realize that my mindset was a problem.

Chapter 8

~

MISSION SHIFT

WHEN MY FATHER informed me that things were beginning to go south between him and Major Domo Guru, and that he was exploring other income opportunities, I knew that it was over for our family in the Amway business. The longtime dream of success, family wealth and financial independence, which we had always clung to during all those years of leanness and struggle, and which had guided our life decisions since getting married, was suddenly evaporating. The promise of care-free retirement which formed the vision behind our struggle had been the only thing glossing over our serious marriage issues. We were now approaching thirty years old. Our twenties were almost history, nearly a decade gone. We had not spent it solidifying our relationship, enjoying meaningful time together, or building a foundation for future happiness. Instead, we had spent the time trying desperately to succeed at a gimmicky direct sales business that no one wanted to admit being in. I could have gone to night school and earned my master's degree with the time and money I had wasted chasing an impossible dream in multi-level marketing. Now, with our Amway venture over with, I faced bleak prospects. Rather than sending my resume to colleges or high schools inquiring upon teaching positions, as I would have been doing as a graduate of a University English program, I was checking the newspaper for material handler and shipper/receiver jobs. By this time, we had three children, and full-time college was completely out of the question. "Online learning" had not yet become a well-known thing. We were caught in a malaise, feeling dislocated but not knowing what to do about it. To add to the stress, my oldest had recently developed symptoms of Tourette's Syndrome. They were severe. We didn't know if he would be destined to live with us as a dependent the rest of his life.

Leaving the Amway network was also the most emotionally draining thing we had experienced to date. It felt like divorce. The decision to admit defeat and walk away was also a decision to step directly into a friendless existence and the nagging feeling that we had betrayed lots of people. Our life had been nothing but Amway for years. We had essentially no life outside of it. We lost communication with most of the people we had been associated with. But there was a silver lining.

Unexpectedly, we received a call from my mother-in-law. They were moving to Florida and wanted to know if we were interested in buying their house. Not at market value, mind you, which we could never afford, but for just a percentage of it. The house was worth close to $150,000. Of course, we enthusiastically said yes. It turns out they had already asked the rest of the older siblings, who had all said no. We were the last they would approach before hiring an agent. For us, it was a new lease on life.

We moved from Rhode Island to North-Central Massachusetts, into Chana's childhood home. I changed careers, leaving Amway and entering a trade, printing, and began learning how to succeed in that. I progressed rapidly, becoming a lead pressman in a large commercial shop in less than five years. Our fourth child, Jane, was born on September 7, 2001, four days before the World Trade Center attack. We did not have television at the time, nor did we have Internet, and

Smartphones had not yet been invented. I remember holding Jane in my arms and rocking her as I paced back and forth in the downstairs hall while listening to the AM mega-station, WBZ-Boston, relay the events in New York City via the radio broadcast, without the aid of pictures or video. I thought, at the time, that we were being hoaxed. It sounded like Orson Wells' War of the Worlds. Later that day, I arrived for my shift at the print shop. My supervisor, upon hearing my doubts about the whole thing, brought me into the customer lounge and turned on the television, so I could see for myself. Every channel had the coverage. The imagery of the passenger airlines striking the World Trade Center was surreal. I saw people jumping from the building to their deaths as the structure burned. I could not believe what I was seeing. It was another shock I would experience in the long run of shocks to my system which cumulatively resulted in me questioning everything I thought I knew about reality.

I tried to focus on my work. The World Trade Center had melted and crashed to the ground. Hundreds of innocent lives lost. There were more deaths on the plane that crashed in a field in Pennsylvania, and again at the Pentagon. My Tupperware bowl of spaghetti and meatballs hissed and spit in the microwave, popping the lid from the heat. When I took it out, I struggled to eat it, since it reminded me of twisted metal and blood at the base of the Towers. What did all this mean? Did these lives matter? What was I doing with my life? I sincerely wondered.

After leaving the Amway business and moving north into my mother-in-law's family home, we wanted the opposite of virtually everything we had experienced over the previous decade. Stable employment, a stable family life and a stable religious community were all attractive to us. Leaving the quick pace of business suits and prosperity preaching, we desired something slower and steady. We found a church about five minutes away, which was Fundamentalist Baptist. The pastor was a kindly middle-aged man who had been raised in the home of an alcoholic father and had committed his life to the ministry at a young age. His wife was a soft-spoken woman who also gave piano lessons.

THERE'S NO SUCH THING AS MAGIC BLOOD

Sunday morning consisted of a Bible study before service, at nine, and all the deeply committed members showed up for that. Following this, the less-committed, more casual members and visitors would trot in for the actual service. After we all sang several songs out of the hymnal, a solo by a distinguished vocalist who had been approved by the leadership would perform his or her magic. You were not to clap after this, but merely say "amen" if you liked it. This would precede a lengthy sermon, which would be "expositional" in style, meaning verse by verse through a book of the New Testament. There was always an altar-call, to save the lost who may be in attendance. You were expected to bow your head respectfully and pray during this time, so that the holy spirit could "convict" the sinner to "repent". The altar-call would be accompanied by a slow, emotionally driven ballad to lure the reluctant from their seats. After all, I had been taught, this was, and always would be, the most important function of the church; *to save the lost.* Chana tied in with several families who homeschooled their children and pulled Jonathan and April out of public school as a result.

My first printing job (prior to the one I was at when 9/11 happened) was also down the road from our house, at an industrial packaging company called Boutwell-Owens. I became the helper for a good pressman working on a beat-up old Mitsubishi six-color sheetfed press which ran paperboard. I liked the job the lead pressman had. He taught me that printing was like sailing a boat on water; it required constant, astute management and oversight. It was an art, and it also paid well, as he earned over twenty-three dollars an hour, which was decent money for a tradesman in the early-to-mid 1990's. For someone making nine dollars an hour, as I was, I was incentivized to learn.

"I want to be a pressman like you if I'm going to work in this trade." I said to him one night, while he leaned over the console staring through his magnifying "loop" to study the registration of the images on the printed sheet. He shot me an incredulous expression, and then smiled. He liked me and had told me so. He was a few years older than me, divorced, with two children. He was balding, fat and his tank top always bunched up at his belly, exposing it and the sweat which glistened on his stomach. He wore greasy, ink-covered basketball sneakers, loosely tied, with shiny basketball shorts. A large, hulking man, when he sat between the printing units to hang the plates, he looked like a giant laundry bag that gets stuffed into the back seat of a small car. I often wondered how he managed to get up again. He probably did, too.

"People go to trade school to learn this, you know. You're starting kinda late. But you're a smart guy, and probably could do it. But why would you want to hang around with a bunch of divorced alcoholics like us?"

"Because if I must work for someone else," I told him, "I want a job that pays well and that I can be proud of. Plus," I added mischievously, "I like the smell of the chemicals." He guffawed. He had a booming and commanding voice, and he immediately turned to the crew on the machine next to us and belted out,

"Hear that, boys? Preacher-man here likes the smell of the chemicals!" They all laughed. Two and a half years later, I was a lead pressman on the flagship press of the largest commercial print shop in Central Massachusetts and was doing well. How I pulled this off is hard to fathom, but it happened.

Before I left Boutwell-Owens, I wound up inviting him to church. His name was Chris. He came, along with his seventeen-year-old daughter, who showed up to our suit-and-dress-wearing, fundamentalist church sporting a tube-top with no bra and tight shorts. She looked like a pin-up model from a muscle car calendar. (When they came to our house for burgers and hot dogs after the church service, she stood behind Chana staring at me while thrusting a Rocket Pop in and out of her mouth suggestively and flicking the end of it with her tongue. She had an issue.) Chana started grilling Chris about my career choice to pursue printing.

"You guys have the world by the balls, Chana," he said, "You don't have money right now, but so what? You have this great house, a great family, and your husband is the smartest guy I've ever been around. If he wants to be a pressman, let him. He'll be a good one. I envy you guys. My life is a fucking mess. If I can help him, I will. I don't fit in at your church, though."

This was true. The church body didn't warm to him at all, or his daughter. No one tried to slow his hasty exit after service, particularly the women, who caught their husbands repeatedly stealing glances at Chris's daughter. This was a discouraging event for me and marked the beginning of the end of my involvement with the Fundamentalist Baptist movement, looking back on it.

I was deeply troubled by how the church had reacted to Chris's visit. Supposedly, the Baptists were all about getting people saved. It was the exalted idea of *the wretched lost coming to Jesus*. In this light, it was unconscionable to me that a truly "lost" family would venture into the matrix of this church's prefabricated gospel presentation and find themselves unwelcome. Yet, that's exactly what happened. *What did this mean?* I had done my part. This was the new "mission", as I understood it. The new "Amway", only for Jesus. I would witness to people through my positive testimony and life choices, develop relationships, and at the right moment, invite them to church to hear the "plan" of salvation. The idea was to get the sinner in an environment in which the majority around him or her were believers and this would create a better chance for the holy spirit to "convict" their hearts. This is how the Baptists conceived of the role of the holy spirit, as they didn't believe in the "sign gifts" pursued by the charismatics and considered such expressions "satanic".

It all sounded so amazing but was not so impressive in real life. I had done the work in the "field" to get him to church, but then it all broke down. It seemed, after all, that "saving the lost" was far less important to these folks than maintaining the façade of social order within the community culture. When push came to shove, being "Baptist" was a bit more important to them than being "Christian".

The church may have believed that Chris needed the gospel, they just didn't want or need Chris, and probably hoped he'd get saved quietly at home and then go to a different church afterwards. And he felt it, for sure. It merely reinforced his already low self-concept, and so he took it in stride. Further, and probably more to the root of the issue, the ladies in the church most definitely did not want his slutty daughter to be regularly exposed to their sexually repressed husbands or their horny teenage sons. They didn't take the time to discover that the girl's mother left her and her dad when she was two years old, never to return, or that her father worked nights to provide a life for them and slept most of the day, leaving her largely neglected. That was not relevant to them. Her presence and her presentation were an affront to what they stood for, so the gospel would have to be put aside for the sake of prudence. Chris had come to church, probably because he liked and trusted me, ignoring his natural reservations, but I was the one left most embarrassed by the experience. I would not be able to revisit the spiritual conversation with Chris again, and when I changed jobs to take a better opportunity, I lost contact with him. I also did not invite people to church anymore.

What the church said they were about (spreading the gospel) did not appear to be what they were truly about. In fact, I am not sure that *they* knew what they were about, but they talked a lot about preserving things. It would take a little more time for me to figure out what they were trying to preserve.

Chapter 9

———— ∾∾ ————

A Christian Caste System

THE HOME SCHOOL group at the fundamentalist church worked wonderfully for Chana and the kids. They had togetherness and unity and generally, even peace. I should have just stopped going to church altogether after the incident with my friend Chris, because I was already dissenting from the groupthink, and was surely bound to disrupt this idyllic arrangement, one which we would never duplicate once I successfully dragged them all out of there because of my incessant and divisive search for truth. I was asking questions that Chana simply was not concerned with. If I had stopped attending the church, I would have been viewed as a "backslider" by the congregants, but Chana would have been happy to live in Fundamentalist-land without me around, and the children would have thrived, for the most part. Her and I have always been far apart in this area. She does not seek to get to the bottom of things, like I do. She wants happy children, simple answers to life and brownies in the oven. I, on the other hand, would rather burn down the world than live a lie. My passion for "truth" provides me with keen insights, but is also rather self-destructive. I am at times reckless in my penchant to air my views without respect to how it will affect my social standing, particularly in religious communities. I am not always, I must admit, reasonable. I learned the hard way that I was in the minority on this issue of challenging the status quo, regardless of the issue at hand, but particularly concerning issues as emotionally sensitive as people's religious beliefs. Most people are more than willing, eager even, to participate in the practice of social and religious rituals for the mere psychological reward of a sense of belonging, even at the possible expense of any real meaning behind them. This is true of people in all social environments, and certainly their religious practices are not an exception to this rule. I had found it just as grating in the business world, as I now did in the religious one. I needed space from this. Time to think and decide how I felt about this dynamic. I wanted to get off the treadmill of social expectations, climb a tall hill, and sit and reflect. I needed perspective.

A couple of years before we quit Amway, I had bought a pair of hiking boots; the expensive variety made of one-piece Italian leather, hand-sewn last and steel shank, the kind favored by serious mountain trekkers. I was proud of them and showed them off to my dad, who scoffed at me and told me I was wasting both my money and my time. He was wrong. From my late twenties until my late forties, the mountains were my second home, and they became the fiber in my emotional and psychological diet which kept me "regular". I spent as much time as I could in them, which wasn't nearly enough. All in all, the mountains provided healing in an important way. I climbed nearly all the major peaks in the northeast, some of which I climbed from every point of the compass. I also got heavily involved as a volunteer trail worker and maintainer for the Appalachian Mountain Club, which stewarded an extensive network of trails in the White Mountains. Spending an entire day working in the soil, digging rocks out of the terrain and building a staircase or drainage structure was pure joy for me. The fatigue it created was glorious and, I felt, godly. Getting stuck in a torrential downpour while in the woods of New Hampshire, with a pick mattock in my hands, covered in mud, was perhaps the most spiritual experience I ever had.

While a member of the fundamentalist church, I led hikes for the youth. On one trip which I led, along with the youth pastor and his intrepid younger brother, I experienced something curious that stuck with me and affected me deeply.

After a successful climb of one of New Hampshire's majestic alpine summits, I was driving the church bus full of tired, cramping hikers on the highway back to the church in Massachusetts. It was a two-and-a-half-hour drive, and I needed to stop so people could use the restroom. I also needed a coffee. In New Hampshire, the liquor stores are all owned and operated by the state, and there are state liquor outlets at the Interstate rest areas. I thought nothing of this, since these rest areas were equipped with separate outbuildings which housed both the rest rooms and the vending machines, respectively. Yet, when I veered into the lane for the rest area, the youth pastor stiffened in his seat and his eyes grew wide.

"What are you doing?" he asked, urgently.

"Taking a bathroom break," I offered, casually, "so that people can use the bathroom."

"There's a liquor store there," he said. I swallowed as I attempted to digest his comment.

"Yeah, there is." I turned my head to look at him. "Is that a problem?"

"Well, yes, in fact. Our church's name is on the side of this van. I don't want our people, or this van, near a liquor store." To his increasing anxiety, I pulled in near the front of the liquor store entrance, directly facing the rest room building. I turned in my seat and told everyone what we were doing and for no one to wander off. No one was to go near the liquor store, I emphasized.

"Relax, dude. The youth group is not here to buy vodka. They just need to go to the bathroom." I shut the driver door and headed to the vending machines.

There was a cold silence between us the rest of the ride home. Eventually, I interrupted it.

"You're awfully quiet over there."

"I get quiet when I'm challenged."

"You talking about the rest stop? I didn't challenge you, you challenged me." I was ready for an argument. He contemplated his response for some time before responding.

"I was challenged by the hike," he said, surprisingly, "I apologize." And with that, the incident was over.

Generally, we got along well, he and I. I really was quite fond of him, as I was of most of the people at that church. They were generally good, decent people. But there were elements of the Fundamentalist Baptist culture and approach that were offensive to me.

On one occasion, I was approached about taking over the leadership of the church softball team. This surprised me, as I had just had a conversation with another member, Tony, about playing on the team for him. He had been running it for years.

"Did Tony back out?" I asked, innocently.

Tony was a middle-aged man with a large family, including his oldest, an 18-year-old attractive and precocious young woman who was feeling her oats a little bit. I had connected a bit with Tony's oldest boy, a quiet, athletically gifted young man, and even took him on some aggressive hiking trips. Tony and his family were a significant presence in both the youth group and the church itself. They lived in the woods off a dirt country road about a half hour out of town, and they didn't appear well-heeled.

The week before the youth pastor asked me about the softball team, I had been invited over Tony's house on Saturday to hang out and watch football with him. I sat on his tattered, stained sofa, with my feet resting on the threadbare carpet, through which you could see the subfloor in a few spots where it had completely worn away. I used the home's one bathroom which was missing paneling on one wall, had no curtain or shade in the window and boasted a box of ceramic tiles in the corner staged for the flooring installation which he would do himself, without help. I had to step over his tool bag to reach the sink so I could wash my hands. As we sat together watching the game, I noticed his hands which were stained with the grease and grime that the soap had not removed. I asked him if he had been working on his car. He told me he had spent the bulk of the morning at our youth pastor's house, kneeling in the gravel driveway replacing the front brakes on the pastor's minivan.

"Side job?"

"Nah," he shook me off while readjusting in his seat, "I can't charge the pastor!" He smiled wryly. "He paid for the parts", he added. I thought about this a while and pressed further.

"So, he offered to pay but you refused?" I asked. He shot me a curious glance before turning back to the game. Suddenly, he hopped up from his seat and pointed at me.

"You want a beer?" He asked.

"Sure," I said. I did not share the Fundamentalist aversion to alcohol, and he seemed relieved when I said yes. He returned with two cans of Budweiser, pressed one into my hand, and said to me as he cracked open the can and plopped back into his seat,

"He didn't offer. I'm happy to do it, though. It's my service to God."

The youth pastor, after having spent a minute deciding how to respond to my question about whether Tony had backed out, finally looked up at me again and explained that Tony was compromised in terms of his testimony and he wasn't comfortable having him represent the church in a public capacity.

Apparently, Tony wasn't spiritual enough to lead the church softball team, but he was more than spiritually qualified to fix the pastor's brakes on his minivan. For free. This elitist mentality among those in hardcore pursuit of the fundamentalist viewpoint could be discerned in other, more overt ways, also. Once, during a Sunday morning Bible study hour led by a congregant, a question was asked about the doctrinal stance of a certain charismatic church down the road from us. The answer was telling.

"I wouldn't know, because I would never darken the doors of their church entrance."

In other words, what those people at that other church thought about doctrine wasn't relevant, because to him, and to so many others within the Fundamentalist movement, those people weren't even *real* Christians. They held only a slightly higher status, in their minds, than Catholics, who were not even considered *saved* at all.

As I was seeking to find my place within the Jewish community, many years later, I was reminded of these exchanges I had while a member of the Fundamentalist Baptist church. Once, I was talking to an Orthodox rabbi about joining his community, and he told me that I should probably go to the Conservative shul down the road, since "they weren't even really Jews, and neither was I if I converted through their movement." He didn't accept my conversion to be valid, you see. So, to the Orthodox rabbi, even though I had official paperwork declaring me to be Jewish and a citizen of Israel, having gone before a legal Beit Din in the process, I was a non-Jew still. My rabbi today (the rabbi of the Conservative shul in question) just laughed when I told him this. He had heard it all before. Elitism and tribalism is not a problem unique to the Christian world, by any means.

Many people I know currently look smugly down their nose at non-Orthodox Jews in exactly this way, however I'm entirely unimpressed by this approach, or by people who cling to such attitudes. Telling other Jews that they "weren't really Jews" was not different than the Fundamentalist Bible study leader telling the questioner that *I don't care what they think. I would never darken the doors of their church.* How was it different? It was the same. It was a group of people circling the proverbial wagons around their pet issues and making others feel that they didn't measure up to the standards being set for them by the elites. It was base, servile and childish. Yet, it was extremely commonplace, and often created great pain for a lot of people, as they were shunned and marginalized from this or that community.

There is an aspect to all this that is important to understand. It is entirely possible for multiple, seemingly contradictory realities to coexist at once. These internal issues which I am pointing out were things which I observed by paying attention and analyzing them, but which were not commonly recognized or acknowledged by the members of the church (or synagogue, as it were), most of whom were genuine, morally upright folks. This was doubly true of the pastors I met and their families. Most of them led clean, restrained lives, tried to raise their children to embrace the same values, volunteered their time to worthwhile causes and worked with intention of doing good in the world. Moreover, and this is quite significant, these families in the Fundamentalist movement, more than any other group I have ever met in religious circles, other than Ultra-Orthodox Jews, had children who were committed to the faith, even after the arrival of adulthood. It does seem as though isolationism and a general policy of segregation from outside groups is a sound method to ensure that one's children will carry on the faith of the parents, and yet, I am not convinced it is a proper approach, regardless. The goal is not worth the method to get there. Nevertheless, despite claims to the contrary by people who have left fundamentalist forms of Christianity or Judaism, it's simply not true that these people are being *psychologically abused*, in most cases. In fact, most of the people at the Fundamentalist Baptist church were happy and are still happy today, and still actively part of fundamentalist Christianity. They aren't complaining. But there's no question that it's an approach that doesn't allow much room for individual expressions of spirituality. Fundamentalism, both in Christianity and Judaism, generally thrives on rigidity and order, and the core of the people who make up these expressions of faith are pleased as punch to remain a part of them. They aren't looking to escape. But this approach clearly doesn't work for everyone, and for some people, it's a nightmare that they can't wait to wake up from. But the folks who find these environments oppressive are most definitely not the majority, which is baffling to those who do fall into that category. They ask themselves, as I did,

Doesn't anyone see what I see?

How could these people be so oblivious to such real issues of on-the-ground prejudice and hypocrisy? I think the answer is largely sociological. Many of them had been raised in this environment, and therefore what seemed an affront to me was business as usual for them. Like the question I posed earlier about questioning one's convictions, their religious environment never occurred to them as a problem that needed fixing. To me, however, who was not raised in that setting, it was unnerving.

I look back on my time in that community and my memories are generally pleasant. I was not a theologian at that point in my journey. I had not analyzed critical scholarship on the New Testament or the claims of other faiths. I just had a gut feeling about things and I let my intuitive sense guide my thinking, which informed me that I didn't, and would never, fit in with these people. It would be okay for a time, but then, it would start to unravel as I continued asking questions and I would be rejected and cast aside. I saw this as inevitable, so I began looking for alternatives. Chana gave me her blessing to do so. She was also convinced that there were some potentially insurmountable issues with the Fundamentalist perspective, but she was not certain it was worth uprooting the family for them. At least not yet. I wanted to see reform. I wanted open dialog within the congregation. This would never happen, of course. I was naïve to think it ever would have.

The Fundamentalists were intentionally creating a "bubble" for their families and did not want it disturbed. This came at a price to both their religious convictions as well as their stated ethics, but they decided, apparently, that preserving their manufactured culture mattered more to them than other extenuating issues. The type of inconsistencies and problems their approach created were left unattended to. They seemed content to leave them to the apologists of the movement to address. A huge mistake, I would contend. The same could easily be said of my later experience with the Ultra-Orthodox Jews, although there were decidedly different reasons in that case. Yet and still, the results were the same. *Fit in or leave.*

From a larger vantage point, it's clear that there are many folks who seem more comfortable in a more rigid, boxy expression of religious faith than a more open, even experimental one, as I've mentioned. This is most interesting to me, and something I've reflected on quite a bit in recent years. Protestant Christians generally have a tortured and dissonant relationship with the concepts of tradition and ritual. They certainly embrace "sameness", but not "ritual", per se. This internal conflict is built into the doctrinal framework of their understanding of the gospel. A foundational tenet of Pauline Christianity is "faith without works", and this will lead, logically, to the denigration of cultic ritual as having no real or eternal value. However, ironically, many Christians cherish their traditions, even though at their deepest moments of reflection, they must acknowledge that these elements, such as the celebration of Christmas and putting up a Christmas tree, add no actual theological value to their faith. So, why have them? This is the crux of the issue I was wrestling with concerning the Fundamentalist approach. Why segregate from other Christians? If other Christians, outside of Fundamentalism, had Jesus in their heart, what more did they need? What more did I need? *What more, for that matter, did anyone need?*

What I had learned from the Fundamentalists was that they believed in the work of the holy spirit, but they chose to define such activity in very starched and narrow terms, relegating the idea to pre-ordained doctrinal positions which amounted to *this is how God works, and not like that.* It seemed to me that the stiffness of their approach was a death-knell to their stated mission, which was supposedly to spread the gospel and save the lost. In truth, as stated earlier, this was obviously not their real goal. They were not evangelists, but *preservationists.* The true emphasis of Fundamentalism was to preserve

American conservative values and 19th-century cultural norms against the rapidly encroaching influence of secularism, socialism, textual criticism, cultural relativism, progressive liberalism and what they termed the New Evangelicalism. Interestingly, in this way, the Fundamentalists shared much common ground with Jewish Orthodoxy since the period of the Enlightenment, who were also, in many ways, zealous *preservationists*, above all other considerations. This is one reason that Artscroll, one of the prominent Jewish publishers of classical Jewish sources in English, censors its content to reflect a more uniform portrayal of the tradition, one which better reflects the editors' biases, rather than the variegated reality which the rich history of Jewish thought represents. Ironically, the term "Orthodox" was invented by the Reformers, not by the Orthodox. Before the rise of the Reform Movement, an "observant" Jew was simply "Jewish".

A mantra you frequently heard in the church was "avoiding the appearance of evil". In this case, "evil" included any activity they viewed as culturally offensive, from mixed-race dating to rock concerts to tattoos. Again, I found common ground with the Orthodox in their approach to such issues once I analyzed it, though within the Jewish world it was expressed differently and through the context of *minhagim,* or traditions of the community. Generally, this was the way to read the room. You were not usually far off if you assumed that everyone was, for lack of a better idiom, *keeping up appearances* as the first order of priority. There is pressure to maintain the standard, and it comes from one's peers. To deny this is to deny reality. It's no different than being on a championship sports team or a crack military squad. You must try to keep up, or you'll be on the outside looking in very quickly.

Fundamentalist Baptists also viewed the emerging popularity and growing influence of rock-band-style worship within evangelicalism in America as a movement that shook proverbial hands with *apostasy.* I simply wasn't convinced that the Fundamentalists had a firm grasp upon what apostasy truly consisted of. Nor did I like the elitism of the worldview. It was as if they were creating a sort of Christian caste system. They had chosen as their primary focus of contention the *outer expression* of many Christian denominations and styles, such as music, and the involvement by their members in the greater culture at large, none of which are core to the theology of the Christian confession of faith, but which meant a great deal to *them*. I grew tired of it all and found it both irritating and needless.

As my printing career progressed successfully, I was hired to be a 2nd Pressman on the flagship press of a large commercial printer in the next town. The man I was hired to replace was middle-aged, slight of stature and slow-moving, hence why they were trying to replace him. He was known as Pastor Dan. Working with him one day cleaning up the press, he told me he used to be a Fundamentalist Baptist like myself, a pastor, but had left the denomination for greener pastures and was reportedly quite happy. He invited me to attend the Friday morning men's Bible study with him at 7am at his new church. I agreed to check it out.

When I walked in with him the following week after our night shift, I experienced a shock: Rather than the three or four men I expected to find sitting in cushioned chairs in a small room with Bibles in their laps, the main fellowship hall had several plastic tables pushed together and no less than twenty-five men jammed around them sitting in uncomfortable metal folding chairs. I could not believe that there were this many men who would show up for a mid-week Bible study at 7am. The enthusiasm was something I had not experienced to that point in any environment which wasn't Amway-related. I was intrigued, and so began the next phase of my journey.

Chapter 10

———— ❧ ————

THE MUSIC NEVER STOPPED

I BEGAN ATTENDING the new church by myself. We had agreed that we would not make a switch unless we were *sure*, since we had spent years building relationships in our current environment.   I carefully read the new church's promotional material and checked out their doctrinal statement of faith. I didn't want to go *too* far on a limb, after all. It all seemed fine, however, at least based on my level of understanding at the time. They were a part of the Calvary Chapel movement, which had begun in Southern California in the 1970's and had achieved fame under its founder, Pastor Chuck Smith, for pioneering the "Jesus Movement" among the hippies of the counter-culture crowd, and also for beginning the musical phenomenon known today as "CCM" or Contemporary Christian Music, which is a recognized commercial market segment of the music industry. It all started at Calvary Chapel in Costa Mesa, CA. Calvary Chapels across the United States start their services with a rather long period of "worship", which for them (and many evangelicals today) means a concert. After anywhere from twenty minutes to an hour of this (it depended upon the church), the pastor would finally get up to deliver his message. This format has subsequently been adopted by most of today's modern evangelical churches. Calvary Chapel believes in expository preaching, which means going verse by verse through a book of the Bible until it was completed. Then, they would start the next book on the list. I liked this approach, which was also consistent with how the Fundamentalist Baptists approached the text. This contrasted with what many churches did, which was to offer topical sermons based on subjects of interest. Calvary Chapel also was known for the casual dress "come as you are" approach to church, and in fact they seem to have popularized it. Very few of their pastors wore the traditional suit and tie as they preached before the congregation, but preferred polo shirts and Dockers, or even shorts and Hawaiian shirts. Today, this is commonplace in many evangelical churches, but Calvary Chapel pioneered the fashion trend. They are on the charismatic spectrum, as they believe in the active presence and exercise of the "spiritual sign gifts", but they have strict rules about how they were to be used, particularly in public settings. And they are "seeker friendly", which was another distinction from the Fundamentalist Baptists.

When Chana finally came to a service with me, she enjoyed the experience. She especially liked the music, which got her moving and swaying and made her happy. She just thought it went on too long, but despite this objection, she preferred it over the staid and restrained choir singing of the Baptist church.

There was also a difference in philosophy at Calvary Chapel concerning the place and purpose of the music as compared with the Fundamentalists. At the Baptist church, the music and singing were an act of obedience to the scriptural mandate to praise God. In contrast, while Calvary Chapel would not dispute this mandate, that was not their chief motivation within it. Rather, they viewed the worship segment of the service as a sort of *marination* of the congregation, preparing their hearts and minds to *receive the word*, as was explained often. It was a type of *sensual foreplay of the mind* and, in their estimation, the *spirit* of the person. The goal was to get them moving about, and to stir them up *emotionally*. The Fundamentalists expressly sought to avoid appeals to the emotions, but the Calvary Chapel folks viewed such call and response to emotional stimulus as literally essential to the experience they were foisting upon the congregation. A worship leader who didn't succeed in getting people on their feet and clapping, putting their hands in the air, and moving all about, at least for a good part of the time, was not going to be a worship leader for very long in the Calvary Chapel movement.

Another interesting feature of Calvary Chapel was the vast network of Christian radio stations that the organization owned and operated. This platform spread the "good news" of Christian pop and rock music while also transforming certain Calvary Chapel pastors and worship leaders into celebrities. Additionally, many worship leaders ended up with major record label recording contracts leveraged from their popularity and from the songs they would write which would find themselves in regular rotation in evangelical worship services. So important was the music to this movement that an offshoot of Calvary Chapel, called Vineyard, developed, which had a heavy emphasis on music and less as much on teaching. As I volunteered at the church during the building project, the church's radio station would be playing nonstop in the background. Everyone had their favorite teachers and often an accompanying collection of their teachings at home on cassette tape, and the array of CCM artists were on full display.

This celebrity culture was evident when it came time to go to spiritual conferences and retreats, as the success of the event was often predicated upon what "big name" Calvary preacher would be brought in for the occasion. In addition to creating a celebrity vibe, the radio station was also the biggest driver of Calvary Chapel "mystique". People would routinely show up on Sunday mornings after listening to the church service being broadcast on the radio, or to the music and teachings being promoted during other time slots. All of this was quite familiar to us, as we experienced this same phenomenon in the Amway business; this celebrity status of the resident heroes of the movement being promoted through the distribution of mass-media.

The worship leader at this church, hand selected and brought in for that role by the pastor, had a real Grateful Dead feel about him, and I loved him instantly. Someone in the congregation had overheard me one morning as I sang along to the band and had complimented my voice and encouraged me to speak to the worship leader about joining the team. I thought that might be fun, so I did.

"You sing?!" He exclaimed, as if he had just won $200 on a scratch ticket. "Man, we need you! Could you come practice with us? I'll introduce you to the team."

"Sure," I said. *That was easy*, I thought to myself. This simple and otherwise innocuous exchange spun off into an FBI-level, paranoia-inducing bad dream which would unfortunately serve as a warning and a precursor of many similar incidents, which collectively drove us out of the movement years later. But at this point, I was loving my involvement with them, and so was my wife. While she missed her home-school group, she was optimistic that another would materialize, and all would be well. That never happened either, it should be noted.

I practiced with the team for a long while, long past the time when it would be considered reasonable, and yet I still wasn't performing with the team during the services. So, I decided to address it and find out what was going on. The worship leader responded to my question after practicing that week with a pained expression and danced on his feet trying to explain the situation to me.

"Everyone is excited about having you on the team, Dave. But sometimes these things require patience. It's out of my hands." He said, gesturing with his open palms to reinforce his statement. I was confused.

"What's out of your hands?" I asked, honestly.

"I love your heart in all this, Dave. That's why I'm advocating for you," he said. *Advocating?* I pressed him to clarify what he meant.

"When Richard asked me to be his worship leader, I told him I'd do it, but that I didn't want the responsibility of bringing people onto the team or taking them off. It had to be his call. So, it's his call. Not mine." I think he probably thought this would end the conversation, but unfortunately for him I had no clue what he was talking about. I had never experienced anything like this before.

"Pastor Rich has to approve of me joining you guys on stage? But *you're* the one that asked me to join. How long were you planning on leaving me in the dark about this?" He nodded again, with the same pained expression he displayed before. I could tell I was treading on shaky ground, and I was making him uncomfortable. But I didn't like what I was hearing. I had not had a single conversation with the pastor about any of this. This has always been a pet peeve of mine. I don't mind volunteering for things to be helpful, but I don't like being presumed upon, and I especially don't like being left in the dark about things which directly affected me, especially when I was volunteering my time. I knew nothing, at this early juncture, about the "Moses model" of leadership employed by Calvary Chapel. It was all extremely strange as I experienced it first-hand; this bizarre, CIA-like leadership structure. Every volunteer leader would be vetted, tested and challenged psychologically in a series of *poke tests* to determine, I was later told, whether a person was a "sheep" or a "wolf", designations which were defined arbitrarily and without your consent. I could not have known, at this early juncture, that I was, in fact, going through a very secretive type of audition. This would become my ongoing experience within Calvary Chapel, in ever-intensifying ways. I pressed my case further.

"Are you saying, then, that Pastor Rich has a *problem* with me? Or is there something else, something which I can personally control, which is preventing me from serving? Am I not a good fit with the team?" He shook his head at this and told me that it was complicated by the fact that I had asked to serve. I blinked hard. This was something beyond the realm of my comprehension.

"What do you mean, because I *asked to serve?*"

"In the sense that you pulled me aside and told me you could sing. *I* didn't approach *you*." He replied. I felt myself shaking my head with incredulity.

"You would never have known I was a singer if I hadn't told you."

"I know," he said, and shrugged. He continued, seeing my frustration. "Calvary Chapel teaches that the pastor is instructed by God as to who to raise up into ministry. He seems to not have any leading concerning *you*, yet. And when a person seems eager to step into a role, especially one that is public and in front of the congregation, it raises red flags. I'm being very frank with you, Dave. That's probably it."

"Red flags," I said aloud. I was at a loss for words, but I recovered fast. "Pardon me, but that's insane. Being eager to help is a *red flag*? What the heck is going on here? What is this?" At this, my friend's face took on an air of concern. He raised his hand as though to stop further comments.

"I hear you, Dave. I'll talk to him. I promise you I will. Okay?" I wasn't smiling. I was bewildered and feeling manipulated by this process. I wanted to tell him to forget it, but I hesitated, shifting my body position around, wanting to turn and leave but not wanting to hurt my relationship with my friend.

"I don't know," I said, finally, "Whatever. Fine." I tried to smile. He nodded, patted me on the shoulder and I went home.

In my van after the conversation, I felt regret at bringing it up at all. I regretted even offering to participate with the team to begin with. I just wanted to have friends. I wanted to help and show appreciation for the church and the ministry in a meaningful way that made me feel useful. I didn't want all this drama; it was giving me anxiety. After a few days passed, I was so distraught over the whole thing that I decided to resign from the team and pursue something else; some other way to serve. I just wanted the stress to be over so I could just enjoy going to church again without having to think about it anymore. But on Saturday night, the worship leader called me and told me I was on for both services the next morning. I hung up the phone, even more confused than before, but also hopeful that the "test" was over. Maybe it would be okay. Richard must not have an issue with me after all.

This emotional scenario would repeat itself many times in my years with Calvary Chapel. It was called, as I mentioned, the "poke test", and it was an actual management technique employed by Calvary Chapel pastors on a regular basis with their volunteers and was also something they taught their volunteer leaders to practice with those they were responsible to oversee. You can imagine the cluster of double-speak and compromised relationships that this created. Through it, they would manipulate and use people, whether intentionally or not, in much the same way that you would be mistreated and abused in corporate environments as people jockeyed for promotions behind your back, except in this church setting they could hide behind the guise of being "led by the holy spirit". Such a strategy could, of course, provide them with a form of immunity from accountability or, more importantly, liability. The "poke test", to be clear, was merely the slang term for a corporate policy of executive secrecy regarding how to handle volunteers and even staff members. You would get your ego challenged regularly, but they would not tell you they were doing it. It was covert. Neither would they tell you if you had passed or failed the test. You would simply be dropped from the project or ministry or position of oversight, or simply allowed to languish until you stepped down from serving of your own volition. Alternatively, if the evaluation was positive, you would be "raised up" (a term one would hear constantly in charismatic environments) and told that the "Lord had his hand on you". If you questioned or debated their decisions, as I was now doing, they would either take immediate action on the matter and give you what you asked for, or censor you, or counsel you to "seek the Lord", and that would essentially be the end of it, from their perspective. If you continued to press the issue, and particularly if you roped others into the situation and tried to build a case for yourself, you would be marked as a divisive person and slowly pushed away until you left the church altogether. It was mind-blowing to experience and humiliating to boot. I watched it happen to many people. And it happened to me. In fact, I got "poked" frequently, because I tended to be a pernicious pain in the ass. This was my first serious "poke", and I was not enjoying it. I felt it was disrespectful, particularly since I was a volunteer. It appears, based upon my later experiences, that they saw potential in me but weren't sure of my motivations. (This was something I learned after entering leadership myself.) I should also mention that this "poke test" procedure was only aggressive in its application when they were dealing with potential ministry partners and was particularly intense if you held aspirations of being a teacher or public spokesperson for the congregation. I fit both scenarios, as I had joined the worship team and had already spoken to the pastor about a pastoral internship. Having me teach Bible studies or even preach on a Sunday or Wednesday evening service was on the table at that point. So, I went through psychological hell. Apparently, I never handled it to their satisfaction either. People who had little talent or potential for growth never experienced this treatment at all and would struggle to accept that it even happens if you were to point it out to them.

My first experience singing with the worship team during the public services went extremely well, and I received many compliments for the two songs in which I sang lead. The next week, however, everything had changed for me. For months, practicing with the team, I had my own mike and was stationed on stage left along with the female vocalist. That was also how I was positioned during the service the first time I sang before the congregation. But the following Sunday, I would not have a mike, and would be standing behind the worship leader, out of view from most of the people, in the back of the stage next to the drum kit.

"I'm not going to be miked up? So, why am I even going to be up there? What's the point?" I asked over breakfast early the following Sunday.

"It's what Richard wants. Like I said, I don't make the rules." He replied, apologetically.

"This is insane. What is that supposed to accomplish? Without a mike!" I repeated this for emphasis, or maybe just so I could hear it out loud, as though the information was too outrageous to be believed.

"You don't have to do it, Dave," he offered, "But I hope you will. Just sing your heart out like you're the only one in the room." He smiled as he said this. I shook my head.

"What will happen to me if I refuse and just sit in the audience?" I asked. He shrugged.

"I dunno. You might be off the team. But that's not my call, like I said. It's up to you of course. I understand if you decide to say no. It won't hurt our relationship at all." I nodded, but also raised my hand up between us.

"I just want it known right now that as of this moment, Pastor Richard has not spoken to me about any of this. I'm trusting *you* here, that you're being honest with me and not deflecting responsibility." I didn't want to question him like this, but I had to be sure. He handled my challenge without offense and with compassion. As a result, for his sake, I agreed to swallow my discomfort and try. I hated every minute of it. I made it through the services without too much fuss. It was the blowback I received from people afterwards that got my goat. People kept asking me what was going on. Some laughed at how ridiculous it was. I felt insulted and humiliated. It was the first public humiliation I had experienced of that nature since the DJ at my first High School dance lampooned me on stage in front of the student body. This development was causing me to be distrustful of the pastor. It was a major wedge in my ability to enjoy the experience of being part of this church, and I was now beginning to wonder if I had made a mistake leading my family out of the Fundamentalist culture, where my wife had been so happy.

Chana advised me to quit the team as she could see it was eating me up. She felt the drama was stupid and couldn't understand why I was being put through it. But I didn't quit, because the worship leader asked me not to. So, you see, I was fully entwined in the web that these

Calvary Chapel leaders weave around people whom they want to test and evaluate. The off-center and tipsy feeling I was experiencing was something that they created with intention. I ended up being a regular member of the team and was on stage with them nearly every week, but I never quite got over the way I had been treated on the way to that status, nor did I ever lose the sense that I needed to keep a watchful eye behind me, just over my proverbial shoulder. I couldn't relax.

A while later, I was volunteering my time at the church. The pastor was working alongside me, and we were separated from the rest of the volunteers. As we spread sheetrock mud over tape lines, he began sharing with me a conversation he had with his mentor. He said he had been told that the church would never really grow until the worship team was solid as a rock. He said the worship team really drove the growth. I was more than a little surprised to hear this.

"I thought it was about the preaching," I protested, "I thought Pastor Chuck claimed that the church grew when he committed to teaching the Bible verse by verse."

He stopped working and turned to me. "Well, yes, in the beginning of the movement that was certainly true. But today, people expect a good worship experience, or they are less likely to come back, whether the teaching is good or not. The music is the key to the participation. Especially since we have the radio station…" he trailed off and resumed working. I just continued to stare at him, stunned. It was beginning to make sense to me now. There was a public narrative and a private one, and it involved radio and worship music as the central hub of how the organization became viable and grew to its current size, rather than the narrative that it grew simply because "God was blessing them". In other words, whether consciously or not, they relied upon their ability to manipulate people's emotions, just like any advertising campaign is designed to do. And that is exactly what was happening during the band's performances. You could see it in the people from my vantage point on the stage. I now knew, also, why I was being interrogated and messed with by the pastor. I had learned from the gentleman who ran the radio station that the church our pastor had come from experienced a massive church split which was started by the worship leader, a man who held tremendous emotional and psychological influence over the congregation. He had many followers. I had a strong and an assertive personality and I made good first impressions. I had a good singing voice. I held aspirations of becoming a pastor someday and had shared this openly and I was, in addition, a talented and experienced speaker. I was in the prime of my mid-thirties, when many people are beginning to ascend to the highest achievements of their chosen field, so I was the right age. Women seemed to be attracted to me. All of these factors combined to position me as a major potential threat to a paranoid, insecure leader who was afraid of being challenged and undermined by his own staff. And there was no doubt about it; Richard showed all the signs of intense paranoia. And perhaps it was somewhat justified, based on what he had previously experienced. The problem ran through my mind in a flash of insight as we worked together on the sheetrock, and I was searching for a way to address my concerns without alarming him. I chose an indirect approach.

"Basically, you're saying that the worship team is the key to the success of your church. That must explain why you oversee it so carefully?" This was a risky question, as I didn't know if he was aware that I knew that he did, in fact, oversee it. I was conscious that I might be throwing the worship leader under the bus, but I had to know. Pastor Rich didn't respond immediately but finished his tape line first. When he spoke, he surprised me.

"You impress me as a man who is pretty serious about his faith."

"Uh, yes, I think so. I try to be. I have often felt that I'm supposed to be a pastor or at least a teacher."

"Yes, I can see that you think like a teacher. I see that. Pray about it. Listen," he continued, turning towards me directly, "ego and sin on the worship team can divide the church. Can you do something for me, privately?" I turned and looked at him. I thought he was about to accuse me of an overinflated ego or something.

"Can you report to me if you notice problems on the team, or members walking in sin? I need to know. Can you do that for me? You don't need to tell anyone about this conversation. It's between you and me. I feel I can trust you for this." I mulled it over for a minute.

"Walking in sin? What do you mean?" I asked, finally. He shifted his weight from foot to foot, planting himself squarely at me.

"It's not a big deal, really. Just let me know about anything you feel may be disrupting or compromising the unity on the team, or hurting the church's testimony," he said. I nodded slowly.

"I'm not a leader on the team, though." I protested. At this, his reaction was swift.

"What's a *leader?* What *is* that, exactly? We are all just servants, don't you agree?" I nodded at him. What else could I do? How could anyone object to such altruistic generalizations?

"Sure," I said and smiled. His face relaxed. We finished our wall and he made small talk the rest of the time. Just like that, the "trap" of the "poke test" had been set. If this sounds like a clip from the "Godfather" movies, you are not far off. It felt a little bit like that, minus the murders and cement shoes.

It was through interactions such as these that I, and others, were kept off-balance and which served to create a Hegelian environment. For those unfamiliar with Hegelian method, it is essentially the strategy of manufacturing conflict between two parties so that they would seek a solution, which the neutral, manipulating party would be happy to provide. They literally wanted the head games, what they termed "poke tests", to create insecurity and even outbursts of emotion, born out of frustration, so that they could evaluate your character and intentions by virtue of your reactions. The explanation was that a "sheep" will just fall over on its side if you "poked" it (meaning they were harmless) but a "wolf" would turn on you, bear its fangs and attack. So, they instigated you, *poked* you, one way or another, and then stood back and watched how you handled it. For the person experiencing it, you felt like you had psychological vertigo. One apparent goal of this was to create a dichotomy in your psyche; they wanted to convince you that you were indispensable to the ministry and yet at the same time so indisputably corrupt as a "fallen sinner" that it would be improper to think that you were worthy of any honor. In this way, the pastor got what he wanted; loyal servants who protected his authority. If you failed to succeed in that role, you would be marginalized and pushed out, or at the least, your service opportunities would be greatly diminished. If this sounds overly cynical, perhaps it is. But anyone you speak to who has lived through it would not say so.

I would learn, in just a few short years, that "worship teams" and "Contemporary Christian Music" in general, were a source of many evils within the evangelical world at large, and not just within Calvary Chapel. Everything from contentious church splits, extra-marital affairs, ego battles that embarrassed the congregation and even disputes over money, often originated from within the groups of people responsible for the music ministry. The CCM world, and thus the mega-church movement by extent, was awash with business interests, moral compromises and usury; issues which should never be deciding factors for a faith community. The worship leader in large evangelical churches in America has become a salaried position rivaling or exceeding the salaries of many pastors. Some evangelical worship leaders of large ministries make six-figure incomes.

From the stage, during a worship concert at one of these churches, I witnessed the level of emotional and psychological influence the worship team had on the congregation. As we strummed the melodic harmonies of any middle-of-the-road worship song, you could watch the people swaying in time, like the citizens of Whoville on Christmas morning in The Grinch That Stole Christmas. Women would gaze into my eyes as I strummed my guitar and sang. Really, they were staring *through* me, and whatever they saw of me was just an illusion that they projected into their spiritual and sensual fantasy. I imagine that this is how sex workers experience their craft. At some level, they must genuinely connect to the client, or else their customer would feel cheated and defrauded, but they reserved an important piece of themselves which you would never be able to touch. It was a transaction, above all else, and the audience was not supposed to be present when you slumped into the couch backstage and enjoyed the afterglow. A junkie never wants to share his needle, after all. It was not difficult whatsoever for me to recognize why pastors and worship leaders so easily fell into sexual flings in the modern evangelical culture. *How could they not?* They were in tune with the crowd, and it was not a joke to be trifled with. A worship leader who was good-looking (man or woman, it made no difference), with a good voice, and a commanding stage presence, could win the hearts and (dare I say it) the lustful imaginations of many in the congregation. They would be singing about Jesus, but many in the audience had shifted their attention to the worship leader. The worship time, in these cases, became celebrity events that the public would attend on its own merits, regardless of the benefits spiritually, real or perceived. And according to the pastor of this church, as I was learning now in a veritable flood of apprehension, this experience drove the growth of the church. Because of all of this my pastor was *compelled* to assert dominance and control over me, whether I was aware of it or not. The risk, from his perspective, was too great to not do so. If I were ever to focus my energies towards establishing myself as a competitor, I could really create a mess. But I had always experienced this in my short life, after all. Ever since the Blue-Eyed Angel raised eyebrows by bringing me, as a seventeen-year-old boy, to her faculty party, I had been wowing some at first blush, and inciting others to jealousy and resentment, unbeknownst to me, largely because I was too self-absorbed to really notice. My problem, essentially, was that I was too stupid and unconscious of my surroundings to take advantage of any of these scenarios. I lacked a "killer instinct". Or, maybe, I simply lacked confidence. Plus (and this was a bad combination) I was confrontational when slighted. I was usually miffed or upset about something, simply because I was a purist, an idealist. I could have gotten away with my naivete if I had maintained a humble posture throughout, but the fact that I never shied away from pointing out the hypocrisy of leaders in authority over me pretty much nixed any chance of receiving a hand up to success, not only in religious environments but also in corporate ones. A more self-confident and practical person would have struck while the iron was hot, and taken advantage of the weaknesses of my opponents, but not me. I would break my own kneecaps rather than out-stride my boss because I was *duty-bound*. Perhaps I'm better for it. I don't know. I suspect if I had been otherwise, I would be both freer, richer, and more morally compromised than I am today.

Later, I contemplated and wondered about this situation and this conversation with the pastor. Was I being "poked" when he asked me to "oversee" the team, morally? Most definitely. Perhaps, I was on the beginning rungs of a ladder which would allow me to ascend in status and which would place me into the inner circle of Richard's closest associates. Or, maybe, I was disqualifying myself from that circle. I only wish, today, that I had never fallen into the madness of it all. Because, by the time I realized what was going on, years later, my family had been split in half, my financial future destroyed, and my life objectives pushed aside to serve the interests of others who, it turned out, were only looking out for themselves.

Chapter 11

———— ❧ ————

THE MENTOR AND THE MAVERICK

MY LIFE CAN theoretically be divided up according to three relationships which have steered it. There is my dad, whose influence over-
shadowed the first thirty years of my life. When my father moved to
Florida in 2001, I took on a spiritual mentor who would have a similar,
dominant effect upon my family and who would occupy this role, with
my consent, for about thirteen years. Then, of course, there is my wife,
whose relationship with me arcs across much of that time and continues today, and with whom I've tried to put back together the broken
shards of a functioning existence with varying levels of success.

The youth pastor at the Calvary Chapel, when we started attending, displayed a radical, damn-the-torpedoes approach to life which I
found fatally endearing, and I started forming a kinship with him. He
became, over the next decade, the closest thing to a spiritual "guru" that
I would ever associate with. As I allowed him increasing levels of authority over me, however, he revealed himself to be a narcissist-type, and was
extremely controlling, as well as profoundly dishonest. Importantly, he
elicited the same dysfunctional response from me as my father always

did. I caved to his manipulative approach and aimed to please him, until it became clear that this was an impossible goal, and he washed his hands of me when he determined I could no longer help him accomplish his goals, but only after I had burned all my bridges to follow him. It would have been nice if he had at least been willing to accept some accountability for the whole mess, but I still don't think of myself as a victim. After all, I'm not. I volunteered for the abuse. This is what many victims need to understand if they are going to successfully move forward. We all get our fair share of raw deals, in one fashion or another. But as adults, we must understand that no one can mistreat us over a long period of time without our psychological permission. It doesn't absolve the people who hurt us, of course, but taking responsibility for ourselves and what we can control is the only way to change the landscape of our lives and experience healing in any meaningful capacity.

Roman had a playful and irreverent manner about him that made him a great youth leader, but there was a darkness to his spirituality, and an undercurrent of controlled rage that lurked just below the surface of his outer demeanor. He was passionate about youth and discipleship and also deeply attracted to helping those who struggled with addiction and were on the margins of culture. He took the radical call of the gospel literally. He wasn't playing around.

One Wednesday night, the youth meeting was cancelled, because his van broke down, and the teens were sent into the main service. Afterwards, when he finally made it to the facility, he described to me a scenario in which satan was buffeting his minivan, causing it to lurch violently as it went down hills, forcing him to call a tow. He confidently assured me that he was being "attacked" by "the enemy" to prevent him from sharing a "powerful word" with the youth. I just had to challenge him.

"That's ridiculous, it's just a machine. It must be something mechanical. There's no way you can convince me that the devil is attacking your minivan." This seemed to affect him, and his countenance changed. He laughed, sheepishly.

"Yeah, probably," he admitted. I studied his expression, which reminded me of a child who just got caught cheating on an exam. I pushed it.

"Why would you blame satan when a mechanic hasn't even had a chance to look at it?" When I asked him this follow up question, he got quiet and his smile washed away, replaced with a veiled, but somewhat threatening look in his eyes. It was a tense moment, but it soon passed, and he regained his composure and told a joke, changing the subject. It turned out his van's transmission had broken down. Satan was not, in fact, "attacking" him. But his analysis was typical of the unhinged charismatic worldview common in such circles and which he embraced in his own unique way. And I took note of the fact that he became moody when I challenged him.

Roman had migrated to Calvary Chapel from a leadership position at an Assemblies of God church from which he had been scandalized and pushed out of. According to him, all those people he left behind were "fried" and "out to lunch". The youth pastor position at CC, therefore, was a rebound role for him. He won my trust by denouncing the excesses of the charismatic movement, yet at the same time he undermined his testimony by relying on bizarre, difficult to believe stories of supernatural visions and encounters with angels and demons as a token of his spiritual authority. His message and personality were completely skewed with inconsistencies.

During a volunteer day at the church, I was working alongside the Assistant Pastor, a man named William. He asked me about my relationship with Roman, I imagine because the leadership could tell we were growing close.

"Has he told you any of his stories yet?" He asked.

"Yes, of course. He's led a pretty radical life." I laughed. William didn't laugh.

"As he would have us believe, sure." He said, reaching his trowel into the bucket for more sheetrock plaster.

"What do you mean?" I asked, cautiously.

"We all have listened to his stories. We roll our eyes. You might think he's the only one on the planet who actually hears from God, and the rest of us are in the audience just waiting for his updates."

I had to admit thinking this myself, to some degree. That is the impression you got listening to Roman, very often. And he was always the hero in every encounter he described. But I had chalked it up to flamboyance and charisma and hadn't thought to hold it against him.

"I'm sorry to be cynical. I've seen guys like him come and go, you know? The pattern is the same: They burn out their welcome somewhere else and get a fresh start here and rise through the ranks, only to wear out their welcome and leave or get sent away. I'm waiting for that with him. But man, these stories..." he trailed off before continuing. "He's a weird...a sort of secretive kind of guy, yet very charismatic. The type of person that draws unstable people to himself. Like groupies..." He turned and faced me, framing my face with his free hand, "Like you. I sure hope I'm not describing *you*. You seem like a sharp guy, Dave. You're a good candidate for internship. Which makes me wonder why you are hitting it off with him. I don't think he'll be here long. I suspect that Richard will send him somewhere else as soon as the opportunity presents itself. If I were you, I'd keep your distance from him."

"Do you guys have bad blood between you? Why are you telling me this?" I asked.

"I'm sorry, no." He looked down, and I thought he was hiding a smirk. "There's no bad blood." He looked up at me again. "I like you and I think you have potential. Pick better friends. That's all. You might just have a future here." I nodded in acknowledgment, pondering his words. I tossed these ideas about in my mind for a few mentally turbulent weeks, but they didn't sit well with me. Will had not built trust with me yet, and I couldn't understand why Richard would allow Roman to have influence over the church's youth if this was truly the leadership's opinion of him. I decided to dismiss his advice as not representing anything but his own slanted take, which is unfortunate, because it turned out he was right. Instead, I drew closer to Roman, and he slowly began to undermine my confidence in my pastor, throwing little digs at him and mocking his perspective on many things when I was alone with him. He sowed the seeds of division and prepared me for what would come next.

I doubt there is a library that could hold the sheer volume of stories cataloging all the spiritual abuse and overt manipulation that people have been put through at the hands of psychotic religious extremists, would all of them to be written down, most of which would fall under the false premise of "building the kingdom of God". What is it about these people that enables them to capture the hearts and minds of otherwise-sane, intelligent people? I am not a psychologist, but I think I was susceptible because of the broken relationship I had with my father. We all have our "headless horsemen" which are riding free through our subconscious minds, waiting for their turn to monkey-wrench our brain's circuitry. In my case, as embarrassing as it is to admit, I spent a good part of my adult life wrestling with feelings of deficiency, failure and insecurity, and I kept finding myself in situations, both religiously and in my work life, in which I became subject to narcissistic people. I don't believe it's a coincidence. It's not as though the world consists of a majority of narcissists. I was just gravitating to them. I was on a subconscious journey to heal what was broken. The trouble is that what was truly broken could not be fixed outside of myself. It was an inside job. *I needed to fix myself.* First, I needed to *forgive myself.* And *accept myself.* Then, I could stop chasing ghosts. One of the "headless horsemen" of my subconscious had placed Roman in the saddle, and I was following him over the cliff of infinity. I had already made the choice, I just had not yet been presented with the opportunity to prove it, but that would come soon. Only severe psychic shock could throw me off that horse once my will or, in Hebrew, my *ratzon*, had been settled, and that would also come, but not for a few more years.

Against all logic, therefore, I believed him. I believed the stories; all of them. He was a classic anti-hero; someone who went against the grain, bucked the system and kissed the ring of no man, not even the Pope (he had a story about that, too), and he did it for the most noble and altruistic of reasons; *he did it for Jesus*. Roman had an anti-hero of his own, and his name was the Apostle Paul. He loved that Paul had the spiritual and moral "courage" to thumb his nose at the founding apostles and their status as "pillars". As Paul famously declares, *"what they are is of no consequence to me...I received my gospel from no man, but from the Lord himself."* This is what Paul says, and it's the perfect synopsis of Roman's philosophy, too. He was not only willing to die on the hill, alone against the world, he was *eager* to do so. But what got me involved with his gambits was that he told me that *I was to him what Silas was to Paul*. How could I let him down? He promised me he would never abandon me or let me leave his side. We were going to serve Jesus recklessly and do mighty work for the kingdom together. I trusted him. It was like a life oath. I clung to that for years even when the church around me that he led was denouncing me and discrediting me. I stood strong on the promises he had made as a brother and friend. Foolish me. I really should have known better. Had I known that his true motivation was to lure my family to Vermont so that my oldest son could marry his daughter eventually, since he claimed that God showed him this in a vision, I would have perhaps thought better of trusting him so implicitly.

Such is the mentality which often develops among religious extremists and their followers. There is a very imbalanced and unhealthy worldview which can overthrow the mind, and which gives the emotions the authority to take over the Command Bridge of one's will. The result of this process is that, rather than critically analyzing things when they stop making sense, you *increase* your devotion. Why? Because *more devotion is possible*. It becomes an end unto itself to become *more* religious. But religious zealots never quite grasp this. All they can see is their zealotry, and it is self-justifying. They become mentally blinded by their mission and sense of duty. Somewhere, out there, there was a heavenly reward waiting for them for their faithfulness and sacrifice. *They just knew it.*

Roman was the most reckless, dangerous type of zealot since his zealotry was born from extreme military training and trauma. (One of my jobs when I served under him was to keep an eye on him so that he didn't go AWOL and revert to vigilante justice, something I never witnessed in the time I knew him but which he claimed were things he had been involved with in the past.) He was the type of zealot that would gladly throw away a good life to live completely on the edge of sanity and sustenance. All that mattered was the *call*. The *mission*. Living on the edge became a goal in and of itself, therefore, as it represented our *destiny*. His advice for me was full of radical rhetoric and bold injunction. A house? It's just a pile of sticks and metal. It's *nothing*. God gives me shelter, not a house. *Forget all that worldly stuff, it's the Lord's problem. You just follow him. He'll take care of your family.* This is how Roman talked, *and* how he lived. It was so simple, and seemingly so pure. It was the opposite extreme which we experienced in Amway, and so it felt like an inevitable journey to take. Like ying-yang.

Don't misunderstand me. There is something inspiring about throwing caution to the wind for the sake of a noble cause. Thousands of brave souls died on Normandy Beach in France for a noble cause. But that was also a *real* cause. But the idea of throwing your life away because of an existentially based spiritual vision of reality is wildly dangerous because to do so, you're selling out to a dream which will never, ever materialize. And the dream was spun for me through stories. Many of which were probably not even true.

Chapter 12

SQUIRREL-TRAP

WE WERE PART of a home fellowship Bible study sponsored by the church and led by an "approved" leader. It met weekly on Thursday nights. Because of my involvement on the worship team, we were tied in to the one led by the worship leader. During our time going through the book of First Corinthians, I was told by the host and leader that Pastor Rich wanted me to teach. It would be chapter thirteen, the infamous "love" chapter, often quoted at weddings. On Sunday, after services, one of the pastor's assistants approached me with a printout. He said they were the transcripts of Pastor Chuck Smith teaching the chapter.

"Richard wants you to follow these notes," he stated flatly.

"Really?" I replied, dripping with sarcasm, "I have an idea...why don't we just play the recording of Pastor Chuck teaching it, then?" I laughed. He smiled weakly.

"It's what Richard wants," he replied, as though that settled the issue. For him, maybe it did.

"Thanks, I'll look them over." I said, and he walked off, satisfied. I am entirely certain that this was another "poke test", and one which I was already destined to fail. My instincts told me to study the passage on my own and present my findings, like a good teacher is supposed to do. I would learn the hard way that I was wrong. The church in America (and Calvary Chapel would prove no different) had a corporate structure, for the most part. It truly wasn't about the word of God, or the integrity of the faith. Rather, it was about maintaining the status quo so things progressed in the ways already pre-ordained in board meetings. Serving in ministry at these highly organized churches was like being in middle management. As the old saying goes, *if you're not the lead dog, the view's the same.* Frustrated, I called Roman and asked his advice.

"What is the Lord showing you?"

"I'm not against Pastor Chuck or his notes, but I'm torn about what to do. I haven't put together the study yet. Why would they ask me to teach and then tell me *what* to teach? It doesn't make sense."

"Because this is how they raise people up. You are representing Richard. If you do a good job it will lead to other opportunities. You may be asked to preach someday."

"I'm not Richard."

"Well, that's how it is, Dave. Tell you what, finish studying and then call me and we'll talk about it." I agreed.

Chapter thirteen of First Corinthians is one of those texts, like Psalm twenty-three, which travels well. It can be used and applied in a great many contexts successfully without any problems. This is no doubt one of the main reasons it was the chapter selected for me to teach. How could I screw it up? Here is an excerpt, for those unfamiliar:

"Love is patient, love is kind and is not jealous; love does not brag and is not arrogant, does not act unbecomingly; it does not seek its own, is not provoked, does not take into account a wrong suffered, does not rejoice in unrighteousness, but rejoices with the truth; bears all things, believes all things, hopes all things, endures all things." (1 Cor.13:4-7)

On the surface, there should not have been a problem with putting

Chuck's notes into my own words and delivering a nice slow batting practice lob over the middle of the plate for the evening's guests. We would all say "amen", have coffee and cake, and go home. Nobody gets hurt, and I stay out of trouble. But I saw a major problem as I studied the surrounding material to gain insight on the text in question. The first problem, and the reason I took the time to study the entire book in an overview as I prepared, was that Calvary Chapel did not approach the texts of scripture in topical fashion, but in expositional fashion, which means that one cannot, using this technique, ever lose sight of the context of the surrounding material when creating an outline. In an expositional approach, the context is king, not a secondary consideration.

First Corinthians is a very controversial epistle, to begin with. It is considered by critical scholars to be one of the seven "authentic" Pauline letters (meaning it was written by Paul and not a forgery like the rest of them. *That's right, chew on that for a bit.*) Paul is ripping people's heads off during parts of this letter. The last half of the book is just as provocative and controversial as the first half. At the three-quarter mark, chapter thirteen sits like an oasis amidst boiling molten lava, seemingly disconnected from the surrounding material, and it certainly does not represent the conclusion of Paul's thoughts. There are still three more chapters to go after it. So…*why is it there, and what is the true message?*

In chapter ten, Paul seems to overturn any notion of Jewish kosher law, particularly in relation to table fellowship, by offering a 'don't ask, don't tell' policy regarding food sacrificed to idols. Basically, he says, *what you don't know won't hurt you, so mind your business.* Chapter eleven is that wonderful passage about women wearing hats in church, or else they will be acting like prostitutes. He also gives rebuke and instruction about the "Christian love feast"; his "divine revelation" of the Lord's supper, which he claims came from a spiritual vision, and not from the apostolic tradition. In chapter twelve, he rebukes the Corinthians for their juvenile and prideful practices of spiritual gifts.

Then comes, finally, the "love chapter" and it proceeds to wax eloquent concerning selfless devotion and fealty. It would be convenient at this juncture if Paul ended the letter, and then everyone could claim (as they do already) that this "love chapter" is the apex of its message. Except, he doesn't do this. Chapter fourteen follows with a hugely controversial text which has divided various parts of the evangelical world for hundreds of years now; the teachings about "speaking in tongues". The material in chapter fourteen continues to rip church assemblies apart at the seams today. Not to be outdone by such mundane topics, the epistle concludes with, in order, an otherworldly dissertation on the nature of the resurrected body after death, followed, no less contentiously, with exhortations about giving over your money to the leadership. *Whew*, and I thought American politics was exhausting. And where might Paul have received his authority for these ideas? If you think they came from Jesus's teachings or from the other apostles, you'd be wrong. He got them from private spiritual "visions". We know this from his own testimony on the matter.

Roman had wanted to know what the Lord showed me in my study preparations. While I'm quite certain today that the Lord (meaning Jesus) doesn't show *anyone anything*, since he's no longer alive, it did occur to me at the time that the chief reason the "love chapter" existed was to help rectify the massive infighting and individualism being reflected in the issues brought forth in the surrounding material. The chapter, therefore, had little to do with the sentiments of a groom and bride on their wedding day expressing a desire to practice sacrificial love towards one another, or to some universal ethic that can be embraced by all, regardless of religious affiliation. (I recently was in a Jewish home that had this passage on a plaque as a wall decoration, and they were not believers in Jesus). Rather, it was clearly meant to reign in and correct rampant individuality within a religious culture which required the subjugation of self in favor of the collective. In other words, to get people to settle down and respect their leaders. This sounded nauseatingly familiar to me. It was, according to my reading, a backhanded rebuke to anyone who was not submitting to the agenda, as it were. And it was also, on a more applicational level, a rebuke of spiritual pride. I shared these thoughts with Roman.

"Personally, I would love the study you have done. It is powerful. But your study is not what Richard is looking for, I can tell you that, but it's powerful, and it confirms things that the Lord has been showing me about you."

"So, what should I do, scrap my notes?" I asked.

"You'll have to follow the Lord," he replied, "Who are you trying to please?"

That last statement haunted me as I made my decision. Roman had made it clear…a true servant will speak the truth, not play a political game. *Damn the torpedoes*, I thought to myself, *I'm going in strong.*

I decided to use my own notes, and not rely upon Chuck Smith. The study was well-received, though it did create a heavy atmosphere. Several people were in tears as I concluded, and there was a rather intense prayer time afterwards. I thought I had succeeded and had made the correct choice, and I felt confident. Pastor Will was in attendance but had been quiet throughout.

As I prepared to put the van in reverse and back it down the host's driveway, Pastor Will tapped on my window. I hit the button and zipped it down. There was a crisp chill in the October air. I could smell the fallen leaves.

"Hey," he said, "That was a powerful study."

"Thanks," I replied, beaming. Maybe I *did* succeed.

"Was that from Chuck's new notes or the older version? I'm not familiar with the new series." I swallowed hard. *Maybe I didn't.*

"I relied on Chuck somewhat, but a lot what I shared tonight was from my own study." I admitted.

"Interesting." He said evenly. "Well, it's such a forgiving passage you could have taught just about anything and made it work, really," he said. I didn't agree with that statement, but rather than argue, I just smiled weakly at him. He tapped my door with his open hand and stepped back from the van and said good night. I zipped my window closed and turned away to navigate the van down the narrow lane.

"What was that about?" Asked Chana.

"I don't think Will liked my study," I said.

"Great," she said, and she cupped her mouth and chin in her hand, staring out the window. She didn't speak another word to me as we drove home. *It was a good study*, I thought. Pride was the greatest threat to love. And spiritual pride among leaders is the worst. I determined, right there and then, privately in my mind as we drove home, without even saying anything to Chana, that Roman was my guy. The rest of these clowns were frauds, and of course I was completely convinced I was right. After all, Roman had told me so.

Exactly as Will had predicted many months prior, Richard announced one Sunday morning that Roman would be leaving our church to take over another Calvary Chapel. For a month or so prior to this, while Roman traveled north to preach to his new community, I had been co-leading the teen youth group along with another man named Doug, who was a great guy and with whom I was becoming friends. Both he and I had teens in the group. It was supposed to be a temporary arrangement while Roman "filled in" for the pastor in Vermont. Privately, however, Roman called me and prepared me for the meeting that would be happening. He had arranged things with Richard, he informed me, so that I would be the new Youth Pastor. Except, when the time came for the meeting, it never happened. Rather, Doug and his wife were introduced as the new youth leaders by Richard the week after Roman received his send-off before the church. I didn't receive as much as a courtesy call, nor any recognition for having filled in alongside Doug during that time. It was as if I didn't exist.

As it turned out, Richard wanted a change of direction, rather than a continuation of Roman's philosophy, which I would have represented. He wanted Christian concerts, festivals, games, entertainment, etc. Roman was all about making the teens serve in ministry and fostering their discipleship. He was about undecorated rooms, plain plastic tables, and long Bible studies. William had been right: I may have enjoyed a future with Richard if not for my allegiance to and association with Roman.

A long-time friend of mine from our Amway days reached out to me about this time about helping him lead a Bible study in his home. My friend had become a Christian because of me after having been raised agnostic, but he was thinking of leaving his current church. His home was over an hour away, but since he was my friend, I agreed. However, I had remembered Roman telling me that Richard wanted a satellite church in the general area of where my friend lived, so I mentioned the opportunity to Richard so that he knew what I was up to. Brett had come to visit our church a few times, upon my encouragement, and Pastor Richard called him up. Before I knew it, Richard had decided to lead the study himself and make it a ministry opportunity of the church. I felt this was presumptive of him, but rather than protest, I asked to remain involved, and Richard agreed. He also asked me to plan on leading the worship at the gathering, and I agreed to do so. I had just started learning guitar and had to practice anyway, so I committed some time to learning some songs for the occasion. I thought it would be fun.

When the night arrived for the start of the study at Brett's home about a month later, Richard invited my wife and I to carpool with him and his wife. We thought that was a great idea. We met at the church, and I asked to put my guitar in the trunk. He became cross and asked me to step inside the church foyer with him alone.

"Dave, I'm really flustered right now. I need you to explain this," he said. I was smiling, having no idea what he was talking about. I waited for him to elaborate.

"Why did you bring your guitar? Why would you presume on me like that? I already asked someone else to do that." I felt my mouth drop open.

"You asked me to do it a month ago. Don't you remember?"

"No, I don't, and I don't think I would have," he said, his face becoming red.

"You most certainly did," I protested, "I can tell you exactly where we were standing in the church after service when you told me. If you hadn't, I would not have spent the last month practicing for it."

"I don't recall that, and I'm very uncomfortable right now." At this, I snapped a bit.

"Richard, I'm sorry, but you most definitely asked me to prepare to lead worship tonight. I distinctly remember it. If you don't, that's unfortunate, but that's on you, not me. Secondly, why would this idea even upset you? I'm part of your worship team, am I not? Wouldn't it be appropriate for me to lead the group in a few songs? Third, I hate to play this card on you but this was a Bible study that my long-time friend asked *me* to lead, and I informed you of it out of courtesy. Now, you're just taking it over. And *I'm* making *you* upset? Your reaction here is beyond reasonable."

Richard seemed unsure of himself. But to keep the peace, I agreed to leave the guitar behind and not make a scene with the ladies. It was an awkward ride to my friend's house. When we arrived, I met a man named Steve, a young guy in his late twenties, who had recently moved east from Richard's home church in San Diego, and had been hand-picked by Richard, unbeknownst to me, to become the church planter for this satellite effort. Steve led the worship. I was stunned, and Brett was confused as well. This had gone from a private home fellowship that I had agreed to lead as a favor to my longtime friend to a Calvary Chapel church plant that I was barely welcome to be involved in.

Richard, nonetheless, was happy with how the evening went and expressed appreciation for me connecting him to Brett. But he did not apologize for the misunderstanding earlier in the evening. In fact, he acted as though our earlier conversation never even happened. Chana and Richard's wife chatted in the back seat on the way back to the church. She did not yet know what was going on. Later that week, I informed Richard and Brett that I would not be participating anymore, but neither of them would hear of it. They both wanted me involved. I reluctantly agreed, for Brett's sake. I tried hard over the following weeks to remain positive and to build my relationship with Richard, but I had really run out of patience for him. I was looking for a way out.

I called Roman to complain about the situation.

"He doesn't trust you, Dave, that's why you're having issues. He told me recently when I was meeting with him that "Dave does what I tell him, but he's not *with* me." That's why he doesn't give you responsibility."

"That's crazy," I said, "When did that happen?"

"It doesn't matter. He's not your pastor. I am. And he knows it." Roman said this with such assuredness that it never occurred to me to call Richard out and question it. I just assumed it was true. There was no denying that I had a special relationship with Roman that I did not enjoy with Richard, but, as usual, things simply weren't adding up. Nothing, thus far, that Roman had told me would materialize had happened. *Nothing*. Why did I still believe him? I was simply trusting him implicitly, with no critical evaluation of what he was telling me. I thought, at the time, that I was a disciple, but this was something other than discipleship. I was ready for the squirrel trap.

"I don't have a worship leader, Dave. Would you be willing to come up to Vermont and lead worship for a few Sundays?" He asked.

"Really?" I was excited. "Sure." Just like that, I had one foot in Vermont.

Chana and I drove up on Memorial Day Weekend. I led worship for the service, and afterwards much of the congregation drove over to Roman's home for a holiday BBQ. Roman grilled hot dogs and hamburgers and I manned the bouncy house for the little kids. There were good vibes everywhere. It felt as right as a virgin walking down the aisle.

On Monday afternoon, after a restful night's sleep breathing Vermont's clean air, Roman and his wife sat down across from us in their living room and we had the "talk". He explained my *calling* to me and how God showed him that I was to serve alongside him in partnership, ministering to the people of the region. This would of course involve closing my business, selling our home and moving to a new state and was, frankly, a lot to swallow. We owned a large split-level home on a quiet dead-end street in north-central Massachusetts with a level yard and driveway, an in-ground pool in the back, a three-season porch, and a full finished basement. Our mortgage was only $800 a month. We had 60% equity in the place. We had it made, and my carpet cleaning business was just starting to take off. We literally did not have a single reason to seriously consider what he was offering us. But the call was everything, or so we had been taught in Calvary Chapel, and Roman was laying it on thick.

He informed me that he had been meeting and praying with Richard every month since taking over the church in southern Vermont, and for six months they had been discussing my potential move to Vermont to serve with him. Light bulbs ignited in my mind. Suddenly, Richard's reluctance to allow me a major role at Brett's house took on a different context. *He knew I was called to Vermont.* It was all falling in line like a puzzle. Roman asked us to pray about it. Only much later did I develop serious doubts as to whether he had any such conversations with Richard. Judging by the fact that we were never publicly blessed or "sent off", I doubt it. Further, I know that God had never shown him my face in any vision, as he claimed. In that moment, though, I had no suspicions or misgivings. The trap had sprung, and I was in the salad days of my prime. There was nothing but optimism and future glory ahead. The past was an inconvenient memory. The present a mere speed bump. Everything was hopeful, and I could not fail.

Chapter 13

———∞∞———

LOCK & LOAD

THE LITTLE GREEN Toyota rattled and clunked up the loose gravel of Putney Mountain Road, a steep, winding and at times treacherous journey. Roman and his wife were in front and, inches behind them, sardined together on the cramped vinyl of the back seat, sat Chana and me. The Toyota had all the charm and comfort of diving headfirst into the recycling bin at a transfer station. It was our first week living in Vermont.

"What?" Said Roman, as he looked at Chana in the rearview. Chana repeated herself, louder, "My sister saw pictures of the Village Center online and told me she wants to move here because it's so beautiful. That was encouraging to me."

"Tell her not to come." I felt Chana squeeze my arm tighter.

"Why not?"

"The beauty is fake. This is a demonic, evil place. It will destroy you if you come without being *called*. Tell your sister *never* to come." Chana looked at me with a slight panic. I just laughed, nervously.

When I had told Richard that I wanted to accept Roman's request to come alongside him in Vermont, I was really inviting him to bless and congratulate me, since I was under the given impression that he already knew all about it. After all, hadn't he been praying with him for months about that very thing? Roman had received a grand send-off complete with a party after services, in which the congregation got to offer their support and encouragement, when he left to take the pastorate of this church. I didn't expect that level of send-off, but I was hoping for at least some public acknowledgement, to quell the questions if nothing else, both in the minds of others and, more importantly, in our own thoughts. We had doubts. When I had approached Richard about sending us, he was thoughtful and measured in his response.

"I would love to have you teach occasionally, especially for the Friday men's group, but I'm unsettled at the idea of you teaching. I've told you this. I can't shake it."

"You've never actually heard me teach though." Richard paused and thought about this.

"You have my blessing, but I'm not going to send you. It's your choice. Sink or swim, I'm not responsible."

This was hardly the ringing endorsement I was looking for. And certainly nothing that would convince my wife to give up her big house with the in-ground pool. She had grown attached to it, which was a minor miracle considering that I sold her childhood home to move into it. If I moved her again, and it wasn't at least as ideal as what she had now, I might lose her altogether. But if she became convinced that God wanted us to move again, she would do it with enthusiasm. We just needed to know. We agreed together that we would not step into anything in Vermont unless God made it unmistakably clear that this is what we were supposed to do. To me, this meant we were not going anywhere because I had never experienced anything in my life in which God made anything *that* clear. In all cases, at some point, I had to make a choice between potential paths. So, when we established such firm parameters, I considered this to be a concession to my wife that we were standing pat. I was thinking of talking to Richard about abandoning the Vermont thing and starting a home fellowship in my house. There were increasing numbers of people going to our church from our area and there was no home group for them to attend. Over the period of a few days, I convinced myself of this, and when I began the trek up the stairs to the church offices it was with the intention of telling Richard that I had changed my mind about Vermont. On the way, I encountered the worship leader headed the other way.

"Dave! Hey man, you're going to be an assistant pastor in Vermont? Without an internship?"

"Uhhh," I said. He patted me on the shoulder and smiled, shaking his head. "Happy for you, man!" then he continued bounding down the stairs. I watched his head disappear and stood in disbelief. This was taking on a life of its own. I called Roman to set the record straight.

"I haven't made a decision yet, you know."

"Of course not."

"In fact, I'm not selling my house. I'm not hiring an agent. Someone will have to come to my front door and ask to buy my house. I need to know this is God."

"Sure. No problem."

Chana was satisfied with my ultimatum. We would stay put, remain part of the Calvary Chapel in Massachusetts, and maybe something useful would materialize in our town. Sanity would be restored.

Later that week, my flip-phone buzzed in my shorts pocket as I was cleaning the carpets in a hotel grand ballroom. It was Chana.

"You're not going to believe this, but Mary Bond just came by. She asked us if we'd ever consider selling our house." She kept talking, but I had dropped the phone.

"I don't think I heard you. What did you say?"

"She wants to come by and talk about it. What do you think?" I wasn't sure what my wife meant by this. Was she inviting me to say no, or to agree?

"Sure. She can come by."

"What time?"

"I don't care. Tell her whenever. I'll get there when I can."

"Okay."

This was getting real. My thoughts were racing on the way home. I felt as though God was facing me directly with my ultimatum and challenging me to put up or shut up, as it were. *No backing down now.* We had paid $169,000 for the place a few years prior. In the meantime, we had put a whole new roof on it, replaced the furnace and all the copper piping, all the carpeting and most of the windows. That was a major investment. But this wasn't about making money, it was about serving the Lord, and God was watching me. *This was a test of my faith*, I reasoned. I somehow settled loosely in my mind upon the number of $235,000 as a reasonable pay off.

When I arrived home, Mary was sitting in our garage with Chana. They had been talking for nearly half an hour. Mary seemed to have full knowledge of the entire Vermont scenario, so I assumed Michelle had filled her in, and she immediately and somewhat rudely asked me if I had any idea what I would sell the house for. Like an idiot, I floated out my hypothetical number and she gasped.

"That's the number Bill and I just got approved for!" *No kidding*, I thought. Mary cackled with glee. It was as if the cards in the deck were marked and we were being played. It seemed obvious that God wanted us to sell our house and move. I practically resigned myself to the idea. This felt extremely rushed but nonetheless I felt spiritually compelled to proceed.

Never during this time of decision making did it occur to me to do any research on real estate values in southern Vermont, housing availability, or even to get a professional opinion about our current home's market value. *We were called to Vermont. God would take care of the details.* Why did I think this way? Because for a number of years, Roman had been conditioning me to think that down was up and up was down and that personal success was a sign of ambition and faulty motives as well as a lack of commitment to the gospel. Didn't he walk away from a successful business of his own and leave it all behind to serve God?

Of course, he did. Why would I, as his chief disciple, expect to avoid such sacrifices? There was no amount of recklessness which was not justifiable in the service of the King. Further, before Roman was in my life, I had spent over a decade in the psychotic and intense direct-sales environment of Amway. The mentality there was very much the same, which truly mitigates Roman's responsibility. I already had the imbalance within myself long before he and I met. Which means, of course, that he didn't create the problem. He merely revealed it. And in any case, he had the sickness himself. In fact, even worse than I did. It was precisely why we hit it off so well. We were like two displaced Knights of Arthur's Roundtable seeking the Holy Grail in the wrong century.

Another thing that I never thought about was that Mary and Bill were intimate friends with Roman and his family. I knew that they had association with each other, however I was not aware at the time of how close they were. For some unfathomable reason, it never occurred to me that Roman had probably called them and told them about my ultimatum of not listing my house. It appears that we were set up. I imagine, today, Roman slapping his knee in hysterics in his house at the idea of sending Mary Bond to my front door. I just assumed, at the time, that God had done the unthinkable and sent a person to my door in answer to my challenge. I called up a real estate lawyer in town and asked him to do the necessary work to produce a purchase and sale agreement. In a week, he was ready to see me. His office was pleasant and bright. I found myself lost in thought, staring at his bookshelves stuffed with endless hardcover volumes of Massachusetts case law, and wondering if he had read any of them. His voice startled me out of my daydream.

"I received the market analysis yesterday. I can't in good conscience complete this sale agreement without at least attempting to talk you out of it." This irritated me but I asked him to explain. He continued, "The current market value is $310,000. You have asked me to write this up for $235,000. I think that someone may be trying to take advantage of you here. You need an agent. No agent would advise you to sell at $75,000 below market, I know that." Here was my test of faith, I thought. I knew that this moment would come.

"It's okay. They are friends of ours. They really need the house." The lawyer took off his glasses and rubbed his eyes before answering.

"I'm sure you also needed the house at the time you purchased it. And I'm sure it wasn't sold to you for $75,000 below market." True. He had me there. "Your friends have other houses to choose from. They are capable, just as you were, of finding a home within their budget. This house is not in their budget unless you give it away. I am all kinds of uncomfortable with this. I think that you owe it to yourselves to list the property with a qualified firm and get as much as you can for it. The timing is right for you to flip this house and make a nice profit. You should do so."

I folded my legs, leaned forward with my elbow on my knee, covered my mouth with my hand and closed my eyes to think. Roman's advice was ringing in my mind. *God showed me that my path is down, not up. This is the challenge of those who serve the Lord. Whose interest matters, yours or his?*

"I really think it will be okay," I said, finally. He sighed and looked at me with a combination of disdain and pity and then rose from his desk. The meeting was over, apparently.

"I'm going to sit on this for forty-eight hours. You go home and talk to your wife. Think about what I told you. If, after this, you still want to move forward, I'll finalize the paperwork. That's my promise. By I insist you take a couple of days to think about it." I agreed, shook his hand and left.

It is quite common in evangelical culture for people put "a fleece" out to gain direction, based upon the story in the Jewish Bible (what Christians call the Old Testament) of Gideon, who put out a woolen fleece in the book of Judges and divined God's will by the dew which fell upon it overnight. The practice, in modern evangelical Christianity, is to challenge God to provide a specific answer for direction about a particular problem by laying out a condition by which you will be bound to the "answer" that you receive. This is what we had literally tried to do by creating the condition that we would not sell our home unless someone came to our house to ask to buy it from us. In our view, this scenario was so unlikely that we felt it would only happen if God directly answered our prayer. So, when the condition was fulfilled, all sense of rational analysis disappeared, and I was left with a divine mandate. Truly, this approach to spiritual guidance is equivalent to flipping the Bible open in random fashion with your eyes closed, placing your finger blindly upon a place on the page and thinking that the verse your forefinger lands on is God's direction for you. Yet, you would be shocked to know how many Christians make major life decisions in times of crises through this very practice. They might as well drag out a Ouija board and use that. A week after my meeting with the real estate lawyer, his packet of information arrived for us to review. We were going to move forward with the sale.

Our last week at the Calvary Chapel in Massachusetts was disappointing, to say the least. Not only was there no send-off, but there was not even an announcement in the bulletin or through the leadership channels. Richard merely mentioned us during his brief comments before the start of his sermon that our family was leaving for Vermont to "serve up there". When we loaded the family in the van after services, it was as though we had never existed. We just left, and few people seemed to be aware of what had happened, since most of our friends in the church either weren't in that service or weren't there in time to hear the announcements. And it had been kept largely secret from the congregation.

We moved our furnishings into storage and took temporary residence with Roman and his family in their small chalet in Vermont. Within days of moving in with them, things got weird. The encouraging, faith-building guy I had grown attached to and who had been in my ear influencing me since I first began bringing my kids to his youth group; the guy who had been my hiking buddy, who was leading me into a new understanding of what mattered in life and how to serve

THERE'S NO SUCH THING AS MAGIC BLOOD

the Lord, started playing mind games with me. He criticized the way we dealt with our children and the way Chana and I interacted and embarrassed me repeatedly in front of my family. It was infuriating and confusing.

I was practicing on his deck for the worship service one week during this period. I had eight or ten songs that I was fiddling with. He came out and stood in front of me until I stopped playing.

"What songs are you playing this week?"

"I don't know. Haven't decided yet."

"Show them to me before Sunday, okay?" This was something new. He had never, to this point, concerned himself with this.

"Why? Is there something in your sermon you want to emphasize?" My question was sincere, but he just smiled and shook his head, walking back into the house. I was left feeling very unsettled. But I pressed on. On Saturday, he brought it up again. I showed him the five or six songs I was considering for the four I would need to play. He started reading the lyrics and mocking them.

"Who wrote this?"

"It's from my worship book. I get songs sent to me every month. I like some of them." He tossed it back to me.

"Nah. Get rid of that. It's fried. I don't hear the Lord's voice in that." I looked at the song sheet. It was one of my favorite new songs. I had planned on leading with it. How did he determine that it lacked the *Lord's voice?* What *was* that exactly?

"Just play three songs. Sing the last one without the guitar."

"Okay, I'll try."

"Don't try. Do." I just looked at him. This was all new. Sunday morning, I arrived an hour before service to tune up and practice in the sanctuary. I typically led the worship alone. Just my voice and my guitar. Near the end of my practice time, as I was putting my guitar on the stand and about to sit down and wait for services to begin, he called me up to the prayer room, which was a nursing mom's room that no one ever used, converted from the former balcony area.

"Pray with me." We bowed our heads and prayed together for the service. I got up to leave when we were done. He stopped me.

"I want you to play without a pick. Just finger pick."

"I don't know how. I just learned how to play guitar less than a year ago. I practice the songs by strumming chords." Roman closed his eyes in mockery, pretending to pray.

"Dear Lord, please help Dave overcome his pride and just do what he's told." Then he laughed. Confused, I went back downstairs. People had begun arriving. I sat in front wondering how I was going to do this. The two songs I played without a pick went relatively fine, though I thought they would have sounded better with a pick. The song I performed without a guitar was a disaster. I started singing off-key and had to restart. People laughed. I laughed. I started again. It happened again. Roman called it off and started the service, laughing at me as he did announcements. I was angry. It was totally unnecessary. I was not a professional musician. I was not skilled enough to change on the fly like he seemed to want me to do and I didn't understand what he was trying to accomplish by humiliating me.

We continued our theme park style drive up Putney Mountain Road in the Toyota until we reached height-of-land and began descending. Chana had an angry look in her eyes now. She had consoled herself about the loss of her house and pool with the thought that her family would be excited to come visit their new home, appreciate the beauty, and maybe some of them might even move there to enjoy it with us. Now, she was told the place was evil and that her family would not belong there.

"You have to have a certain mentality to live here." He continued, "It's not like anywhere else. There's no support. No structure. You are alone here. Just you and God. That's it. In most places, churches have cute little mottos, like *love God and love people*. It's not that way here."

"What's the motto here?" I asked.

"Lock and load."

I laughed out loud, repeating the words *lock and load* under my breath. Chana didn't laugh. She clenched my hand tightly and frowned, as if she realized that we were in a log ride that would head over Niagara Falls and she had no way to get off.

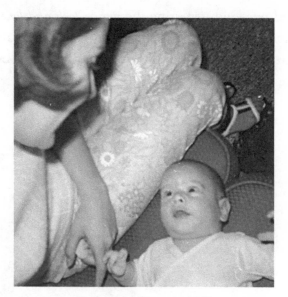

Author with his mom, 1968

Maternal grandparents, 1967

Author, age 9, setting off on his homemade raft, circa 1977

With my family and paternal grandparents, circa 1984

With my sister, circa 1985

Author with his wife, circa 1990, during the "Amway" period

Celebrating our conversion to Judaism at synagogue, Feb., 2020.

Chapter 14

───── ∾∾ ─────

DON'T WORRY ABOUT THE SEPTIC

"SO, YOU'RE GOING to Vermont. You are going there as a servant. You know that, right?"

"Of course." I thought, *here comes the Calvary Chapel lecture about titles and humility.*

"Make sure you bring your toilet brush." This was a Calvary Chapel idiom used often and it connoted the idea of being a servant.

"They don't have a toilet," I said. Richard chuckled. "As I've heard."

The church building in which I'd be serving, built in the 1800's by President Taft for his brother, who was a pastor, had no running water or proper bathroom. There were no "toilets". At least, none that could be "scrubbed" with a brush. In the back of the large fellowship hall was a narrow door which opened to a tiny step-up platform with a hole carved into the plywood that led outside. Under the hole was a blue 55-gallon polyethylene drum which would catch the poop, paper and urine. A vent pipe captured much, but by no means all, of the odor. In the winter, it was wise to wear your coat or at least your hat, as the little alcove was not heated. Every week, some elderly and small children would miss the hole entirely (probably because they could not lift themselves high enough to sit on the platform) and their urine would run down the front of the platform and collect on the floor, convalescing into a moving yellow puddle which would spread under the door and into the fellowship hall, where we served food after service. It was rich. I spent most of my time before and after the service with a cleaning bottle and paper towels. When a small child did this they would giddily tramp through their own pee and track it across the hall and back into their classroom. Many of the small children in this congregation went shoeless during services. With no running water to even wash one's hands, hand sanitizer was worth its weight in gold.

The old-timers acted like this was normal. In fact, they took pride in it. People would visit our little church from out of town (being a tourist area, this was almost weekly) and the old-timers would approach the attractive yuppie mother with the yoga pants and large diamond ring, and ask if she had taken her darling, effervescent children to the bathroom yet, and if she needed direction. The mother would politely ask where the facilities could be found. The old-timer would then point to the little wooden door which swung somewhat violently on the rusted metal spring (causing it to *fwap!* against your rump before you had fully entered the room) and smile gleefully at their latest victim of Vermont humor. The old-timer would chuckle under their breath as they waddled away. Most of these poor folks never came back for a second visit, particularly if they stayed long enough for the cream cheese sandwiches on Wonder Bread or Jim's recycled coffee, which he made by simply adding an additional pot of water to the same expired grounds. (This was a strange practice considering we had an abundance of coffee but only a few gallons of potable water on hand). You could tell that this had happened because the guests would grimace, and then examine their disposable Styrofoam cup to try and figure out what they were tasting. It was then that the locals would look at the guest inquisitively, saying something like "Is there a problem with the coffee?" To which the guest would say, "No, it's great thanks." I would then watch them try to find a way to dump the coffee without appearing rude. It would usually end up in the poop barrel. They slapped their hands clean of the crime immediately after the little door went *fwap!* Everyone knew the score. We would see the taillights of their vehicle a few moments later as they pulled out of the gravel parking lot. The old-timers were always happy to see this and would point and smile. *No church was going to grow on their watch.* Of course, these guests that showed up in the fellowship hall after service were, in fact, the hardy ones, since they had managed to survive the psychological beat-down that Roman would call a sermon. Many high-tailed it out of there before they ever got downstairs to taste the recycled coffee or step through urine puddles.

One of my jobs at the church, during the entirety of my tenure there, was to roll the poop barrel out from under the indoor outhouse when it was full, and then cover and seal it and replace it with an empty barrel. Not infrequently, I would get sprayed with human poop while rolling the barrel as it sloshed around and flipped upon itself like a wave pool, splashing back into the container. This was because the alcove was not tall enough for me to stand upright, and I had to lean my face over the barrel opening to gain the leverage to move it. I learned the hard way to take my time and to keep my mouth closed. I don't think that this is what Richard had in mind when he told me to "bring my toilet brush", but it was close enough for my taste.

Septic systems and poop, in general, are a bit of a sport in Vermont. A common method of building a septic tank in Vermont is to dig a hole, bury an old car or truck in the ground, run a PVC pipe through the back window of the vehicle and then cover over the whole affair in sand, gravel and soil. It was also common to have it running directly into a stream or river. Predictably, the septic pipes are not mentioned in the postcards.

Finding a home proved more difficult than we first imagined. Roman perceived that my wife was struggling mightily with giving up her home in Athol, especially with the bleak prospects we found ourselves facing in the southern Vermont housing market. He decided he needed to "pastor" her on the issue. He built up her hopes to a fever pitch one night by telling us over dinner that a minister friend of his in Dover was selling his "huge" ranch which also had plenty of land and breathtaking mountain views. Chana got so excited that she started calling her sisters to tell them the exciting news. She seemed encouraged for the first time in several months.

It was a long, winding ride about forty minutes away. Roman repeatedly looked in the rearview to reinforce the notion that this was a "huge" house, and his wife would smile and giggle in the seat next to him each time. Chana clutched my hand tightly, concerned.

We arrived, finally. Toddler bikes and other dirty toys were strewn about the small front yard which was more dirt than grass. The house was in a gully, surrounded by trees and had no view. A smelly yellow lab ran around the Toyota, barking wildly. The small front deck and steps were roped off and listing dangerously, needing repair. The exterior needed painting. It was also tiny, no more than a thousand square feet. I assumed that we were meeting someone here who would escort all of us to the actual house, but instead, Roman looked at us and smiled devilishly.

"This is it!" He said and hopped out of the car.

"You go," Chana said. She turned away, upset and disgusted, still in the Toyota. I waited for her for a moment or two, but finally just went in. This was a non-starter. I stood on the back deck with Roman's wife after our brief tour, while Roman hung inside talking with the owner.

"Chana didn't want to come in?"

"Can you blame her?" Roman's wife lowered her head and made her way back to the car. Chana cried herself to sleep that night. A home did finally come onto the market in Newfane. Chana saw the listing in the weekend circular. We called the agent and were told that there were already two qualifying offers on the property. We needed to move fast if we were interested. It was a modified chalet on a dead-end private road on a mountainside about two miles from the center of town. It had a pond, a rough-hewn garage and a partially finished walk out basement. Only one bathroom. But it had a large great room with a massive center fireplace and open concept main level, including a wonderful side room with large windows and a small wood stove that was homey and inviting. If we bunked the boys and girls into the two upstairs bedrooms, it could work. It was in our price range, too.

We made a full-priced offer, and it was accepted contingent upon the inspection and title search. The sellers had been long-time members of the church before Roman had taken it over, and though they no longer attended, he knew them well. He felt it was an obvious "God thing" and offered to do the home inspection for us. He wasn't a licensed inspector but had been a plumber's apprentice years previously, and it would save us $600 to have him do it. During the inspection, while Chana and I and the kids walked the grounds and visited the pond in the back, I noticed that Roman and the owner were spending an enormous amount of time under the huge back deck discussing something. I was curious but waited until we were back at his home to ask about it.

"It's a great house," he said, "but it has a few issues. I can help with most of them. My question is, do you want the house?" I nodded. "Chana liked it."

"You can get your deposit back easily if I report what I found. But if you want the house, I won't bring it up."

"What do you mean? What are the issues?" He put his arm forward, palm up on the table, and used his fingers to number them for me.

"The roof leaks. Mark said he fixed it, but I don't believe him, because I know him. That will have to be looked at. The electric panel is a snake's nest. Looks like he did a lot of it himself and he is not an electrician. He did install a Generator and a Gen Box for it, so that's good to have." I didn't know what a Gen Box was, so I just shrugged. "But those aren't the main issues," he said.

"There's more?" I was growing alarmed.

"There's an issue with the septic. Seems it's a failed system. He has a gray water pit in the back under the deck. People put in gray water pits when their septic is no good. It diverts all the gray water and only allows septic waste into the system. The pit was overflowing and running down the embankment when we arrived."

"So, we probably shouldn't buy this property then." He put his hand up and smiled.

"Do you want the house?"

"Well not if we have to fix every damn thing in it, no. Sounds like a bad deal."

"Do you like the house? Do you want the house?"

"Well, I'm trusting you. If you say the issues can be fixed, then yeah."

"Then, don't worry about the septic. And don't say anything about it to Chana, the Realtor, or anyone else. I'll handle it."

"Okay."

"I'm serious. If you say anything about the septic you won't get the house." I nodded in agreement.

We bought the house, but not before my pre-arranged financing fell through and I had to scramble at the last minute to find new financing, which I did, albeit at a terrible interest rate. The $800 mortgage I had in Athol became a $1,600 mortgage at this new place, which was less than half the size of the house we had left behind. I was going backwards in life. But that's okay, since *down was up*, if you recall. It turned out the roof had not been fixed, the electric was a problem (the kitchen overheads caught fire one day) and the "gray water pit" in the back was, in fact, the septic itself, which had completely failed, and raw sewage was running out the opening that the owner had created for overflow so that it ran down hill into Smith Brook, contaminating the stream. We had to manually pump out the septic tank every month for several years, and it always smelled like sewage in the warmer months. Roman told me he misunderstood the septic situation because Mark had lied to him. He did help us by building an actual gray water pit which helped a bit, and I was thankful for that.

Eventually, we bypassed the septic altogether by investing in a composting toilet, which didn't work. The composting system was designed around a natural composting method which was self-contained in the home. This failed nearly right away, as the system appeared to be designed to work only when no one used it. For some time, we had to pee in a five-gallon pail and only use the toilet to poop. It was disgusting all the way around. And we had one bathroom for seven people. Despite several other attempts at repair, including a local contractor volunteering to put in a new leech field and tank for us (which wasn't done correctly and failed within two years), the septic was always a problem, and ultimately prevented us from selling the property.

The house was perched on the edge of a dirt right-of-way which was owned by our neighbor across the street and shared by our neighbors at the top of the hill. The first day we moved in, while the moving truck was still in the driveway, our neighbor up the hill maneuvered his backhoe down the hill and started digging a trench at the end of our driveway in front of our house. It was about a foot deep. I went over to ask what he was doing.

"Not your concern," he replied. "Don't screw with it. It's for drainage." I looked at the ditch, which would no doubt cause our Buick LeSabre to bottom out every single time we drove over it. I looked back at him.

"This is something. Do you always make a point of digging trenches at the end of people's driveways the day they move in? Just curious." He didn't laugh.

"This here's not your driveway. It's mine. You just get to use it. If you don't like it, you can use your own right-of-way." He pointed off to his right, down the hill, where a faint go-cart track could be discerned between the trees near the power lines downhill from my garage. "That's yours. It's on your land." I was mystified.

"Don't you think you should introduce yourself to your new

neighbors before digging trenches at the end of their driveway? That's all I'm saying."

"You aint very sociable, are you now?" He replied. He shook his head and continued digging. I waved to get his attention again.

"I want you to stop digging, please. As soon as you leave, I'm going to fill this back in, so you're wasting your time."

"Don't you touch, it, ya hear?!" He was serious. I nodded my head. *These were our new neighbors*, I thought. I left him to his fun. I had a truck to unload. I'd have my son fill it in before we had to bring the truck back the next day. The "road", as he called it, was his most carefully guarded possession, even though it wasn't actually on his land, but belonged to our other neighbors across the road. It also constituted our legal right-of-way, according to our deed, so he was wrong to restrict us in any way. *He called the shots*, though, or so he thought. This road would be the source of several police reports, a violent attack upon my wife and daughter, several letters from lawyers and the reason I spent nearly all my spare time solidifying the property's original right of way, the one our neighbor had pointed to, which I rebuilt from a cart path to a well-groomed, smooth driveway. This ended up benefitting my neighbor when Hurricane Irene swept through the region, and his right of way was completely washed out. That's because, thanks to my experience building drainage structures in the White Mountains, my road was built to withstand the deluge and escaped largely unharmed. I called them and told them they could use our right of way to get back and forth until their road was fixed. This, of course, didn't stop their grandson from nearly running over my young daughter Jeanette in the driveway by barreling up our driveway at forty miles per hour in his truck, so fast that she could barely run out his way. This nearly resulted in people getting shot. It was such a wonderful place to live. The year after we moved, I was told that this young drunk redneck had dropped dead suddenly in his home from a brain aneurysm. Never, before or since, had I been so happy to hear of someone's death. I think I danced at the news, and still smile today when I think of it. The son of a bitch was lucky I didn't take his head off several years earlier with my shovel after he threatened my wife and daughter. You had to be there to appreciate the feeling. He was truly a complete waste of human flesh.

When we moved out of the area, we rented the home rather than sell it, because the septic was bad. By the time we moved south to Georgia, the person we bought the house from had moved back into it with the intent to rent to own. We walked in this in good faith by not charging full rent in exchange for maintenance and upkeep by the renter, since he was a general contractor, and had promised to fix everything. He did nothing. And every other month he had an excuse as to why he couldn't pay the rent on time, or in full, or at all. It was an ongoing battle. Eventually, he found a lawyer who let him know that he could outlast us if he just stopped paying, and that's exactly what he did, forcing us into bankruptcy. Such a scumbag.

Following Roman into the dirty, dangerous waters of religious extremism had led to a loss of financial security and a feeling of desperateness and estrangement. But at least we knew that Jesus loved us. *The Bible told us so.* And Jesus could be trusted to bless our efforts to serve him, as we could plainly see.

Chapter 15

———⚬⚬———

THE MOSES MODEL

DURING THE BEGINNING of the Covid-19 event, I took a part time job at a grocery store to help supplement my income while my business sagged through the spring, stocking shelves in the grocery department.

"Shalom!" I heard this from behind me. I turned and a tall, thin, older man with long white hair and a matching beard was smiling at me. I smiled back.

"Shalom!" I replied.

"You Jewish?" He was looking at my kippah.

"Yes, sir." He drew a few steps closer so he could lower his voice.

"Do you know who your Messiah is? It's Jesus Christ! Do you know Jesus?"

"Thank you, but I don't believe in Jesus."

"That's because you haven't met him," he replied. I sighed. *Should I tell him?*

"I actually wasn't born Jewish. I used to be a Christian." His eyes widened and he stepped back.

"You left the faith to become Jewish? Or are you a *messianic* Jew?"

"Look, I respect your passion and what you think you're doing for me, but I told you I don't believe in Jesus." I tried to say this evenly without a trace of attitude. He was undaunted.

"Well, listen. What's your name?"

"David," I said, and he smiled.

"Great Jewish name," he said, and I nodded. "Listen, you must never have been born again. I can understand losing belief if you haven't been born again. But, man," he raised his arms in dramatic fashion, "When I experienced *that*, I could never go back. Never! Jesus is so *real!* That's what you need, man! You need to be *born again*!" His face exploded with enthusiasm.

"Actually, I was born again radically in college." I added air quotes for effect, "I dedicated my life to Christ. I even served as a pastor for a number of years." After I said this, the excitement drained from his face and was replaced with horror. He shook his head in disbelief.

"How?" he said. I shrugged in response. He continued, "How can you taste of the truth and walk away? Man, I'll pray for you, but I hope you haven't committed the unpardonable sin."

"I'd love to discuss it with you sometime, but right now I'm on the clock and I need to get back to work." He shook his head and waved me off. I felt sort of bad. But his mentality is typical of many who are brainwashed with the Jesus story. There are only two types of people in the world for these folks: The *saved* and the *lost*. In my case, I was a special kind of lost, at least to him. If ever I get the opportunity to talk to him at length, I will explain to him that in life sometimes, there are experiences one can have which transcend the psychological orgasm called being *born again*. Such spiritual or psychological highs eventually become like dusty photo albums you pull out and look at occasionally when you feel nostalgic. But when you have lived through the depths of trauma and abuse, becoming *born again* is ultimately just another rebound relationship which must be held in suspicion.

Roman sat with me on the glacial erratic, which is a huge granite boulder, overlooking Townshend Dam. He had asked me to take a hike with him so we could talk. It was a crisp, early fall day, and the water in the lake in front of the dam glistened. A few solitary row boats sat motionless, with thin lines of fishing poles extending from the end of small human figures within them, so far away that they looked like seagulls over the ocean sky. It was my first year in Vermont.

"Do you know about Pastor Romaine?"

"Can't say that I do," I said. He tossed a pebble off the ledge and adjusted his posture.

"Romaine was there in the beginning, with Chuck Smith. He refused a title. Didn't even have an office. But all the guys that were raised up in Calvary Chapel, guys that are famous today, you know, many were discipled by Romaine, not Chuck." I looked at him. He continued, "Chuck teaches that Calvary never really took off until he had Romaine. It wasn't the music, like everything thinks. It was the relationship Chuck had with Romaine."

"How so?"

"Because Romaine was the *tough love*. He would put the young, ambitious pastors in their place. If he saw two pastors gossiping in the hall during the service, they'd high tail when they saw him coming. It really is what allowed Chuck to be effective. He didn't have to be *that* guy." I nodded as he continued, "It's what most Calvary Chapel pastors lack. Richard is still looking for that guy. It's a position in Calvary that only the leaders know about. It's called Second. It's not an official title, but it's a position of tremendous honor that very few people have the humility to walk in." He looked at me squarely, "And that's who *you* are, *here*. You're my Second. That's why you don't have a title. You'll *never* have one. I prayed for a person who could fill that role. It's desperately needed here." He turned away and rested back on his elbows, "And I'm glad it's you," he said. I didn't have a clue what he was talking about and had never heard of a leadership position which was a secret, but it seemed like something I should embrace?

"I thought I was your Assistant Pastor," I said. He shook his head and laughed.

"No, it's much better than that. Any pastor that comes here, or is raised up here, is *under* you. You are *me* to the congregation. You have my authority, like Joseph in Egypt."

What he didn't tell me, was that the position of Second, since it wasn't official, was also prone to manipulation. Anything he told me to do, as his "undercover" representative, he could either claim or deny responsibility for. The reason a position like this could even exist was because of the Calvary Chapel method of leadership.

Calvary Chapel operated, in its church government, under what they termed the "Moses Model", which was somewhat loosely based (they would claim closely based) on the story of Moses in the Torah, or the Books of Moses, as they are known in the Christian world. Essentially, this ministry distinctive assumed that the pastor of the local assembly was the one selected by God and, therefore, the one who had the authority to speak on behalf of God to the congregation to which they were "called". In other words, the Calvary Chapel Senior Pastor was, in essence, Moses to his congregation, and anyone who came against the leadership, authority, or even the teachings of the Senior Pastor of *any* Calvary Chapel, was, for all intents and purposes, participating in the rebellion of Korah. (Korah, a Levite, rebelled against the leadership and authority of Moses and was subsequently swallowed into a fissure in the earth, which opened to Hell, along with all aligned with him.) In this light, the pastor of a Calvary Chapel congregation was obligated to pray for, and seek out, those individuals (always men) who would support and enhance his vision and leadership. (In the corporate world, these are people that we call "yes-men"). When one of the leaders under the Senior Pastor felt they were "called" to go start their own church, they would go to the "Moses" of their congregation who would (if he liked them, or perhaps even if he didn't) ask them to pray about it and to write a "vision statement". This was, essentially, their job application for a promotion, to be "sent" off to try and accomplish the vision, which typically meant a church plant. This was called *being sent*, officially. The term meant that the leadership (read: God) had endorsed them. If you weren't *sent*, it meant you didn't have a *covering*, which also meant you were potentially out of God's will if you decided to leave on your own. The cool part was that, even if you succeeded in being *sent*, you would receive zero financial support. After all, if God were truly with you, then you should thrive on your own, right? No, you were entirely on your own. *Lots of luck; be sure to write.*

This was the Calvary Chapel model and environment, and Roman militarized the expression in such a way that only a masochist could succeed in his version of the program. One way he walked out the Moses Model was to claim that anything I felt that God had showed me through study and prayer was invalid unless God *first* showed *him*, since he was my Moses, and Moses always received instruction before the people did. This is the way the Moses Model operated, in practical terms, under Calvary Chapel leaders, generally, and specifically for me under the men I served.

The corporate ladder within this program, unofficially of course, was a system of tests. There were the above-described poke tests, but there were also the most important tests of all; the *loyalty tests*, which, if you failed *them*, then your progress would forever cease. And, just like the evaporating morning mist of a pleasant Vermont summer morning, your career in ministry would have reached its end within the Calvary system. Such was my fate, ultimately, and this sad end had already befallen two leadership couples, unbeknownst to me, before I arrived in Vermont, both of whom ultimately felt that the only solution was to completely relocate to another part of the country, since staying in the same state was too risky. After all, Roman might talk to them again. Roman was apparently thinking that the third time would be the charm. But, at this juncture, sitting above Townshend Dam, I was all full of love and hope and trust, as I knew deep inside that Roman was not like my father or my Scoutmaster or Pastor Richard, but that he *understood me*, and wanted the best for my life. In fact, I was literally desperate to believe this, and that, of course, was my problem. I was a grown adult with a family, yet my daily existence in Vermont was at the edge of my psychological seat, always with halting breath, trying to settle into a security that would never materialize.

It was this perspective, and my willingness to buy in, that enabled me to go along with a vast array of insane scenarios and tasks. One thing which didn't help matters was that Roman would routinely (without my knowledge) call my wife at home and press for inside information as to my attitude, my conversations at home and my job. My wife was constantly upset with me in ways that I never understood because he would routinely do this, as it made her feel that something was wrong, or else why would he have to "check up on me"? My son Ari witnessed this repeatedly and he cites it today as a major reason why he lost trust in Roman's leadership and, by extent, the church itself. This intrusiveness would extend to public shaming, such as the ride home from the Boston men's retreat one year, with both my sons and two other members of the congregation in my van, when Roman announced before everyone that my wife, (my sons' mother, I must emphasize), *had lost too much weight*. I stole a glance at him while driving.

"She's lost too much weight?! What the heck are you talking about?"

"You'll see," he said.

"What do you mean, *'I'll see?'*" Roman just shook his head and looked out the window for a moment before answering.

"Your wife is very good-looking, okay? And she's lost weight. She's *too* good looking. She needs to gain weight again." I'm not entirely sure why he told me this or what his purpose was for doing so in front of my sons, since I was too angry to pursue the discussion further. My sons sat silently in the back while this conversation transpired, saying nothing, yet I know they heard the whole thing. There were many other similar situations, too many to try to catalog and useless to try.

One consistent theme which was reiterated both from the pulpit and through interaction, was the idea of "coming under authority". It was a big deal to Roman, and he also had a novel and eccentric manner of measuring the concept. A neutral observer would rather term his idea as "blind obedience". Walking in this proved particularly difficult when ethical boundaries were stretched or altogether violated, such as when Roman began privately counseling my oldest son, while he was still a minor and living in my home, to escape our home and to get out from under our tutelage. He also began grooming him as my replacement, all without informing me, even telling my son that I was like Balaam; a scandalous charge. I discovered it one day in casual conversation with my son. I confronted Roman about the issue at church one weekday.

"The Lord told me you'd have a problem with it. Said you'd be jealous," he said, nonchalantly, while painting trim in the sanctuary.

"The Lord told you I'd be jealous, huh? I'm not, and yet it occurs to me that you proceeded anyway, didn't you, despite the Lord's warning?" I waited for his response, but he just kept painting.

"Hey, I'm talking to you." He stopped and looked at me condescendingly, as though this were a formality he would merely tolerate but not engage with. I proceeded. "How would you have reacted if I did something like this to your son? Huh?" The answer is that he would have murdered me. Yet, he had no issue taking nonconsensual license with mine. "All I'm saying is that you have no right to do this with Jonathan without telling me first, and I should be briefed on the process as it develops. That's *my son*. I'm still responsible for him."

"Are you finished?"

I left the church, angry. It was really the first time I had confronted him in this manner and left the encounter unsatisfied or upset. It was an omen of what was to come.

Yes, it was a tough job to be Second. The expectations and standards were high, as well as inconsistent. I never really knew where I stood, or exactly what was expected of me, because it was fluid; it seemed to change daily. One day, a few years into my tenure, I was brought into his office at the church. He needed to "prepare" me for something.

"My brother is moving here," he said, "He's used to being in charge.

He's been an Assistant Pastor for a long time of a church much bigger than this one. I want to assure you of something."

"Okay," I said. He lifted his hands, palms open and facing down, in front of me, with one about six inches above the other, imitating a scale.

"He thinks he's here," he said, indicating the higher hand, "and he thinks you're here," indicating the lower one, "but you need to know that you're here," he moved the higher hand again, "and he's down here." I nodded.

"Okay," I said.

"He claims God told him he's called here but God hasn't shown me anything about him like he showed me about you. I just want you to know the score because it's going to be a rough ride." I was ready, so long as he had my back. I could handle it.

Before his brother arrived, I was the worship leader, the only acting elder, and the only real assistant that Roman had. Of course, none of these roles were official, as the only person in the church with any official authority or title was Roman. When his brother arrived, he immediately assumed for himself the self-appointed role of being in authority over me, like Roman had told me would happen, and Roman informed me that his brother felt threatened when he sensed that Roman and I had an advance arrangement. I saw no evidence of this, but I took his word for it. After all, he was his brother. As part of this "rough ride", I was demoted from leading the worship team, and his brother was given the role. He was also given the official title of Assistant Pastor, whereas I remained without an official title, as I had expected. But things did not get better over time, and I was sensing something was wrong. About a year later, I vented my frustration with my predicament.

"I have tried and tried to build a relationship with your brother, like you asked. He just resists all the way. He no-shows me at appointments, badmouths me to people in the fellowship behind my back. I mean, it never ends. How long do I have to put up with this?"

"I know it. I see it, believe me. It's *him,* not you. I've given him roles and responsibilities so that I can pastor him. He won't listen to me otherwise." This reassured me for a time, but things started to go sideways. Whereas I used to meet with Roman weekly, privately, to discuss the fellowship and some of the issues we were facing, in time, after his brother arrived, these meetings stopped. I didn't understand why, but didn't think too hard about it until, one day, Roman started a Sunday service by bringing several men, including his brother and my eighteen-year-old son, up front before the congregation and introduced them as the leaders of the church. I was not included in this, even though I was present, sitting in my normal spot in the back row where he wanted me to sit (for security reasons). A couple of the men on stage had no previous association with any significant role in the fellowship, and hardly ever attended anything besides Sunday morning services. Most of the people in the church who had been there for any length of time had their heads on swivels stealing glances at me in the back row, trying to figure out why I wasn't up front with the others, since people had known for years at that point that I was Roman's right-hand man. I questioned him about it after service. He smiled and shuffled his feet.

"I knew you'd be having this conversation with me. God told me." he said. *God told him. It didn't take a psychic to discern that this was coming,* I thought. Anyone in my position would have desired an explanation. He just looked at me, smugly. I continued, "What's going on? You don't really talk to me anymore." He pursed his lips.

"I have no idea what you're talking about."

"What do you mean? All those conversations we had about me coming alongside you. I sold my house cheap and sold my business and moved here because it was the *call.* That's why we're here. I can't turn back. I bought a one-way ticket. I want to know what's up. We used to meet just the two of us every week."

"Well, you know what happened to the woman with the issue of blood, right? Where did she go with her issue? To Jesus. You need to take your issue to the Lord, like she did." And that was it. That was the answer. This created a fight between my wife and I, as she wanted to know what I did to get demoted. But the only proof I had that I was of any rank at all were my private conversations with Roman. There was nothing in writing. It appeared, ultimately, that he had led me on. He had asked unwavering commitment and loyalty from me, but it seemed that in his mind, at least, I was still being evaluated even after I made the commitment. At some point, he apparently made the decision that he'd rather work with my son and his brother than myself, because I simply got boxed out of everything and had all my responsibilities taken from me, with no explanation for any of it. And I never got anything back. But it took me a long time to figure this out because I had been working with the presumption that I was *alongside* him, as Second, with nearly equal authority, only without a title. After all, this is what he had told me. As I continued to try to walk in my presumed role, I began having friction with some folks because Roman was not backing me up. In my last year there, I confronted him again.

"God told me to take my hands off you. That you belong to Him."

"What does that mean?"

"Ask the Lord. Get alone with him. He wants to talk to you." It was the last time we spoke of such things. Our relationship was effectively over, but I didn't yet know it.

Everything deteriorated quickly once I fully realized that I had been pushed out. Just before an extensive building project commenced at the church, near the end of my time there, Roman unexpectedly asked me to oversee a particular floor repair situation and to see that it was completed. I asked my friend Greg, who was going to be selected as the General Contractor for the upcoming project, to do the work. We rode to the church together after grabbing some tools from his home. When he and I arrived, Roman's brother was already there, working on the same project. Since he was also a contractor by profession, I felt it was foolish to try and stop him just because I was supposedly "in charge", as I had no similar skill. So, I let it go. When his brother was done, I went and reported to Roman, as he had asked me to keep him informed. He became visibly agitated.

"You blew it," he said. I was incredulous. *Blew what*, I wondered? He came into the hall and Greg proceeded to tell him that he would fix what his brother had done (it hadn't been done correctly, apparently) and not to worry, but Roman just stared at him with a blank expression and walked out. I followed him, angry. When I finally was alone with him and out of earshot of others, I laid into him.

"Would you mind explaining to me why you take such pleasure in being such an asshole all the time? I'll remind you that Greg and are I volunteers here. I do my best, always, but your attitude *sucks*, and there's no excuse for it. I'm embarrassed for Greg's sake, if not mine." After I said this, he poked at the floor and remained silent for a minute. I wondered if I had truly made an impact on him. Finally, he spoke without looking at me.

"I just want someone who will do what I tell him. That's all I want." I was ready to explode. This was one of the last private conversations I ever had with him while a member of that church.

The stress and tension finally came to a head one Tuesday night at the men's meeting. Another man, named Grant, who had been se-lected as an officer for the Board, had discussed with me privately his concerns about Roman's suggestive and problematic allegorizing of the Bible, as he constantly implied to us that he was in the role of "Moses" to our group and that we were "children in the wilderness." We prom-ised each other we'd speak up the next time he spoke like that. On this particular evening, all the leaders were there. By this time, I was not the same person that had moved to Vermont eight years previously. I had become jaded and skeptical. The trust had been broken between myself and Roman, and I was now highly suspicious of his motivations and his character.

We all sat around the long, white plastic table, with our coats still on in the chilly hall, our Bibles open before us. Roman began to tell us, as he had done on other occasions, that if we ever left the covering of the fellowship of the church and of his personal leadership, that God would surely destroy us, the way he destroyed the Israelites in the Wilderness. We needed to stay within the fold if we had any hope of God seeing us through life. I looked at Grant, and he lowered his eyes. And that was it for him; he lacked the courage to speak when the moment came, but I had seen and heard enough. Nearly eight years previously I had recklessly walked away from a fantastic situation in Massachusetts to move to Vermont to answer the *call*. In Central Massachusetts, I had a business which was maturing, a beautiful home, and a promising future. I left it all for the woods of Vermont, all because of a crazy spiritual spell which had been woven over my heart and mind by this crazed extremist whom I had grown, at one point, to love and trust. It was a spell born out of a desire for brotherhood, and of a friendship I thought I had but which was apparently not real, and a spiritual destiny I thought was mine to grasp but which had never truly been available. Now, the spell had been broken, the fantasy had unraveled, and I was not fooled anymore. I was *angry*.

I looked around the table, at the people in attendance, studying the faces and reactions of the men. Every single man there, including Roman, had left the church where their faith had been born and had moved on, in some cases multiple times, before landing here in southern Vermont in this church, participating in this group and hearing him tell us that he, as their pastor, was the gatekeeper to our spiritual health. But if Roman was correct in his perspective, all of us should have been destroyed long before this night, since we had all left our "covering" ages prior. Yet, here we were, alive and well, and listening to this nonsensical drivel about what God had planned for our lives and futures. I turned to face him again, but I had to tap my forefinger on his Bible to get him to look me in the eyes.

"Hey. I have a word for you. And you need to listen close to what I have to say." He responded with that unstable gaze he would often show, the one that had violence just below the surface; that lurking part of his personality which caused me to have to leave my house at midnight and rush to the hospital after an offended congregant had attempted to take his life with a metal pipe to the head, just so I could prevent him from going after the man and depositing his body into the Vermont woods in vengeance.

"I'm not here to see if you're okay. I'm here to make sure you remain okay." He smiled, wryly, his forehead stitches still bleeding.

"You know me well," he said.

But during this moment at the men's study, I wasn't interested in making sure he was "okay". I was intending to light him up.

"You're not Moses. Got it?? You aren't fucking Moses!" I slammed my hand on the table for effect. Out of the corner of my eye, I saw his brother jump in his chair, "You sit here and talk about coverings and staying where you're called, but both you and everyone else here has come from somewhere else." I looked around the table at each of the men before continuing. "You know that guys? This isn't where you started. It's not where any of us started. And it's not where any of us are headed, either." I turned back to Roman, "You're full of *shit*. You know that, right?" Roman, in his classically deflective fashion, placed his palm upon my open Bible, and spoke slowly, and condescendingly.

"Are you concerned about your place of leadership in this church?" I laughed aloud at this.

"No!" I threw his hand off my Bible and closed it. "Maybe you'd like to share with these guys all the things you've told me privately over the last seven years, huh? Maybe you ought to do that." I stood up with my Bible in hand and marched out of the fellowship hall.

"Have a blessed night," I heard him say this behind my back as I was walking out.

"Fuck off," I said without looking, being sure to slam the door behind me. I didn't step near the church again for nearly six months, nor did I make any attempt to speak to him. In turn, he made no attempt to reach out to me. I decided to accept a printing job at a commercial print shop north of Burlington, a little under three hours from where we lived. I was intending on making my escape.

My son, Jonathan, who has always been a peacemaker, tried to talk me out of leaving. But I knew the score. Of course, I should have known up front that this was the ending we could expect. The pattern had been set for me as a child with my Scoutmaster. Roman merely reinforced the narrative:

"I don't want you to talk to anyone in Massachusetts about what I'm doing with you. They are going to want to know. You'll get calls. I'm already getting calls. But it's between you and me. It's not for anyone else to know. Let all those relationships go. You don't need them."

Yes, I had heard all this before as a young boy. I had been told again and again by Mr. Beck, *'Never tell anyone about this or bad things will happen to you'*. All mistreatment and abuse has as its core tenet one key element: An intentional misuse of power.

Early in my time with Roman in Vermont, we sat together on his front deck, and he was straining to see into the darkness of the treeline near the brook.

"You see those eyes there?" I peered into the void.

"No, sorry, I don't."

"There are demon eyes. They are watching us. See them? They are bobbing up and down." I didn't see them, and told him so, with disappointment. He grimaced.

"When you're ready to step into your role, you'll see them too."

It's crazy to talk about it now, but it was as if I had spent a decade existing in some type of half-light; neither day nor night, but now I finally had the proper illumination to see properly. In the end, though, it was hard to let go. He had been my confidante in Massachusetts when I felt that Pastor Richard didn't understand me. He had believed in me. He had pastored my children. We had been hiking buddies. We laughed at the same jokes. We were going to run the roads of ministry together and our families would grow old side by side. He had encouraged me to step into things that Pastor Richard justifiably didn't approve of, and I had done so, following his counsel at the expense of all other voices. But none of this was enough to save our relationship, and

I felt quite sad about it when the truth finally settled in. As painful as it all was, I couldn't allow myself to be angry forever, and I knew it. It wasn't all his fault. In fact, since he has never openly admitted culpability, I doubt he views hardly *any* of it as his fault. I'm convinced that he also thought, at one time, that things would work out just as he had said. I really don't believe for a minute that he intended for things to go the way that they did. Perhaps he felt, at a certain point, that he had made a mistake in asking me to come north to Vermont and didn't know how to tell me, and probably wasn't comfortable with the implications of that realization.

The two of us had shared important things in common. Both of us had rejected our father's hard-driving, business orientation of life for a more altruistic focus. Both of us wanted to cut to the bottom of the bullshit and live for what really mattered. Both of us had felt deceived and lied to by the society and culture we called home. Roman had left the Marines depressed and angry because of the things he had experienced and the lies he discovered that our country was telling its citizens, and he decided that nothing else mattered except Jesus. He took the mission of the gospel very, very seriously, and by combining his religious zeal with his military training and background, became a cultic religious extremist, but to him, it was nothing more than commitment. Most importantly, he isn't responsible for my life or its problems. Yes, he was an extremist who lived on the edge, but I followed him to that very edge. *That's on me.* He had a certain worldview, one which very few people could embrace. I tried to live on that razor's line with him, but I fell off. The trick, now, was to stop the fall before we had nothing left to hang on to.

Chapter 16

———— ✺ ————

SOMEONE ELSE'S STORY

DESPITE THE DIFFICULTIES of my experience in Roman's church, there were some valuable things which came from it. There was one thing that he did, particularly, which had a major impact upon me. He decided, in my first full year there, to start a men's group, one which I was supposed to eventually lead, in which the curriculum would be a continuous verse-by-verse study of the books of Moses, known as the *Torah* by the Jews, which were the first five books of the Bible. For seven years I participated in, and at times helped lead (my anticipated role, as you might have guessed, never materialized) this Bible study on Tuesday nights at the church. It was the most important component, in the mind of Roman at least, to the entire ministry. At first, I didn't catch on to what he was seeking to accomplish with this study. In hindsight, though, I see it. He desired to raise up leaders, and what better way to expose the men of the church to the Moses Model of Calvary Chapel than through the books of Moses? For me, however, this repeated, intensive journey through the Torah, even though it was presented through the lens of Christian dog-ma, had a transformative effect upon my thinking.

A curious thought dawned on me somewhere during our first journey through these books, which I had previously read but had never *studied*: These were the sacred texts of Judaism and of the Jewish people and related to an eternal covenant that God made with Israel at Mt. Sinai. This event had occurred over 1,500 years before Christianity was even a thought in anyone's mind. I became increasingly uncomfortable with the fact that we were appropriating these ancient scriptures for our own personal application when they, technically, *didn't belong to us*. Or did they? I was struggling with this. Didn't Paul declare that we were, by virtue of Christ's atoning work, "grafted in" to Israel? Wasn't Jesus the "King of the Jews"?

The thought of two major religions sharing the same scriptures yet with fundamentally different views of them was a puzzle piece I could not stop fiddling around with. I began to gnaw upon the problem the way a piece of gristle gets lodged between your teeth and you spend all day playing with it with your tongue in the futile hopes of dislodging it. It irritated me. How could this be possible? What did the Jewish people think of these books? How did *they* interpret them? And how would this be different from what *we* were doing with them? After all, wasn't Jesus all through the Old Testament? Or so I had been led to believe. *Why didn't the Jews see him too?* There was a book on my shelf at the time titled something along the lines of "Jesus in every book of the Bible". I think I had been carrying it around since my Fundamentalist Baptist days. I picked it off the shelf and read it. Jesus was here, Jesus was there, Jesus was *absolutely everywhere*...typologically of course. But he even made personal appearances, according to Christians, such as the "angel of the LORD" who confronted Joshua as he readied to take the nation across the river to Jericho. Some even contended that it was Jesus who called out to Moses from the burning bush. I found that this was the lens that most evangelicals approached the Old Testament with: *What can we learn about Jesus by reading this?* But this approach no longer worked for me. The Jewish people didn't have the New Testament. How could Jews, consequently, encourage themselves in their relationship with God if they *didn't have Jesus?* One could fairly wonder how it was possible that Judaism even existed anymore if Jesus was truly the promised Jewish Messiah. It certainly appears as though Paul thought that all Jews would eventually know Jesus and accept him, at least if you read his comments on the subject in some of the later chapters in the book of Romans. And yet, clearly, they had not done so. So, here we were as evangelical Christians, some two thousand years after the beginning of Christianity, still proclaiming Jesus as the Jewish King, and the people he belonged to (the Jews) had continued to reject this claim for the entirety of that time. This was amazing to me, and the more I read and studied the Torah, the more amazed I became. Only, as we continued year by year through these books, my sense of amazement changed. Instead of wondering why the Jews still rejected Jesus, I began to wonder why Christians weren't studying these books as priority reading. Further, I began to have suspicions that our Jesus-centered perspective was blinding us to some things. I wondered aloud at times, *what are we missing here?*

This question, originally merely a peripheral concern, took on center stage when Roman asked me to teach the twenty-seventh chapter of Deuteronomy. Amidst the words of this somber chapter, were the following:

"Then Moses and the Levitical priests spoke to all Israel, saying, 'Be silent and listen, O Israel! This day you have become a people for the LORD your God. You shall therefore obey the LORD your God and do His commandments and His statutes which I command you today.'...And all the people shall answer and say, 'Amen'...Cursed is he who does not confirm the words of this law by doing them.' And all the people shall say, 'Amen'." (Deut.27:9-26, edited)

It seemed apparent that Israel was going to be judged according to their covenantal faithfulness to the Law. As I pondered this, it made sense to me. It seemed only fair. And fairness mattered a great deal to me in my conceptions of spirituality and of life in general. After all, I was an avid football fan. When I watched a game, regardless of who I might be rooting for, I was okay with the outcome, provided it was a fair contest. If, however, I discerned that the referees were an unjustified influence on the game through bogus or inaccurate calls (or non-calls), I would feel miffed, or even violently angry, because *justice had been thwarted*. No one likes to see a scoundrel win an honor he hasn't earned. It violates our basic sensibilities of right and wrong. We want justice. We want equity. It makes perfect sense to us to punish wrong-doers and reward people who do right. It's balanced and it's honorable to do so. The reverse is a travesty.

I realized, in studying the books of Moses, that the selling point of the Christian gospel was also one of its weakest attributes, and this was the concept of "free grace" through the *magic blood* of Jesus. It sounded wonderful, and certainly was attractive to people who had really made a mess of things, *but was it true?* Did the Christian gospel of "not by works but by grace alone" hold up to scrutiny? Was it not plausible that Ted Turner was correct to call Christianity a "good loser's religion"? I wanted to believe that it *did* hold up to such scrutiny, but *how?* Why didn't Paul's allegory of the child of promise and the child of the bondslave in Galatians (representing the free grace in Christ versus the Law) find an adequate representation in the Torah that Paul was citing? Were the Jews, then, nothing more than the punchline of a giant cosmic joke? The paid-out villain in a predictable white-hat / black-hat scripted drama? Apparently, the Calvinists thought so. Contrary to Paul, we find no place in the Torah where the Jews are told to "obey the Law until Jesus comes", or even anything remotely resembling his Galatians argument. Jesus was said to have "fulfilled the Law for our sakes". So, he fulfilled the Law. If so, *so what?* What did that do for me, exactly? According to the Torah, absolutely nothing! It truly puzzled me, as I studied Deuteronomy twenty-seven, that God would give such stern warnings to his chosen nation about what would happen to them if they strayed from obeying his laws and yet fail to mention that there was a "get-out-of-jail-free-card" waiting for their descendants, but one which they could not access yet, and wouldn't even hear about for over fifteen hundred years. Worse yet, was the commonly held Christian view that the Law was given to prove to the nation *that they couldn't keep it*, to compel them in exasperation to cry out for the *magic blood* of Jesus, or so the traditional evangelical message goes.

Also, it violated everything we learn about life growing up. How reliable was a religious perspective which failed to uphold known truths by which all people had to live every day? Some things were immutable and accepted by all people. Such as the idea that murder is wrong, that incest is wrong, and that stealing is wrong, for examples of what I mean. Yet God, supposedly, could not even see these blights on your character if you had the *magic blood* of Jesus attributed to you. Not so for the Jews without Jesus. Nope; if they weren't willing to get vaccinated with the *magic blood* of Jesus, they would still have to live under the strictures of the Law. *And good luck with that!* How was this fair? For that matter, most people would agree with the Ten Commandments as being solid moral and ethical principles, even if these same people denied that they were "laws of God". Are the consequences of wrong behavior no longer in effect because of Jesus? Did Christians really believe this nonsense?

In real life, the law doesn't change today, just because I fulfilled it yesterday. The speed limit remains the speed limit, no matter how many times I obey it. It's still sitting there, in all its killjoy power, waiting for me tomorrow. Supposedly however, as a Christian, once I assent to the message of the gospel, I can speed everywhere and break every law on the books without true accountability, because I have a "get-out-from-under-the-law-free-card".

The notion, in this respect, that Jesus is the only one who ever kept the Law perfectly and never sinned sounds wonderful, but even if he did so, how does this accomplishment annul the Law? There's no provision in the Torah by which the Law's power is annulled by virtue of a person keeping it perfectly. What a ridiculously unbiblical, yet universally held, Christian belief.

In addition, on what biblical basis did all things in life center upon one's religious confession that "Jesus was Lord"? What if we never made such a confession? Was our life now meaningless? Were we nothing but an organic lifeform that was here today and gone tomorrow, in lieu of such a testimony? What of the issues of right and wrong, in general? Did merit and performance mean anything in life? What was to be esteemed? What was to be denounced? Who was righteous and who was wicked and how would one define these ideas?

As I contemplated the history and status of the Jewish people (and I began to do so only as I began to study the Torah) I had to ask all these questions and more. Were God's covenants real? What did they mean? Were they still in effect today? How did the Church reconcile these ideas? Was it true that Christianity was a form of "completed Jewishness", as the Calvinists understood it, or was Christianity simply a parasite that was justifying itself by leeching the authority of the Jewish scriptures and the promises God made to the Jewish people, just to commandeer them for their own purposes?

There was an elderly woman whom my wife and I befriended when we first moved to Vermont. Her name was Winnie. She was a stubborn old Vermonter who had come to faith late in life. She had stood up one Wednesday night at church in response to Roman's exhortation that God wanted them to change so that He could accomplish his work in the valley. "We don't change!" She protested, "Vermonters don't change!" She looked around the sanctuary at her peers, "But I'm willing to try!" It was a glorious moment. It seemed to epitomize the whole religious experience and objective entirely. After all, if your religion, whatever it may be, did not inspire you to change and to grow and to become a better person, than what good was it? But, considering the gospel and the Christian understanding of how a person became "right with God", why would this noble objective of personal improvement be necessary? Why would anyone need to work to "change" once they come to faith in Jesus? Isn't Jesus's *magic blood* enough? *You mean, there's more?*

Winnie was an amateur artist. She painted a small watercolor, a print of which we have hanging on our living room wall today, which was her attempt to show all the most meaningful places she had lived in her lifetime, from her childhood home on a local mountain, to the home near the city, to the apartment attached to her friends' home in which she spent her final days. It was an artistic expression of her longing to make sense of her life's journey; of the memories and experiences that can feel so randomized and, at times, cruelly disconnected.

Winnie went to the hospital one day for a health evaluation, which included x-rays, as she was complaining of pain in her chest and difficulty breathing. The doctors told her that there was a spot or two in her lungs that were concerning and could mean cancer. She began early treatment, but her health deteriorated rapidly. It turned out, a month or so later, that what was originally thought to be a spot of cancer, was the only spot in her lungs *not* infested with cancer. It metastasized quickly and she died much sooner than any had anticipated. At the funeral were people I had never met; relatives who were not religious, and who had moved out of the area many years previously. The gravesite ceremony was somber and perfunctory. Our consolation was that we believed her spirit was in heaven. But what of the others? What if they had no such belief? What was *their* consolation? What of the Jews who died in the Holocaust? What of *them?* What was Jesus to do for *them*, most of whom had never had the opportunity to hear the gospel? No, the victims of the Holocaust must not, I imagined, be dependent upon such a fragile happenchance as believing in the gospel of Jesus, could they have been? I wasn't sure I wanted to be attached to a belief system that thought sending Holocaust victims to hell for lack of a confession of Jesus was okay. Winnie's art portrait of her home betrayed the lack of authenticity of the Christian gospel. When she looked back on her life, she rightly targeted the benchmarks of merit as being her physical stopping points throughout her life, and the people which inhabited these scenes, not the religious conceptions she happened to ascribe to, which are inherently arbitrary in nature. Our lives consist of the things we *do*, right and wrong, and the experiences we have while doing them. We are human beings, not doctrinal statements.

"What kind of Christian are you?" Said the older gentleman at the head table, and his wife blushed. I had received an impromptu invite to an awards banquet in which this man's son was being honored as an exemplary citizen and businessman in a town in far northern Vermont. I had been invited to sit at the head table, not that I deserved it.

"I'm a non-denominational Christian," I answered, hesitantly. He became impatient.

"Yeah, I get it, a *Jesus follower*, but what kind?"

"I am not sure what you mean." He had caught me off-guard.

"What do you think of Paul?" He offered this as a change of tactic.

"What do you mean?"

"Paul wasn't a Christian!" He declared, finally, impatient for me to catch his hint. *Well, alright then.* I wasn't entirely sure what to say to that. It seemed rather far-fetched.

"What do you mean?" I asked, repeating myself as much to buy time as anything. I was thinking he was drunk and unhinged, and I was becoming a bit agitated with his ambiguous approach. I thought to myself, *Get to the point, man!*

"Paul was a Pharisee! The Christian Church didn't exist yet!" I had to pause. He had made a good point there, saying that the Church didn't exist in Paul's day. I asked him what he was studying that led him to such a thought process. He scribbled a note on a piece of paper and handed it to me. It read "FFOZ".

"Fozz?" I said, saying it as a word, "You mean like Fozzy Bear, the Muppet?" and his wife, who I wasn't aware was listening to our exchange, chuckled.

"Just look it up. And here's my email address." I handed him the scrap of paper again after he motioned for me to give it back and he wrote it down. His granddaughter was performing in a ballet at a local college in a week. He invited me. I went with my daughters, and met him in the lobby during the intermission, where he handed me a duffel bag full of study materials, including a commentary on the Torah by a "Messianic Jew". By this time, I had already sent away for a complimentary magazine by the organization, which was "First Fruits of Zion". I gave it to Chana to check out. She read it cover to cover, and she liked what she read. One of the things in the issue was the concept of the "kingdom of God" being on earth, and not in heaven. This was, though simple and straight out of scripture, revolutionary to us. And it made sense. For years, we had been indoctrinated in the idea of a "rapture" of the elect, and this concept being presented of the kingdom of God on earth, while a major departure from that, made more sense to us. Based on this, I picked up the massive commentary on the Torah that my friend had given me and looked at it. By this point, we had plugged into a local fellowship about five minutes away in our new town; a non-denominational Christian church which had a heavy emphasis upon music, and which displayed strong charismatic leanings. They welcomed us in, however, and this counted for a lot. But it wasn't going to be enough for us. We had come out of an intense ten-year cult-level experience, and I was questioning the very roots of my faith at this point. When my oldest daughter and son-in-law decided to follow us north and move into the same town, it became imperative for us to explore a coherent spiritual direction together. We had agreed to start doing a family Bible study together. The messianic commentary looked attractive to this end.

Initially, I felt that it would be best to just follow the commentary together and discuss it. We all sat in our living room in the condo, staring at each other, and my family looked to me expectantly. I opened to the first page of the commentary, which started at the first "Torah portion", which is the first section of the book of Genesis. We had no idea about the "parsha cycle" of the Jewish world. We also had no good reason to not start at the beginning of the Bible, just as we had done for years in the men's group. There were some Hebrew letters and then an English translation to the title. It spelled "Bereshit". I had never heard this term before and didn't know how to pronounce it. I looked at my family and stated, matter-of-factly,

"Tonight, we are going to begin with the study of "Bear-shit.""

"Really?" said my daughter April.

"Yeah," I said. After a moment, everyone laughed nervously. I had no clever comeback. It was unredeemable. But we proceeded, and the deconstruction of our Christian faith officially became unstoppable.

Chapter 17

GETTING BURNT AT THE STAKE

WE HAD BECOME, as Paul McCartney famously composed, a *band on the run*. Leaving Roman's church brought a temporary feeling of freedom and liberation, but it was replaced rather quickly with a sense of displacement. We were now dislocated from the identity which had defined us for many years, and we had left pieces of our family behind us.

One of the difficult parts about creating a new life for yourself as an adult is the carnage of ripping yourself out of previous environments into which you have settled. People are not marbles, but interactive beings. We cannot just remove ourselves from one location and deposit ourselves somewhere else without consequence. We leave little pieces of ourselves embedded in each other, like battle shrapnel. Fortunately, we didn't leave *everyone* behind when we moved north. Our son Ari and our two youngest daughters came with us, and six months or so after we left, our oldest daughter and her family followed us and moved into a condo a few hundred yards from where we lived, which was helpful.

However, what made it more difficult for us was Roman's posture towards me after my departure. A month or two after moving away,

I had called to try, once more, to open a positive line of communication and to mend fences between us. After all, he was my oldest son's father-in-law, and I felt this was in everyone's best interest, regardless of my own emotions in the matter. But he was unwilling to engage about our relationship or to address the pain I had experienced or even any of the events of our eight-year tenure in southern Vermont as leaders in his church. I didn't need an apology, just honest dialog so we could reestablish relationship and begin to approach a sense of closure. All he would tell me was that "God had told him that I needed to be under authority". However, I did not believe that God had told him anything of the sort, primarily because that's how Charismatic Protestants tend to operate; God is always telling them *this* and telling them *that* and giving them a "word of knowledge" about some other thing. It's rather tiring. I had to remind him that he was not my pastor anymore. He ended the call shortly thereafter and didn't leave the door open for further conversation. In fact, that's the last time I've spoken to him.

When I listen to the many stories of people who have deconstructed their faith, there is a common denominator among most: We typically experienced a moment of shock, during which our perceived spiritual security got rocked and became unstable. The shock is related to a major relationship going south, a divorce, the death of a loved one for which there is no reasonable explanation, the betrayal of a close ministry partner, or perhaps, an unassailable point of doctrine which was never supposed to be threatened that suddenly gets destroyed, such as the loss of belief in a core teaching of the religion. Any or all of these can conspire to shatter our equilibrium. The walls of our spiritual house, which before were solid and impenetrable, become as translucent glass and we begin to survey our surroundings for the first time. Then, the questions begin to pour into our minds. This was certainly true for myself, and by extension, my family. The fervid nature of our experience in southern Vermont had quite literally set us up for deconversion. We merely needed to have the door nudged open a bit and the path would lay before us. But we didn't see it quite yet.

One point of contact where this struggle manifested, for me at least, was in Paul's letters, which were a snake's nest of contradictory and problematic ideas, once I began to look at them from a place of jaded suspicion. Consider this…

"…Do you think lightly of the riches of His kindness and tolerance and patience, not knowing that the kindness of God leads you to repentance? But because of your stubbornness and unrepentant heart you are storing up wrath for yourself in the day of wrath and revelation of the righteous judgment of God, who will render to each person according to his deeds: to those who by perseverance in doing good seek for glory and honor and immortality, eternal life; but to those who are selfishly ambitious and do not obey the truth, but obey unrighteousness, wrath and indignation. There will be tribulation and distress for every soul of man who does evil, of the Jew first and also of the Greek, but glory and honor and peace to everyone who does good, to the Jew first and also to the Greek. For there is no partiality with God…for it is not the hearers of the Law who are just before God, but the doers of the Law will be justified." (Romans 2:4-13).

This citation from Paul's letter to the Romans (the ultimate Christian text for the foundations of Christian theology) clearly illustrates that Paul was either very confused, or perhaps simply dishonest. When we analyze this passage, we notice several things: First off, we are unsurprised to see Paul portray sinners who remain "unpunished" as being those who are benefitting from the mercy and tolerance of God. This is because God is allowing them to continue, arrogantly, in their sin, and withholding their just punishment, which they deserve for their behavior. This is what we would expect from any self-respecting fire-and-brimstone preacher. In fact, this passage was used repeatedly in my experience by the Fundamentalists as a form of exhortation for a sinner to repent and stop "storing up wrath for themselves". But after this verse, the train goes off the rails of standard Christian doctrine.

"…the righteous judgment of God, who will render to each person according to his deeds; to those who (do good)…eternal life…but to those… who do not obey the truth, wrath and indignation."

Here we see that the *magic blood* of Jesus has failed to make a difference. Instead, we notice an entirely different reality at play: God, according to Paul, is going to reward people who do right with *eternal life*, and those who do wrong with *misery and pain*. (Doing = *works*, for those who are slow on the uptake). Note that, lest anyone think that this is merely Paul painting a picture of the futility of being "under the Law", as most assume (Christian theology cuts and pastes and imposes ideas found in the books of Galatians, Ephesians, and elsewhere into their reading of Romans, preventing them from seeing this contradiction), we must reconsider. Paul, in several places in his writings, refers to being "under the Law" as a condition of being Jewish. But in this passage, we find that Paul makes no distinction between Jew and Greek, telling us that all people will be judged the same way; according to their deeds, even going so far as to conclude his statement by telling us that only *"the doers of the Law will be justified."* Well now, that's something. Especially when one considers his statement in the following passage in Galatians, in which he says unequivocally, *"Now that no one is justified by the Law before God is evident; for, 'The righteous man shall live by faith'".* (Galatians, 3:11-12)

If I am to believe Paul's statements in Romans chapter two, then I am quite right to expect *justice* from God, meaning punishment for evil and reward for righteous behavior. Surprisingly, however, that is not the message preached in church. Rather, we hear the exact opposite: that God is not willing that any should perish, but that all should receive the *free gift* of eternal life, and that this is based on *mercy*, and not our *merit*. That message is more consistent with what we see in the citation in Galatians, as well as this,

"For by grace you have been saved through faith; and that not of yourselves, it is the gift of God; not as a result of works, so that no one may boast." (Ephesians, 2:9)

Of course, this famous passage is contradicted entirely by the epistle of James, which says,

"But prove yourselves doers of the word, and not merely hearers who delude themselves..." (James 1:22) and of course, more to the point,

"What use is it, my brethren, if someone says he has faith but he has no works? Can that faith save him?...Even so faith, if it has no works, is dead, being by itself." (James, 2:14,17)

Is it any wonder that Martin Luther petitioned to have the book of James taken completely out of the Christian Bible? It really pisses down the back of the whole "salvation through faith by grace alone" narrative so critical to Protestant Christian theology, and we should note here that *Sola Gracia*, or "by grace alone", is one of the five *solas* at the core of Martin Luther's theology, and underpins much of modern evangelical thought.

These theological contradictions (and that's precisely what they are, make no mistake) are just a small sampling of the many internal contradictions in the official Canon of the New Testament. There is also no paucity of doctrinal bandages which apologists have constructed and applied which serve to bind up the bleeding wounds of the religion's incoherent self-concepts as represented in its own texts. The varieties of arguments are legion and traverse all denominational perspectives. One of the most popular gambits is finding a creative way to reconcile Paul with James, even though church tradition has informed us through early church commentators that they hated one another, even telling us in one account that Paul attempted to murder James (Clemetine Regognitions).

Most importantly here, we are left to wonder if the passages in Romans chapter two and James chapter two are, taken together, evidence of fissures in the theological fabric of the Christian testimony of its own story and confession as the religion developed, as they serve to completely undermine the Christian concept of atonement and its perceived source for attaining righteousness, which would be (according to nearly all Christian groups) the *magic blood* of Jesus, attained through belief in him, by grace alone, and not by works of righteousness. After all, if it can be demonstrated that there is any viable path for the attainment of personal righteousness before God other than via the *magic blood* of Jesus, than the entirety of the gospel message is open to charges of fraud, and the Jews (as well as everyone else) are correct to reject Jesus as a "savior". Why is this problem not routinely pointed out?

It turns out that there is a powerful conceptual idea which has served to protect these contradictions from being exposed and which has largely prevented challenges to Christian Atonement Theory which passages such as I have cited should naturally raise, and that is the presumed "divinity" of Jesus.

Officially, the doctrine of the Trinity was not a doctrine of the Church until well into the 5th Century, which is rather hard to believe for most Christians when you inform them of this sober fact, particularly if they have, like most, been told that a person must believe in the Trinity to be saved. This is astounding. How did Christianity make it for over four hundred and fifty years without it's go-to dogma to whip everyone into theological conformity? No matter, once this idea took hold, it wrapped its philosophically maddening tendrils around the Church's collective mind until, with the exception of the Jehovah's Witnesses and Biblical Unitarians and a few other outlying groups, it became synonymous with the fundamental core of Christian understanding.

My study of the Trinity doctrine was happenchance, and unintended, but when I was done evaluating it, and had rejected it, I was most of the way out of Christianity. I just didn't know it yet. That's how central the doctrine is to the entire structure of Christian belief today. Once the dogma of the Trinity fell, all the other dominoes followed, until finally, the *magic blood* of Jesus went *poof!* and I was left with a bag of air where I once had a religious identity.

It began with our family Bible study through the book of Exodus. In Exodus 4:16, as God is exhorting Moses for his confrontation with Pharaoh alongside his brother Aaron, he tells him this,

"...*He shall speak for you to the people; and he will be as a mouth for you and you will be as God to him.*" (Exodus 4:16) In the Hebrew text, the word used for God here was *Lelohim*, which unlike Elohim which means "judges" or "God's court of judges", *Lelohim* meant "as a master" (Rashi). Now, I had been taught within Christianity that Elohim was proof for the Trinity, as it stood for "three-in-one", and it was found in various places in the Jewish Bible, "hiding in plain sight" as Christian apologists will often say. However, it turned out that, in Jewish tradition, there were far more names for God than Christians could possibly conceive of. Interestingly, in Exodus chapter twenty-one, which is part of the "parsha" called *Mishpatim*, the word Elohim clearly connotes a man being brought before the "judges". *Mishpat*, itself, means "judgment" in Hebrew, so *Mishpatim* meant "judgments". In Jewish understanding, I would learn that in the opening chapters of Genesis, in which God says,

"Let us make man in our image..." (Genesis 1:26), that this was to be read as God consulting the "court of heaven", a concept found throughout Jewish sources. But in an evangelical mindset, that's not what it meant at all. It was, within the Christian perspective, the Father talking with Jesus and the Holy Ghost. In fact, I had heard numerous Bible teachers tell me that it was Jesus who created the world and everything in it, by permission of the Father, which was a tall drink to down in one shot, but why not? If you're going to believe that a human being, Jesus, whom the gospels claim was born of a woman and died like any normal man, pre-existed creation, why not believe *that, too?* Heck, let's also believe he defeated Thanos long before the dub-philosopher villain appeared in Infinity Wars. The thinking, after all, is consistent.

As I prepared to teach Exodus chapter four, I realized that Moses being "as God" to Aaron (and also, by extension, to Pharaoh) meant that Moses was representing God as his *agent*. There is no Christian or Jew today (that I know of) who thinks that Moses was God, or that he "ascended to the right hand of the father" after redeeming Israel. Yet, the text tells us that he is "as God". This is the Jewish concept of agency. The same principle is obviously at work in the New Testament concerning Jesus, but Christians don't apply the same standard to Jesus as they do to Moses, even though he has the same role as Moses. In fact, Jesus's ministry, particularly in the book of Matthew, is literally patterned after the story of Moses. So why the double standard? Why is it that Jesus is divine, but Moses is not? They both have a miraculous birth and miraculous rescue from harm, they both are sent to rebuke the leaders of the day and to redeem their people, who are oppressed. They are both "called out of Egypt". They both perform mighty miracles before all, and they both ascend and disappear rather than die and lie forever in a grave. Additionally, both Moses and Jesus fail to witness the final entry into the Promised Land, which for Moses is the land of Israel, and for Jesus is the Great Messianic Redemption, which has become synonymous in modern evangelical circles with the Rapture of the Church, and the descent of Jesus on the clouds.

The difference, as I studied it, was that the divinity of Jesus is something which appears to have developed over time. How much time? That's debatable. However, the earliest writings of the New Testament are believed to be the authentic letters of Paul, written decades before the gospels. Even if we are to include *all* the letters of Paul, including the ones of disputed authorship, we nonetheless never find an instance in which Paul conflates the identity of God and Jesus, with the notable possible exception of Colossians 2:9 (but then, Colossians is considered a forgery by many scholars today). Clearly, and indisputably, in Paul's understanding, Jesus is a separate entity altogether from God. Paul never calls Jesus God, and he never speaks of anything resembling a Trinity. Likewise, in the synoptic gospels, Jesus is very much human. He's not divine. The exception, of course, is the gospel of John, which seems to portray Jesus as divine at many points, but even in John the testimony is inconsistent and fails to support trinitarian imaginations, such as in chapter fourteen;

"...I go to the Father, for the Father is greater than I." (John 14:28)

Or, in a similar vein, there's this...

"...I ascend to my Father and your Father, and my God and your God." (John 20:17b)

So, Jesus, who was supposedly God, *had a God?* I was deeply concerned about what I was seeing. I was leading Bible studies, and I wanted to teach accurately. I did not want to be accused of heresy unless I could stand firmly on my convictions. If Jesus was merely a chosen agent of God who spoke the words of God, then that is not the same thing as actually being God. It would make him exactly like Moses. And Moses did not fail in his mission because he was a mere man. Why, then, would Jesus fail if *he* was a mere man? Why was the Church afraid of this possibility? I was following this trail as far as it would lead, and the Trinity was falling apart by the day. I got my son in law Ben involved in the research, and we discovered that his brother attended a church which was a Biblical Unitarian church, meaning they didn't believe in the Trinity, or in the divinity of Jesus, which separated them from the Arian church, which didn't believe in the Trinity, but did believe in Jesus's divinity, and also the Oneness Pentecostals, which didn't believe in the Trinity, exactly, but did believe that Jesus was everything, including God, Creator, and any other transcendent title you wished to give him. We started diving into everything we could get our hands on about the Biblical Unitarian perspective, which appeared the most agreeable to a Jewish one. Conceptualizing Jesus as simply a *man* appeared to remove the barrier that stood in the way of our proper understanding of the Jewish conception of a Messiah, which in Judaism is a *man* who arises from among his brethren and leads them into the Messianic Age by reclaiming the dormant promises of the Davidic line, not a *man-god* who descends from and then ascends back to heaven.

A humorous but nonetheless accurate way to understand the logical pretzel that the Trinity concept creates, is to ponder the idea of Jesus, as God, praying to *himself* (as it were) in the Garden of Gethsemane for the strength to be released from doing his own will. Think about it. I did, and it made my brain hurt.

Once I realized that it was impossible for the Trinity to be true, the concept shattered into a million jagged pieces. Suddenly, the Jewish conception of the Oneness of God took on a significantly richer and different meaning than any idea which I had held in all my years within Christianity. Interestingly, I learned that around the same time that the Trinity doctrine became the official doctrine of the Church, the Pope made it a crime (punishable via excommunication) for anyone to pray the Shema, which is the central affirmation of faith for all Jews; something that is recited at least three times a day by Torah-observant Jews. Not a coincidence.

This led to my conclusion that when Christians claim to be monotheists, they do so in ignorance. I asked myself at the time; *was the divinity of Jesus the lock that held shut the door dividing Christianity and Judaism?* Was this the key to reconciling early Christianity with Judaism? I would learn that there was a lot more which separated the two faiths besides that, but I had not worked that out just yet. Suddenly, Jewish sources became of much greater interest to me and Christian sources were now being viewed with increasing suspicion, because virtually all Christian scholarship and apologetics centered around the Trinitarian model and (at least) the divinity of Jesus as the Son of God.

Around this time our family voted, after a meeting with the pastor, to leave the charismatic church near our condo, simply because the environment was not something we could comfortably embrace. It was too music-oriented and the dancing in the aisles was a bridge too far for us. Also, there was a non-stop narrative in this church about Jesus-as-God. This was really a shame, because the pastor was an awesome person and great friend and who really understood the entire point behind religious environments. But we were, as a family, far too intense for him and his church at that point. We had been through too much trauma, and were too hypersensitive, to deal casually with so many triggers to our spiritual sensibilities. We left there for a Baptist church up the road which turned out to be a Calvinist church with a Baptist name.

We tried hard to fit in at our new home. We walked the streets caroling with them at Christmastime. We had the elders over our home to hang out and get to know us. We joined a home group. I even went to a men's retreat. But I was in for another fall, and so was my family. I had started an email exchange with the pastor concerning a message he had preached in which he cited the Sin Offering in Leviticus as an example of Jesus's perfect work of atonement, comparing the Sin Offering with Isaiah chapter fifty-three, the famous "suffering servant" passage so often quoted by evangelists.

I was unfortunately, and unadvisedly, convinced that if I approached our new pastor from an intellectual front, engaging him in stimulating discussion on the Bible, that I would endear him to myself as a person who was serious about his faith and warm him towards the idea of considering new perspectives. I was very wrong. This was the start of an important learning lesson for me. At this point (and unfortunately for some time afterwards) I held the opinion that most people were interested in the *truth*. This desire should (in my conception) result in a willingness by others to suspend preconceived notions to explore new angles so that they may better understand alternatives. "Argument for the sake of heaven" is a rabbinic principle held dear by Torah scholars. I had already embraced this ethos, but I was about to have cold water splashed on my theological face. Instead of being inspired by my long email discourses, the Calvinist pastor decided to do an investigation of my background, to find out where on earth I had come from and why I was in his church. I received an unexpected email from him one day, shortly after the men's retreat which I attended. He told me he had discovered my blog, which had some material that he found objectionable and he wanted to schedule a meeting at the church to discuss it with not just myself, but our entire family. This was ominous. I had promised my family when we first started attending that I wouldn't create controversy at this new church, and I really didn't intend to, but here we were, and my family wasn't happy to hear of this. Nonetheless, we stuck together and agreed to the pastor's request.

At the Saturday morning meeting, it seemed as though the goal of the pastor (and his chief elder, who was present) was not to engage in a discussion, but rather to humiliate me and put me in my place before

THERE'S NO SUCH THING AS MAGIC BLOOD

my wife and children and, I suppose, to let me know that he was very much in charge here, and that my opinions were neither welcome nor appreciated.

"You make some interesting, and I would say heretical, statements on your blog that we believe violate the fundamental claims of the gospel of Jesus Christ, which would make you an apostate. I scheduled this meeting so you can address these issues and correct them before your ideas create problems in our community."

"Gee, thanks," I said. Ignoring my sarcasm, he immediately proceeded to read an excerpt from an article I had written about the eternal covenants of God which questioned the need for Jews to accept Jesus and become Christians to have a proper relationship with God. He stared at me crossly.

"Yes or no, David. Do you believe that Jews need to accept Jesus to be saved?" I smiled and looked down. This was a set up. My family tensed as they anticipated my answer.

"That's an unfair question," I said, finally.

"It's yes or no."

"Okay, well I have questions, too. Can you show me anywhere in the Jewish Bible where the Jews are commanded to believe in a guy named Jesus? Didn't God promise to see them through, based on the eternal covenants he already made with them?"

"You're not answering the question."

"No, I'm not. Here's another: Are the Jews who were slaughtered in the gas chambers during the Holocaust burning in hell today because they didn't believe in Jesus? Yes or no?" He grimaced and looked at his elder.

"That's different," he said, turning back to me.

"Yes or no." He didn't answer, but rather he looked down, uncrossed his legs, adjusted his seating position and recrossed them with the opposite leg before flipping a page in his notes. I guessed correctly that he wasn't going to answer me. Instead, he quoted from another blog I wrote challenging the Trinity.

"You realize that belief in the Trinity is paramount to your salvation, and part of our statement of faith at this church, and I would like to add, just about every church you'll ever attend?" He stared at me expectantly until, merely to encourage him to continue, I grunted audibly and raised my eyebrows at him. He took the cue.

"So, how do you justify this blog you wrote in which you denounce the Trinity? Are you just trying to start arguments?"

"The Trinity developed over centuries and isn't in the Bible." Again, rather than engage with my statement, he wiped his hand over his face as if trying to cleanse himself from what he was hearing.

"You aren't a Christian, then."

"That's how John Calvin reacted to Michael Servetus," said my son-in-law, Ben, interjecting. The pastor put his hand up to silence Ben.

"Yeah, he burned him at the stake for challenging the Trinity," I added, finishing Ben's thought. At this, the pastor's eyes grew wide, and he leaned forward towards me in a threatening manner.

"Jesus would burn *you* at the stake!" I heard my wife and daughter gasp. My daughter April, normally a quiet, non-confrontational person, spoke up.

"I'm sorry, but we have done nothing at this church except be model citizens. We have participated in everything and have not been controversial. All we want is a community, and none of the things you're talking about have been part of our involvement here. Are you saying that we aren't welcome here?" The pastor turned towards my wife, daughter, and son-in-law.

"I want to know if you believe the same way as David." They all either nodded or said yes. He clapped his hands together forcefully. April jumped in her chair.

"So, here's the deal. You can continue to attend, but none of you are to share any of your beliefs with anyone. And as for you, David," he turned directly to me, "You are not allowed to discuss anything concerning your theological beliefs with *anyone* here at this church. You aren't to talk to any members, period. You may attend, but you must be silent. You cannot promote your blog or your home Bible study, or invite anyone to it, or even to email anyone about it. I would also prefer you remove all references to it from your Facebook page, since there are those in the community who interact with you there."

I stood up. My family stood up with me, as everyone felt insulted by this clown-show.

"We are leaving. The tone and intent of this meeting have been clear. You don't want us here. Good day." We all said our goodbye. It was tense and awkward. A few hours later, the pastor called me, with an apologetic tone. I was alone in my van.

"Hey, I feel you guys left with the impression that we wanted your family to leave. It's not true. It's simply important for you to know that what you are teaching is not something we can embrace. We needed to address it before heresy spreads in the fellowship and creates problems. It's not personal. We like your family."

"What I'm *teaching*? I'm not teaching anything at your church. And I have the right to free speech and to have different opinions."

"Well, I just wanted you to know that you can still be part of our community. We should have another meeting so everyone can talk through it."

"Thanks a bunch. But I think I'd rather run myself through a woodchipper." I hung up.

A month or so later, while grocery shopping, I ran into one of the elders shopping with his children, the same elder whom we had broken bread with at our home several times. I said hi to his son. I heard him say under his breath, "Don't talk to him", as he physically steered his brood into the opposite direction, away from me. Nor did he return my greeting.

"Nice to see you," I called after him. He didn't turn around or acknowledge me. We didn't exist anymore.

Chapter 18

~

JESUS AND THE SABBATH QUEEN

THE PURSUIT OF God. That is largely what drives the human heart towards religious devotion. And what drives the intellect's engagement is the need to try to make sense of it. The idea that there's a supernatural force, or being, whom we call God, from which spring our origins, our root, and that someday in a certain transformative process that is yet unknown to us, we will reunite with this *source of life*. What's more, the idea that this being cares about us and is actively overseeing and working in our lives, is a singularly powerful notion. This concept alone is enough for most people to continue coming back to the spiritual well, time and time again, regardless of how many times they are left with empty buckets. A word, a glance, a song, a teaching comes their way, and all is renewed as hope springs alive once more. They never stop looking for validation that their longing is justified. If we fail to understand this search for significance which burns in the hearts of most people who are involved in religious activities, we will never understand religion itself in any meaningful way, or why we are so easily pulled into so many unexpected directions in the process of trying to figure it all out. Nor will we understand how it is that people can be blind to so many logical inconsistencies regarding their beliefs.

Religious devotion is, after all, not a simple matter, but represents a synergy of emotion, intellect, and soul. But when it comes to the religion of Christianity in particular, which has so much of its perceived authenticity literally stolen from the Jewish Bible (while simultaneously dismissing Judaism as passe), the problem of comprehension becomes acute. Christians should not pretend to have a true connection to God unless they have at least attempted to understand the connection that the Jews already enjoy, and have enjoyed for many hundreds of years before Christianity even came upon the scene. This is precisely why people such as Rabbi Tovia Singer, founder of Outreach Judaism, are so important to this discussion, and why so many people who are Jesus-followers don't like people like him. Or me, for that matter. Because we throw ice water upon the romantic fantasy people have of Jesus, who personifies the very pinnacle of what they believe their spiritual hearts are longing for. But people like Rabbi Singer, who has devoted himself, as an anti-missionary, to knowing the scriptures and history of Christianity intimately so that he can defend Judaism and Jews against Christian missionaries and Christian claims, are of fundamental importance to maintaining the integrity of Jewish identity in the face of religious syncretism. Many people don't like the anti-missionary approach, and consider it needlessly contentious, but these people fail to recognize how crtitical it is for anti-missionary perspectives to have a place at the table when the faith discussion between Judaism and Christianity crosses religious boundaries. It's similar to the scenario that you would face if your seventeen-year-old daughter started dating a twenty-five-year-old drug-dealing gangbanger. She might be smitten with his bad-boy masculinity, but you know better, and you would feel compelled to stand in between them. You might even threaten to call the cops if she fails to listen. And you know that your daughter will hate you for it. But you must do what you must do. That's what anti-missionaries like Rabbi Tovia Singer do. They stand between the

Jew and the Christian missionary like a knowing father who must play the bad guy to protect his family from harm. The insults and thrown tomatoes are part of the price of playing this role. One of the biggest problems that anti-missionaries deal with is that many Christians aren't self-aware that they are missionizing. This is especially true with the Messianic Christian sects; the Christians who syncretize Jewish teachings and practices with their faith in Jesus. These people, generally, are not self-aware of the genuine threat they pose to Jews and to Jewish community. Rather, in many cases, they wrongly believe that they are being helpful.

There are major problems which are created when well-meaning people attempt to syncretize the two faiths of Christianity and Judaism by minimizing or explaining away their very real and insurmountable differences. Scholarly attempts have increased in recent decades to try to reframe the conversation about Christian origins with a new perspective; one which places Jesus and even Paul into the milieu of emerging Rabbinic Judaism of the Second Temple, pre-Talmudic era. Scholars such as E.P. Sanders, David Flusser and others after them have attempted to "Judaize" Jesus and Paul, largely motivated by a desire to combat classical Christian attitudes of "Replacement Theology" and thereby reduce Christian antisemitism. This is a worthy goal, but these efforts have often had an unintended and undesirable effect. For one thing, this movement has influenced the creation of missionary groups such as Jews for Jesus and One For Israel, both of which are Christian organizations which seek to use the concept of a "Jewish Jesus" as a tool to make Jews (mostly non-religious Jews, as it happens) attracted to the Christian gospel. They take scholarship which is meant to reduce Christian antisemitism and exacerbate the original problem by throwing the "Jewish Jesus" directly into the face of Jews as an evangelistic tactic, and some of these Jews become Jewish-Christians as a result. While the people in the Church celebrate this, the Jewish community mourns the assimilation of their own away from their community and resentment justifiably builds against Christians, as it has throughout the last two thousand years by all such efforts. Thus, rather than mitigating the problem of antisemitism, these organizations merely reinforce Replacement Theology, which is the Christian presumption that Jesus and Christianity are the "fulfillment" and therefore the "replacement" of Judaism and traditional Jewish religious perspectives.

Essentially, there are two novel but related movements that represent extreme cases of religious syncretism which arose from within the Christian Church during the last forty or fifty years, and these are the Hebrew Roots movement and the Messianic Jewish movement. (It's important to point out that these movements did not arise from within the Jewish world, despite the suggestive names). Hebrew Roots, while popular across the United States, is basically, in most of its forms, cultish. Members of this movement typically reject many of the obviously pagan elements of mainstream Christianity, such as the celebration of Christmas and Easter, and adopt Jewish holidays and what they call "biblically kosher" standards, which are not *kashrut* as a Jew would understand, but are based upon whatever can be clearly read from the text of the Torah itself, apart from Jewish law. Hebrew Roots groups come in many different flavors, but essentially, they attempt to follow Torah while rejecting the authority of the Rabbis of the Jewish tradition, particularly anything to do with the Talmud or the Oral Law, which most Hebrew Roots people consider to be the intentional efforts of the Rabbis to obscure the truth of God's word. So, Hebrew Roots folks reject both the Church and Rabbinic Judaism, simultaneously. In this, they share some similarities with Karaite Jews. Yet, they still hang on to Jesus. It's highly problematic.

The Hebrew Roots crowd must be carefully distinguished from Messianic Judaism, which boasts multiple branches. The Messianic Jewish movement is (again I speak in general terms) unassociated with Hebrew Roots, but Messianic Judaism nonetheless still maintains many elements that qualify as anti-Judaism. Messianic Judaism self-identifies as a form of "fulfilled Judaism", in quite the same manner that Reformed Theology views the Church as a fulfillment of Jewish ideals, only in this case they adopt Jewish religious practice and eschew traditional Christian norms of religious identity. Essentially however, regardless of the ways they define their own movement, it is quite literally a new form of Christianity which garners its authority, not from the Jewish world, but from the very scholars and commentators (as mentioned above) which have attempted to mitigate Christian anti-semitism through religious syncretism. Most Messianic Jewish groups are also evangelistic and openly attempt to proselytize Jews, though some do so more overtly than others. Their biggest sources of membership are with intermarried Jewish couples (meaning one spouse is ethnically Jewish and the other is not) and disgruntled evangelicals. Messianic Jewish congregations offer a syncretistic option for these people. Approximately 85-90% of the Messianic Jewish movement adheres to traditional evangelical Christian doctrines, such as the Trinity, the Rapture of the Church, and so forth, while outwardly appearing to practice a watered-down version of Judaism. In practice, it usually results in a strange mix of Orthodox Jewish ideology with largely (in most cases) liberal, Reconstructionist Jewish styles of worship and community, infused with a Christian evangelical tone and doctrinal flair. Most of the movement's enthusiasts hale from two distinct wings of the evangelical world: The charismatic (primarily Assemblies of God) and the Southern Baptist. Messianic Jewish enthusiasts from the charismatic wing of Christianity tend to form different styles of community than those from more conservative branches, but all of them, generally, subscribe to the core tenets of Christian faith and would be unashamed to participate in traditional Christian services and sing the same songs, and in fact most do exactly that from time to time. Simultaneously, most of the participants have never actually spent any meaningful time in traditional Jewish space. This is because the vast majority of those who practice Messianic Judaism are not Jewish. I should add that no form of Messianic Judaism is considered part of the normative Jewish world, nor are they even close to establishing that level of status.

One of the more prominent organizations leading the Messianic

Jewish movement is First Fruits of Zion, and this was our door of entry. At the time (still being believers in Jesus), this organization seemed to us to have a balanced view of things and we felt that we could hang our proverbial hat on their hook with confidence, and distance ourselves from the extremist, tin-foil-hat elements of the movement. FFOZ is subtle and nuanced in their attempts to missionize Jews, *but they certainly do this*. However, I didn't really see how until I left the messianic world altogether and viewed it from inside the Jewish community. They have their allegiance firmly placed within the confines of their financial backing, which are mostly Christians seeking a more Hebraic approach to Christianity, as well as Christian organizations who would like nothing better than to see the normative Jewish world accept Jesus as Messiah, such as Southern Baptists.

To their credit, First Fruits of Zion exposed us to a positive presentation of Jewish Oral Law, with their own spin on what they call a "Judaism fully centered on Yeshua". They preferred this name for Jesus, as they claim it's the name "his mother called him." Whatever.

We had attempted to start a home fellowship after we were kicked out of the Calvinist church, but as it fizzled out, I found myself leading online Bible studies and was developing a modest following. It was an outgrowth of an invitation I had accepted to be a teacher for an online community. While that organizational relationship ultimately ended, I continued leading studies with those who wished to do so. A couple of my students lived north of Atlanta. I knew that FFOZ had a top employee who led a messianic congregation near there, and one of my students was offering to rent their small house to us while they reestablished themselves in another country. Simultaneously, I had also become frustrated with my inability to stabilize my business in northern Vermont. The sparse population as well as the lengthy winters made it challenging, and I was actively exploring my options. I knew that the Atlanta region was an ideal location for me to rebuild if I was going to stay in the home services business. We decided that if the window of opportunity opened to us, we would attempt to move.

Shortly thereafter, it did, and we ended up moving out of Vermont. My daughter April and her family would follow us to Georgia a year later, almost to the day.

Our family was desperate for change and a fresh start. We had a lot riding on this move south. It seemed a lifetime earlier that we had walked away from our beautiful home in Athol, MA with the in-ground pool, sun porch and the YMCA down the street. Embarrassingly, we had gone from being full owners of Michelle's childhood home, to buying the home in Athol, to owning the chalet in southern Vermont with the failed septic that we couldn't sell, to being renters, to now moving into a nine-hundred square foot shotgun shack in the Deep South, three days drive from our nearest family. We were going backwards economically, but we had renewed hope notwithstanding. We would plug into the Messianic Jewish congregation and try to learn what Judaism was all about within a physical community and rebuild our lives. When we passed the sign on the highway announcing that we had crossed the North Carolina border into the Peach State, our hearts began to beat faster, and the chatter became more urgent. It was exciting. Not so much for our cat Tigger, who bemoaned nearly every mile of the trip.

Significantly, my wife and I had very nearly filed for divorce the previous year, going so far as a trip to the courthouse to file papers officially, shortly after we were thrown out of the Calvinist church. It seems that this was one hit too many for us and we were beginning to think that we should just go our separate ways. Religious extremist rigors and expectations had sapped both the romance and energy out of our relationship. But we still loved one another, in spite of the problems, and ultimately we decided we weren't willing to give up on the marriage even though it had suffered so much damage, and there had been so much lingering pain as a result of our failed religious experiences and financial decisions. The question remained, however: *Where did we belong? Did we belong anywhere?*

At our lowest point, it was only the fact that we were in rather desperate financial shape which truly prevented our divorce. For her part, since she had not worked outside the home for twenty years, she was in no position for me to leave, unless she was prepared to apply for welfare. And I felt strongly that we were on the cusp of turning the corner and having blessings flow our way if we could just press on. Nothing had gone the way we had hoped thus far but I was confident that we had finally found the right path. However, some of this mentality that I embraced was, looking back, a holdover from my previous charismatic brainwashing and not grounded in rationalism. Without sharing the same boundless confidence, Chana rode my faith like a beaver trader in a leaking canoe during the dangerous spring swell of a mountain river, clinging white-knuckled to the gunwales as it careened dangerously towards submerged rocks, and we decided to try again under those conditions, and hope for the best, as they say. Our track record for creating peace and harmony was not stellar and had affected the entire family. Thankfully, today, those issues have subsided, aided greatly by our family's deconversion from Christianity. The absence of a Jesus-centered worldview, rather than creating a hollow void, has promulgated a sanctuary of normality and reasonableness which has settled everyone down. Surprise, surprise.

The hardest part of moving south, of course, was leaving parts of our family behind. It was incredibly difficult and emotional for us. Our son Ari was most deeply affected by us leaving Vermont, as he had moved north with us but now was engaged to a girl and couldn't follow us south, and Chana couldn't stop crying when we said goodbye to all the grandchildren, which totaled five by now. I had promised her that we would visit, but who's to say what the future would bring? There were no guarantees. Our nuclear family which remained was Chana and I, and our youngest children, Janey and Tara, who were nearly sixteen and ten, respectively. We set sail with the compass pointed south.

We decided, as planned, to plug into the messianic congregation after we moved. My other Buford student arranged and hosted an Erev Shabbat dinner with the messianic "rabbi", the one who worked for

FFOZ, and I spent the evening talking with him. His congregation, which he wasn't the founder of, but had inherited, had a Torah scroll, an expansive Christian-Jewish library and their services resembled a strange combination of Christianity and Judaism. It wasn't an authentic Jewish service, though they tried in some respects, but how could one expect to have that when most of the members were evangelicals and not even Jewish? The facility was a commercial space in a business park, it lacked a kosher kitchen, and the readings from the New Testament that were inserted into the traditional Sabbath liturgy were over the top. But we wanted it to work so we tried to adjust. Within a few months, the "rabbi" asked me to teach from the pulpit, which I would do on numerous occasions before leaving. Once more, as on other occasions, I was becoming a leader in our new environment, and the drama would soon, almost inevitably, follow.

Friday night was where the action was in this fellowship, at the monthly *chavurahs* and weekly get-togethers with members. I enjoyed many hours of high-level intellectual discussion with the people of the congregation. The rabbi extended kindnesses to us and tried to make us feel welcome. He even took the time to visit us at the Children's hospital when Tara broke her forearm. (I was not yet conscious of the fact that he did so primarily because I was a supporter of FFOZ. I would learn this too late.) I was thriving, personally, but my girls felt out of place there and were not making meaningful connections, which put a damper on Chana's excitement about it. The messianic congregation was not a healthy family environment. Many of the people had shaky marriages, uncertain spiritual identities and because the congregation pulled from such a huge geographical area, it was hard to connect with members consistently. Chana floated the idea frequently about going back to regular church, and there were, of course, no shortage of options close by in Buford. There was literally a church on every corner, which was something we had never seen before in New England. I even tried to attend a couple of Christian services locally, via invitation, but I just couldn't stand it. I was too far down the Jewish path to be able to enjoy an evangelical church service with its childish, pedantic approach to the Bible. I remained hopeful that the girls would warm up to the Jewish thing, and the rabbi eventually put me in charge of the youth program and so I thought that at least my youngest daughter Tara would start to become more engaged, even if our daughter Jane was already mentally preparing for college and didn't care one way or the other.

In our second year in the deep south, we moved across town to a larger home in a quiet neighborhood. The high-water mark of our involvement in the messianic church was an Erev Shabbat gathering at our home to celebrate the arrival of my daughter April and her family, who would stay with us for a couple of months while Ben found a job and they found a home to live in. Over forty people packed our home for a raucous and joyous evening of celebration. There was a buzz about everything. We all felt we had finally found our people and everything would be great. But it was not to be, and soon after, things would begin to fall apart around us, again.

When I had arrived in Atlanta, I didn't really understand all the issues affecting the Messianic Jewish landscape, and they were significant to the point of threatening its very existence going forward. I started figuring things out quickly though, and what I learned formed the final pieces of the puzzle regarding my abandonment of Jesus. Particularly, there were things I had started to notice as I participated in Shabbat every week which I had failed to pick up on when we were in Vermont. And, to add to this, I decided to start attending services occasionally at a traditional Jewish shul in Atlanta, which was eye-opening for me, to say the least.

Friday evening included a ritual called "Kabbalat Shabbat", which was a custom which has origins in Jewish mysticism around the end of the 16th Century in Safed, Israel. It is the celebration and welcoming of the "Sabbath Queen". The Sabbath was already firmly entrenched in Jewish thought as a "bride" in Talmudic times and even far earlier. In the Kabbalah, the onset of Shabbat on Friday night was considered *divine feminine*, and the role of women on Friday night reflected this. The women baked challah and prepared the meal while the men prayed at synagogue (at least in most observant Orthodox homes this is the tradition) and finally, the women enjoyed the honor of welcoming Shabbat by performing the candle lighting and its blessings, after which the husband would take over the duties of the ceremony, which included the blessing of the children and the beautiful *Eshet Chayil*, which is when the husband praises his wife before the children and any guests, reciting Proverbs thirty-one, personified in her honor. It is romantic and heartwarming. On Erev Shabbat, observant men shower or bathe before the onset of Shabbat, put on clean clothes (some have a tradition of dressing up), as do the children, and the evening is especially holy between husband and wife as they are (in Chassidic tradition) to make love at the end the evening, if possible (provided that the woman is not in her monthly time of separation). Additionally, during the Kabbalat Shabbat prayers, all participants recited, or sung, repeatedly, during the *Lekha Dodi* prayer,

Come, my beloved, to greet the bride; let us welcome the Sabbath...

As I reflected on this, it became a problem for me. It was clearly antithetical to Christian understanding, and yet messianic Christians which we were friends with were eagerly embracing the Kabbalat Shabbat ceremony as a ritual appropriate for Christian practice and as an additional part of the movement of getting back to the "roots" of the original Christian faith, despite the anachronistic nature of this application.

The problem, of course, is that within Christianity Jesus is the son of God, and the Church is his *bride*. This is self-evident and accepted by nearly all Christians around the world. Yet, this paradigm creates a major problem for Christians attempting to adopt Jewish practice. In Jewish understanding, and in the Bible itself, plainly stated, *Israel* is the son of God, and the Sabbath is her *bride*. God gave the Sabbath to Israel as a marriage gift, and as a token and perpetual reminder of the covenant. It was both a wedding gift and a symbol of fidelity. The ritual of circumcision was the mark of ownership, the wedding ring, as it were, but the Sabbath represented the corporate experience of what it meant to be a Jewish family. To summarize simply, in Christianity the people of God are the Christians, are they are married to Jesus. The Jews, in most Christian ontological narratives, are *also* the people of God, in a technical, though diminished sense, having been now "set aside" for a future purpose (according to the Dispensationalists, such as most Baptists) or have been "replaced" (according to Calvinists). In the Bible, however, the people of God are Israel and they are married to the Sabbath, not to a man-god like Attis, Zeus or Jesus.

"So the sons of Israel shall observe the Sabbath, to celebrate the Sabbath throughout their generations as a perpetual covenant. It is a sign between Me and the sons of Israel forever..." (Exodus 31:16-17)

Jesus, therefore, represents a *substitute* for the biblical reality presented in the scriptures of Israel. He is an *imposter*, a counterfeit. This doesn't mean that Christians are considered idolaters by Judaism (they are not), but it's very wrong for Christians to appropriate Jewish covenantal identity as having been inherited by the Church. This is religious syncretism and, by extent, heresy. In Judaism, and in the Jewish Bible, God doesn't require an intermediary to "run interference" for his people in the Bible. He tells the people to worship Him alone. And when he gives a gift of marriage in the form of a covenant ritual such as observing Shabbat it is a blessing to all the people and something they can cherish forever and pass down to their children; something they can *do*, something they *must* do, which is real, tangible, and physical, and which encompasses the entire family, indeed, the entire community. In Christianity, the only inheritance that is waiting for the believer is a *concept*. Something ethereal, dogmatic, theological in nature. The concept of *Jesus*, and the security of an afterlife that is bartered not by covenant or via association with the family, but individually, through a confession of belief. A much different paradigm. And why, pray tell, would any man, Jew or non-Jew, want to be *married to Jesus?* Additionally, the Sabbath is a marriage gift to the Jew *particularly*, and not to the whole world. It is the exclusive right and privilege of the Jew, and not part of some universalist salvation story. They may share this blessing with others, for sure, but it is most definitely *theirs* to share, and no one else's.

Give me Shabbat, please. I'll take Shabbat as a wedding gift from God over Jesus. I'll take the candle lighting, and my wife, and my children, and my extended family and friends, and the physical reality of the Shabbat meal and ceremony over the pagan ritual of the Eucharist representing the "broken body and blood of the Lord" decidedly, unreservedly and with prejudice.

The disconnect is very real, yet in the ever-promising world of religious syncretism, it becomes obscured. When I tried to reconcile the Christian concept of the Church as the bride of Christ with the Jewish understanding of circumcision and of Shabbat, and found that it couldn't be done, I realized that Christianity had built a metaphoric house of cards out of flimsy material, and it had finally fallen apart before my eyes. There was really, at that point, little for me to wrestle through for my deconversion away from Jesus to be complete. A few quibbles about atonement and some questions about the resurrection and ascension, and the door would be closed on the discussion.

Rabbi Mark Kinzer is a messianic Jew who has relations among the Cardinals of the Vatican, and who published *"Post-Missionary Messianic Judaism"*, in 2005. Kinzer, a humble man, proposed the concept of "Bilateral Ecclesiology", a bold innovation in Christian understanding of Jews and Judaism, which attempted to square Christian doctrine about salvation with the biblical covenants God made with Israel alone. The primary objective of the book is to argue that the practice of Judaism by Jesus-followers is a justified practice on its own merits and not merely as the gambit of Christian evangelists seeking to proselytize Jews. And further, the book argues significantly that Jews have their own, unique path to God and to their atonement which is independent of the Christian gospel. In other words, *Jews don't need to become Christians*. According to his understanding, Paul's declaration of Israel's "partial hardening", as the apostle describes in the later chapters of Romans, makes room for the current theological tension between Judaism and Christianity, without annulling the covenants God has made with Israel, despite traditional Christian claims through the centuries. This theory was presented to me as a viable alternative by friends within the messianic movement who could see that I was leaving Jesus and was considering formal conversion to Judaism. I took the time to analyze it, but ultimately, while I applauded Kinzer's attempts at bringing forth a bridge of healing between the Church and the Jewish people, the truth of the matter is that Kinzer's concession to the Jewish religion merely calls into question whether he believes in either Judaism *or* Christianity. While it's appreciated that he acknowledges the covenants of God, one cannot soft-pedal the gospel of Jesus Christ by making exceptions for the very people the gospels go out of their way to castigate and condemn for rejecting it. For any self-respecting Christian, it's like trying to pull the rug out from under your own feet. Also, by claiming allegiance to Paul's reckless and baseless declaration that Israel has been "hardened" to the gospel, how then does Kinzer expect to explain how Jews are able to get "saved" by accepting Jesus, which thousands of Jews reportedly do every year? Have they had their eyes shut (hardened) by God or not? Is it truly a matter of eschatology, as the dispensationalists claim? Or is it, as I believe, a cheap Pauline trick of theological sleight-of-hand? It would seem to me that anyone who reads the New Testament honestly would see the obvious attempt by its writers, whoever they were, to make a distinct separation between the new faith of Christianity and what we understand to be Judaism, and they do so in starkly unmistakable ways. If a bilateral solution to Israel's and Christianity's path to God is valid, why on earth would Paul and the other apostles have worked so hard to convince their fellow countrymen of their need to accept Jesus? It would seem a needless waste of time if that were the case and Kinzer's theory is correct. They should have, rather, left their fellow Jews alone and focused on the Nations. But that's not what happened, as we know.

Of course, Kinzer's argument, which is largely endorsed by the Roman Catholic Church today, does represent *major* progress in Jewish-Christian relations, after two thousand years of persecution. But really, the debate he raises is merely the off gassing of centuries of Christian argumentation about the nature of salvation, the nature of covenant and the efficacy of Jewish identity apart from Christ. For most of Church history, Jews have been considered *damned*, and are only (in this framing) allowed by God to exist to wander the earth as vagabonds for an example to the rest of the world of what the fruits of unbelief look like. In fact, it is this precise attitude that Hitler embraced in his "final solution". The only possible hope for the Jew, according to mainstream Christian doctrine, is for them to accept Jesus as their Messiah.

But there is a better solution to the problem than what Kinzer proposes. Rather than giving the Jews a pass on Jesus through "Bilateral Ecclesiology", what if Judaism has already done this for Christians? Judaism, after all, already has a simple plan of "salvation" (to use Christian framing) available to non-Jews that doesn't require Jesus or the religion of Christianity in any capacity, and this Jewish concept has rolled along effortlessly regardless of any fancy scholarship of the last fifty years. Judaism, after all, is the only major world religion (excepting Buddhism) that doesn't insist that people convert to it in order to have a relationship with God. Judaism teaches the Noahide laws, which are the seven basic rules of morality laid down and given to Noah, and which contain many subsets and ethical expansions, none of which, however, require a person to be circumsized, become legally Jewish, or to adhere to 613 Jewish commandments to gain status before God. Just be a righteous person, basically, and you'll be fine. It's incredibly accessible. Nothing else is required, unless one is to include, as some do, a form of proxy attachment to the Jews, through support and association.

The fact that a conspiratorial theory such as Dr. Kinzer's "Bilateral Ecclesiology" is even considered necessary as a form of *theological therapy* for the "Jewish problem" should be a red flag to anyone paying close attention that Christianity's claims are unbiblical.

I had kept some of these thoughts to myself as I worked it out. But more and more, I viewed Messianic Judaism as a poor-man's counterfeit of true Judaism. Messianic Jews and the non-Jews alongside them had decided that they liked the Torah. They wanted to practice Judaism, at least at some level, but were not welcomed in traditional Jewish space. But they were emotionally and/or theologically incapable of letting go of Jesus along the way, so they hog-tied him and forced him to be part of their Jewish charade and began calling Jesus their "rabbi". Apparently, they still felt they needed his *magic blood* to make their Jewish fantasy work.

Chapter 19

———— ❧ ————

There's No Such
Thing as Magic Blood

I STOOD THERE, alone, in the carpeted hall at one of the oldest Conservative synagogues in Atlanta, staring at the artifacts displayed behind the glass case, many of which had come from Europe, or from the founders of the shul, who were now deceased. These ranged from "crowns", which are decorative "caps" designed to cover the handles on a kosher Torah scroll, to Holocaust-era yellow stars, worn by Jews under Hitler's Third Reich as state-imposed identity markers, to decorative plates from Israel. My vision clouded as I had begun to weep, unexpectedly. I was overtaken with a certain nostalgia and I could not immediately explain what I was feeling. Today I can. It was the conscious awareness of a *people*, over that of a *theology*. I teared up as the significance of this idea settled in my heart, creating thunderous hammer-blows in my chest as it raced to catch up with my thoughts.

The year before we moved to Atlanta, I had ordered a DNA test kit from Family Tree and promptly sat on it. I never even opened the package. I was afraid to. At that point, I knew already that a DNA test did not determine a person's Jewish status, because membership in the Tribe was not merely determined by bloodlines, but also by choice, through conversion, and citizenship had to be proven if there was doubt. It was entirely different than converting to Christianity, for which all that was required was a statement of belief. When you convert to Judaism, you are not merely accepting a religious practice or a set of beliefs. You are joining a nation. My DNA test was of no value to this process. So, I set it aside. Then, one day, Chana asked me about it. No, I hadn't sent it in. She insisted I do so. Said she had a premonition, for lack of a better word. A month later, the results came back. They indicated that I was a descendent of Conversos who fled Spain during the Inquisition. Not proof, mind you, but an indicator. However, it was enough for Chana. She believed that it confirmed her premonition, and she felt that I should convert. She woke me up to tell me this one night. The frankness and shocking nature of her words gave me goosebumps.

"Yes," I heard myself mutter aloud, "I suppose so." She fell back asleep. I did not. As a messianic Christian who had become disillusioned with the Jesus story, I was at a critical point in my journey. How could I join the Jewish people, for real? No qualified *Beit Din* would approve my conversion to Judaism as an actively confessing Jesus-follower. And this was, of course, the rub for messianic believers; they loved Torah, to one degree or another, but were not willing to throw Jesus into the recycle bin to make the full commitment to become part of *Am Israel*. So, they created their own community outside of both traditions. Many of them went further, such as FFOZ, by adopting the posture that they were "right", and that their mission was to convince the rest of the Jewish world that they deserved a place at the family table, something which, thank God, has never, or will ever, happen. So, was it possible to become "unsaved"? Did I need to worry about such things? I certainly felt like the Jesus story was not relevant to me anymore on a personal level, and I wondered what this meant. *Who was I?*

Evangelicals often ask each other, "When did you get saved?" You are expected to know the answer to this question. Even better if it involves a "story". But how is such an idea possible, if Jesus's *magic blood* spans the eons, and is not restricted by human initiative or effort? Does it atone as advertised or not? How can I say that there is one moment in which his blood is "powerful to save my soul" and yet still another in which it is not? Who gets to decide if I am "forgiven"? How can I know? Of course, if the story itself is a myth invented to accomplish objectives that are now obscured from our understanding or care, then one could understand why the story showed up on the world scene when it did. After all, the New Testament was written entirely in Greek and no authentic fragments of any New Testament texts can be dated earlier than the mid-2nd Century, though most scholars believe the earliest letters of Paul to have been written in the mid-fifties CE, about twenty to fifty years before the gospel accounts, give or take, and about the same amount of time *after* the person his letters extol, though all of this is, of course, conjecture on the part of scholars. The story itself surely appears to be of Roman, and not Jewish origin, and its central drama seems to center around the building tension between the Jewish and Roman territorial interests and the impending destruction of Jerusalem and the Jewish Temple by the Romans in the bitterly contested Roman/Jewish war of 66-73CE, immediately after which the earliest gospels are believed to have been written. But Christian theologians through the centuries have never allowed such inconvenient truths to dissuade their zeal and are quick with an alibi as to why it would be that the earliest Jewish Christians would produce religious propaganda in anything but their native and most ethnocentric languages of Aramaic and Hebrew. Maybe we should concede the possibility that the Roman, Greek-speaking world had other plans for this "Jewish" Jesus portrayed in the New Testament's pages; plans which had little to do with Jewish sovereignty over Israel or the messianic ideals of the rabbis. The universalist salvation message of the New Testament does not have in view the job of the expected Jewish messiah, which is a major reason why educated Jews through the ages have always rejected Christian claims for Jesus.

In a similar vein, the New Testament contains such oft-quoted verses as this one,

"If we confess our sins, He is faithful and righteous to forgive our sins, and to cleanse us from all unrighteousness." (I Jn.1:9)

This was a verse I memorized as a new believer in my discipleship class with my friend Jon. It was a key verse for me for many years, offering a promise that whenever my conscience felt seared by guilt because of my actions, or my attitudes, that I could repent, "going boldly before the throne of grace" to seek forgiveness and restoration. It is not a verse that any Christian associates with obtaining salvation, such as the famous John three-sixteen passage. Rather, it is nearly unanimously applied, regardless of the branch of Christianity in question, to a person who is already within the fold. Then, one day, it occurred to me that this statement by John is quite inappropriate, if in fact Jesus accomplished a "finished" work on the cross of Calvary. Did he or did he not achieve atonement for my sins that day as his *magic blood* drained from his body and he died? If this atoned for all my sins, both prior to my knowledge of him, as well as all my sins (and the sins of all humanity) for all time, then what, exactly, was the benefit of confessing "sins" to "purge myself of un-righteousness" *after* coming to belief in him? If his shed blood was efficacious to purify the world, including myself, then why wasn't everyone purified? The implications of this question, once I asked it, grew like a monster in my closet until, like the little boy suffering from the recurring nightmare, I had to walk right over to the light switch, flip it on, suck in air, and whip the closet door open to face my doom. *Was I "saved" or was I still "lost"?* I was driven to study the Jewish ideas on atonement so I could get the story straight. I had to know. It seemed to me that if I needed to continually go before the "throne of grace" for guidance, forgiveness and restoration, that there was not very much validity to the whole *salvation by grace without works* narrative. It appeared that this practice of continual confession through prayer to restore "right standing" put me squarely back into a presumed Jewish framing of justification by works of righteousness (leaving aside any discussion of covenantal status for the moment) and that, as such, I was no different than a Jew who still lived "under the law", as Paul said in Romans explicitly, and Galatians implicitly. And if I was going to be held to account for the law and its moral imperatives (as it clearly states I will be in Romans chapter two) even after being washed in the *magic blood* of Jesus, then the Jew under the Sinai Covenant was in fact far ahead of me, in both spiritual understanding of and in relation to God, since the Jewish sages were ultimately the authorities on how to properly obey the Law. After all, it was their book, and not ours.

I had been attracted to Judaism, initially, because of my profound disappointment with Christianity, and ultimately through my study of Jewish commentaries on the Torah and by my study of the Talmud. The depth of thought and the breadth of testimony of the Jewish intellectual tradition was mind-expanding and quite freeing compared to the assumptive dogmatism of my Christian experience, and I didn't need to look beyond these avenues to know that I had found what I was looking for. Along the way in my Jewish studies, many ideas I had carried with me from evangelical perspectives were melting away before the onslaught of ideas within the rich Rabbinic tradition. One of the most important of these was the conception of atonement, and perhaps the biggest earthquake to my understanding was the result of experiencing Rosh HaShana in a Jewish community. There is an iconic refrain during the liturgy for the holiday:

> 'Remember us for life,
> O King who delights in life,
> And write us in the book of life –
> For your sake, O God of life.'

Judaism doesn't celebrate death. It celebrates *life* because we are living people, not dead people. Christianity, by contrast, appears to one who is not indoctrinated into it from childhood as a *death cult*. It banks its promises within the death narrative of its greatest hero. The paradigm is not unlike the many pagan mystery cults which flourished in the ancient world. In Judaism, however, everything is about the world of the *living*. Yes, there is a mysterious and complex (even contradictory) tradition concerning the *Olam Haba*, or Future World, but the bulk of the tradition deals with the stuff of living, breathing souls, not disembodied ones floating in the ether. Ironically, it is perhaps because of this emphasis that Judaism boasts a much healthier and robust approach to the topic of death and goes much farther than Christianity to remember and honor the dead. One would perhaps think the opposite, but in fact Christianity's emphasis upon the soul's destiny *after* death as the sole purpose of *life* prevents Christians from dealing with the reality of physical death in a holistic manner. Rather than celebrate the life that a person lived, the focus among evangelicals is typically upon the destiny of the person's soul.

I discovered, and this was a shock to me for some reason, that Rosh HaShana was a celebration of the anniversary of *creation itself*, and in this way was relevant to all humanity, at least in the Jewish imagination. Why had I never heard of this before, especially since Rosh HaShana was in the Bible? No Christian teacher had *ever* dealt with Rosh HaShana in their sermons; at least none that I had heard. As Rabbi Jonathan Sacks, of blessed memory, writes in his commentary on the holiday,

"The ten days that begin on Rosh Hashana and culminate in Yom Kippur are the holy of holies of Jewish time. The atmosphere in the synagogue is intense. You can almost touch the Divine Presence. Isaiah said: "Seek God where He is to be found, call on Him when He is close" (Is.55:6). The rabbis wrestled with this verse. What could it mean? God is the God of everywhere and all time. He is always to be found, always close. The verse seemed to make no sense at all.

This was their reply: "These are the Ten Days of Repentance between Rosh HaShana and Yom Kippur" — meaning, God is always close to us, but we are not always close to Him. He is always to be found, but we do not

always seek Him out. To sense the closeness of God needs some special effort on our part. To reach out to the Infinite in finite space, to meet the Eternal in the midst of time, to sense what ultimately lies beyond the senses, requires a focus far beyond the ordinary.

It needs a drama of holiness, enacted in our holiest place, the synagogue, at the holiest of times, Yamim Nora'im, the Days of Awe." ("Ceremony & Celebration: Introduction to the Holidays", pg.1, Sacks, Maggid Books, 2017)

When I finally experienced Rosh HaShana in legitimate Jewish space, it was one of the most emotional and profound experiences of my life. To be shoulder to shoulder with hundreds of Jews, young and old, packed like sardines into this modern synagogue, all belting out the songs and prayers in unison, and in Hebrew, none of them missing a note or a word but completely in step with the cantor, was surreal. The building vibrated with life and power, and I could not stop crying. Many of these people hardly ever attended shul during the year, but when the High Holidays came around, the call was powerful, and they were there, with tallis and yarmulke, to be accounted for. They were not a group of *believers*. What they were was a *people*, a *Tribe*. And their membership in this fraternity had nothing to do with Jesus or his sacrificial atonement, or any Jewish equivalent of these ideas.

That is getting ahead of the story, however, because the very first time I experienced the holiday, long before this event I just described, I was in the messianic synagogue, and the shofar was blown by a Christian, who believed in the Trinity and in the idea that Jesus was his Savior who atoned for his soul through *magic blood*.

Sitting in participation at the messianic church/synagogue during Rosh HaShana was somewhat uncomfortable, but not beyond the pale of the Christian imagination. After all, the ideas of neutralizing the enemy (HaSatan) who sought to make accusations against God's people was most certainly not an idea foreign to an evangelical mindset. Talk of "rebuking Satan" was rampant in evangelical circles. However, seeing the leaders, and some of the participants, all dressing in white from head to toe, after the Chassidic tradition (which has been largely main-streamed in the Jewish world) was unnerving. What did this mean? Were these messianic Jesus-believers virtue-signaling their "purification in Jesus"? Were they, in fact, *anticipating* such purification? Or were they simply, and blindly, mimicking the Jewish manner of practice, without regard to the true meaning behind the ritual? I believe, for most of them, the latter was the correct answer. But in what way did they find this behavior appropriate? Beyond the obvious play-acting which was happening, this raised questions in my mind which came to a head during the Yom Kippur ritual which followed a week or so later. Not the least of these being a wonderment as to how the sin atonement provided by the *magic blood* of Jesus squared with the atonement concepts presented by the biblical High Holidays of the Jewish faith, and why supposedly Jewish Christians of the 1st Century would conceive of such a connection to a murdered leader named Jesus. I had suspicions that any "Jewish Christians" in the 1st Century were probably Hellenized, and not loyal to the ideal of emerging "Rabbinic Judaism", as the messianic Christians were claiming, because no Jew that was knowledgeable of their own faith would make such a connection to their soul's eternal destiny as Christianity claims in the New Testament concerning Jesus's death, burial and resurrection.

Rosh HaShana marks the Jewish New Year and the calling to account of all Jews for the year which has passed. It is not the Day of Atonement, which is Yom Kippur, but, rather, Rosh HaShana is the Day of Repentance, when God is declared King, corporately, and the people begin a period of collective repentance and reconciliation. When the shofar blows, it is believed to negate the accusations of the Accusing Angel against God's people, enabling them to seek restoration without hindrance. The judgment which follows on Yom Kippur is determined on Rosh HaShana. It has nothing to do with the blood atonement of a Messiah-figure. As it turns out, the Messiah, in Jewish thought, has absolutely nothing to do with blood atonement at all.

This is an enormously difficult concept for a Christian, or anyone raised in a Christian-oriented culture, to understand. It certainly was difficult for me, and I failed to recognize the problem for some time. The Messianic Jewish leaders had attempted to convince us that Jesus was a Jewish rabbi teaching and practicing a messianic version of Orthodox Judaism. The truth is that Christianity is just a Judaized form of an ancient mystery religion, and therefore has little to do with Rabbinic ideas, despite whatever parallels one might extract from the Rabbinic tradition. Those parallels are circumstantial and coincidental, not prescriptive.

Immediately following Rosh HaShana are the Days of Awe, a time of intimate reflection for Jews to contemplate their deeds, their devotion, or lack thereof. The Days of Awe are an encapsulated representation of the forty days and nights that Moses pleaded with God on Mt. Sinai, entreating Him for mercy and forgiveness upon the people, *corporately*. It's the greatest act of intercession and prayer found in the Bible, culminating with the famous passage of Exodus 34:6-7, in which God passes before Moses, after tucking him into the cleft of rock, from where Moses sees God's *"back parts, since My face cannot be seen"*. What Moses records of this experience is known as the Thirteen Attributes of God's Mercy, and they form the basis for *Selichot* prayers, the deeply penitential prayers uttered (depending upon one's tradition) throughout the month of Elul, or at least during Yom Kippur. The Days of Awe climax with the holiest day of the year, Yom Kippur, or Day of Atonement. Jews fast for 24 hours from not just food, but water, as they are medically able. It is a structural and physical form of *teshuvah* (repentance).

The actual Temple ceremony of Yom Kippur has obviously not been performed since the Romans destroyed the Temple during the Roman-Jewish War of 66-73AD. Even were this ritual to be performed today, there are no clear lines which would connect Jesus to it. Yet, Christians do so boldly. This past week, as we prepared for *Pesach*, a woman at my wife's workplace, knowing she was Jewish, gave her a red ribbon to put on her door, as a form of witness to Jesus's representation of the "scarlet thread of redemption" found (according to Christians) in the Passover story. I think the woman thought it would be a good testimony for Jesus that also honored Jewish tradition. My wife thanked her for the sentiment, but gently rebuked her for not having a clue what she was talking about. The woman walked away a bit confused.

For one thing, in Christian understanding, Jesus is "slain from the foundations of the world" as the "lamb of God" for the sins of all humanity. Yet, this immediately breaks down at a fundamental level if we are to equate Jesus with either the Passover Lamb, which doesn't "atone" for *anyone,* or with the "scapegoat" of Yom Kippur, since the sins are placed upon the goat which is *sent away,* not the one which is sacrificed. The Christian interpretation of the Day of Atonement betrays a complete ignorance of both the Yom Kippur ritual and the sacrificial worship system, generally. The Christian view is also barbaric in its conceptualization, basing its understanding upon the pagan idea of sacrificing "one of their own" to the gods as a form of appeasement. The fundamental concept of sin-atonement in Judaism is not, primarily, found in the ritual purification which is achieved through the sacrificial worship system. Rather, it is rooted in the dual concepts of *repentance* and *forgiveness.*

Christians have no understanding whatsoever that there is even a difference between the ritual purification provided through the Temple worship system and the basic atonement achieved through the Jewish understanding of repentance. If there was not a significant difference between these ideas, Judaism would not have survived the destruction of the Temple, or the failure of the Jews to be able to rebuild it. Christians typically conclude that God allowed the Temple to be destroyed because Jesus has now "replaced" its purpose and function, based on explicit inferences from the book of Hebrews. However, if this were true, in any sense, then why does the book of Acts display the core leaders of the early Jewish-Christian movement participating actively in the Temple worship system? We see James instructing Paul to present animal sacrifices as a token of his allegiance to Judaism as he completed a *nazarite vow* (See Acts

21:17-26). If Jesus fundamentally replaced this system, wouldn't it have been prudent for the earliest disciples of Jesus to distance themselves from its active practice? One would think.

I had learned by this point, and this cannot be emphasized enough, that Judaism is not a salvation-oriented religion but represents a relationship with God established through *covenant*. In this sense, how is a Jew to get *saved* when their security is established by a covenant that God himself has promised to uphold? And if this is true (and biblically speaking it is most certainly true) how in the world does Jesus fit into any of this? Why would a person such as Jesus in his New Testament role as the risen Christ be needed or even *anticipated* within Judaism? Why would a Jew who understood their own faith even *look* for someone like Jesus? More to the point, what is he supposed to accomplish for them by getting killed? What Jews were looking for during the 1st Century was not a self-sacrificing, atoning redeemer-figure who takes the proverbial or literal "hit" for their "unrighteousness", but a military commander and spiritual leader who could rally the people to help them overthrow Rome, just like the nation was looking for when they asked Samuel for a king during the days at the end of the period of the Judges. But a human sacrifice to create atonement for sin?? How utterly pagan an idea!

A more disturbing question, perhaps, is why the Messianic Jewish movement was attempting to participate in these covenant-centered rituals that pertained to Jewish covenantal exceptionalism to begin with. Framed another way, why would any Jewish believer in Jesus spend all year looking forward to the renewal and restart of the cycle of the Jewish calendar; of the soul-renewal of the High Holidays themselves, if Jesus somehow rendered the entire process irrelevant? This fact is acknowledged by the writer of Ephesians, who declares that followers of Christ represent "One New Man", creating a physical distinction between Torah-observant Jews and the community of Jews and non-Jews who made up the Jesus sect. This is also why Paul's argument against circumcision and kosher observance by Jesus-followers is important to Christianity, because these doctrines created the needed separation between the two vastly different conceptions of one's relationship to God that Judaism and Christianity offer. And if Jesus had rendered these quaint ancient rituals passe, how did they make sense for Jesus-followers to participate in such outdated modes of worship alongside Jews? After all, there was no "blood atonement" in them. There is nothing in either Rosh HaShana, Yom Kippur or Pesach which rely upon blood atonement. The Jewish people were not forgiven, according to the Bible and the Jewish tradition, based on any animal or human sacrifice, but through their repentance; their *teshuvah*.

Perhaps one reason for the confusion among Christians, at least when it comes to the Day of Atonement, is based squarely in the perversion of understanding of the Yom Kippur ritual in the Bible by Christians through the centuries. Specifically, I'm speaking of a twisting of the idea of the "scapegoat".

One must ask: What is the Yom Kippur ritual about? Why are the sins of the Nation symbolically placed upon the goat that *isn't* sacrificed? The great sage of Israel, Rambam (Maimonides) says this in his Guide for the Perplexed,

"There is no doubt that sins cannot be carried like a burden and taken off the shoulder of one being to be laid on that of another being. But these ceremonies are of a symbolic character, and serve to impress people with a certain idea, and to induce them to repent – as if to say, we have freed ourselves of our previous deeds, have cast them behind our backs, and removed them from us as far as possible." (Guide 111:46)

As Rabbi Jonathan Sacks explains in his commentary on Leviticus, the term "scapegoat" was invented by William Tyndale in his 1530 translation of the Hebrew Bible into English, the first such effort made. The term became synonymous for Christian theologians with the *passion* of Christ, "dying for our sins", and yet ironically, as Sacks explains, the ceremony of Yom Kippur appears to be a blatantly obvious protest against such "human sacrifice". It is precisely the "scapegoat" idea promulgated by Tyndale which is categorically denounced by Yom Kippur, and yet, in the hands of people not versed in Torah, it becomes a dog-whistle for *tribal justice*. He says,

"More than this, we can now see that the institution of the scape-goat in biblical Israel was itself a protest against human sacrifice, wide-spread in the ancient world. Two features of the High Priest's ritual were crucial: (1) that the sacrifice was an animal, not a person, and (2) that it was not an occasion for denying responsibility by blaming the victim, but to the contrary, an acceptance of responsibility in the context of repentance and atonement." (Leviticus: The Book of Holiness, Covenant & Conversation: A Weekly Reading of the Jewish Bible, Sacks, Maggid Books, 2015, pg.257)

As Sacks goes on to explain, the people's relationship with God is also maintained through the ideas of repentance found in the prophetic literature. As this passage illustrates explicitly,

"Return, O Israel, to the Lord your God… Take words with you and return to the Lord. Say to Him: Forgive all our sins and receive us graciously, that we may present the fruit of our lips." (Hosea 14:1-2)

I've heard Christian pastors quote this passage, but yet we should notice that it has no mention of a human intermediary performing "sacrificial atonement" as part of this "return". No, it involves words, and actions. It nowhere implies Jesus, or anyone else, as our "scape-goat". Atonement in Judaism has always been about the returning of the soul to God, and much less about sacrificial rites.

God's people returning. This thought is what made me weep in front of the glass case at the synagogue. The Jews were not held together as a people based on a belief in a dogma or in their allegiance to any person or doctrine. There is no authentic form of Judaism that is entirely centered on a single individual. If there is any identity to be found in Jewry beyond the practice of Torah observance, it is one of common experience, forged in the fires of testing, suffering, shared joy and meaning, all of which are born out of the wellspring of a *shared covenant*.

But what about the Passover event? After all, wasn't it obvious that the blood that the Jews spread upon the doorposts and lintels of their homes in Egypt represented a typology of the shed blood of Jesus, enabling them to escape the death angel of the last plague? So self-evident was this parallel, that most Christians for all of history never for a moment have stopped to analyze the fallacy of this presumption.

The story goes like this in children's church: Jesus is the Passover Lamb, and it's therefore his *magic blood* that is being spread upon the doorposts and lintels of our lives when we trust in Him. The results of this are simple and straightforward; those who have the *magic blood* applied to their lives are now safe…they have life everlasting. But (gasp!) those who do *not* have the *magic blood* applied to their lives are lost and will die a torturous death of eternal torment and suffering. This heavenly reality, according to the Church, will divide even the closest of families, and will separate the sheep from the goats in the apocalyptic end of the age, leaving all those who have refused to place the *magic blood* of Jesus on the doorposts of their lives completely, and tragically, outside of God's loving care.

It's because of this narrative, this falsified parallel, that Christians associate the *magic blood* of Jesus with Passover. The idea is that each lamb killed and eaten by the people in Egypt that fateful night of Passover typologically represented the pre-incarnate Jesus, "slain before the foundations of the world" on their behalf. Makes sense, doesn't it? Well no, actually, it doesn't make any sense at all. And apparently, this Christianized idea never occurred to Moses either, or else he surely would have mentioned such things in his instructions to the people.

As it turns out, there was nothing whatsoever about the Passover event that had anything to do with saving Jewish souls, or anyone else's soul, for that matter. It was a plague; the final, horrific plague upon the Egyptians, which paralleled the awful decree that Pharaoh had levied against the Jews a generation earlier. The blood on the doorposts wasn't magic, nor was it a type of talisman that granted them protection, like some grisly spell from a Harry Potter story. It simply was a physical indicator that Jews were living in the house. The sheep was a sacred animal to the Egyptians; *a god*. Slaughtering the lamb was an affront to the Egyptians. God, through Moses, had literally instructed the Israelites to slaughter and eat an Egyptian god. The blood on the doorposts had no magic or atoning qualities but was merely a sign of obedience and identification. And not everyone in the house was at risk in any case, whether the blood was on the door frame or not. Only the first-born was in danger. That was the plague's promise, remember? Even if the Christian appropriation of this event could somehow be justified, comparing Passover with the *magic blood* of Jesus, it breaks down at that simplest of levels. Christians are taught that the *magic blood* in the story protected the Jews from death. But, as we see from a plain, literal reading of the text, it only protected the first-born. Again, there is no concept within Judaism by which the Jewish soul is rectified to God through the shed blood of animals. (Or of people!). If the blood of the Passover lamb had magic qualities when applied to the doorposts of Jewish homes, then why was this practice not continued when the people settled the Promised Land? More so, if it's critical to the "salvation" of the Jewish soul, why is it not promoted as such? In fact, the only time of year in which the health and safety of the Jewish soul is in question at all is on Yom Kippur, and the High Holidays, at no point, have anything to do with blood atonement.

The Jewish concept of sin atonement, contrary to Christian dogma, has little whatsoever to do with sacrifice or even with blood, even though it's clear that there is blood all over the worship system and its rituals. In fact, there are no worship offerings prescribed in the Levitical, sacrificial cult which atone for intention sin. Not one. Rather, atonement in Judaism is based in the fundamental concept of *measure for measure*; the notion that God is righteous and rewards righteousness while punishing wickedness. It is typified in the story of Abraham found in Genesis:

"Shall I hide from Abraham what I am about to do, since Abraham will surely become a great and mighty nation, and in him all the nations of the earth will be blessed? For I have chosen him, so that he may command

his children and his household after him to keep the way of the LORD by doing righteousness and justice... " (Gen.18:17-19)

In Jewish thought, precisely because God is presented as being fair and just, nothing may be swept under the rug concerning his judgment. No sin is unaccounted for, nor is any good deed ignored. And it certainly would not be fair to send an innocent person to an eternal hell for simple ignorance of a Christian gospel that is not even in the Jewish Bible. Nor is it fair to punish a decent person because they fail to assent to a dogmatic creed. In fact, the idea of an eternal hell doesn't even exist in Judaism. I have been shocked, in various dialogs with Christians, to learn how many of them believe that Jews who died in the Holocaust are (unfortunately, they point out) going to spend *eternity in hell* because they never heard about or accepted Jesus before being starved to death or gassed to death during Hitler's "final solution" to the "Jewish problem". Atrocious.

In Judaism, nothing in life is supposed to be wasted or ignored. Everything matters. In Judaism, all Jewish souls are one. All Jewish souls derive from *one soul*. They are all sparks of the same root, in much the same way that all of humanity is similarly connected to each other. Every Jew alive today is intrinsically connected to every Jew which has gone before, including the generation which stood at the foot of Mt. Sinai to receive the Ten Commandments. Covenant faithfulness is a generational question. It includes the concepts of cultural and generational memory, meaning and accountability, and yes, even the idea of reincarnation, which is a big part of Jewish spirituality, at least for Torah-observant Jews. But one thing that it doesn't include, in any shape, conception or expression, is *magic blood*. Even the blood that the High Priest is to sprinkle on the Golden Altar in the Holy of Holies on Yom Kippur is related to ritual purification, and not atonement for one's soul, as the Bible clearly illustrates.

Jesus, we may someday learn, was a real Jewish guy who taught some cool things. But one thing I had learned beyond a shadow of doubt by this time, was that the Jesus presented to us in the New Testament was clearly a fictional character, and certainly not connected to Rabbinic Judaism whatsoever. What the gospels, as forms of literature, represent is up for debate. This much was clear: They weren't a representation of *history*. And further, Jesus certainly wasn't a Jewish Savior, whether he was real or not. His character and accomplishments, as portrayed in the Christian scriptures, are directly tied to a *pagan mystery cult motif*, with Mosaic overtones painted over the basic pagan model.

I learned, of course, that there was no such thing as *magic blood*. The man Jesus, if he even existed in history, could not have "atoned" for anything related to me or my life by dying an unjustified death two thousand years ago, any more than I can flap my arms and take off like a bird. It is ludicrous to think such a thing is possible. *Magic blood* was an invention of Christian theologians to explain why I needed to be a Christian. It is really that simple. It is part of the initiation rite; a concept that involves *gnosis* and which creates a sense of membership in the cult and its rituals.

Paul's Jesus, and the Jesus of Christian tradition, is a celestial being who accomplishes celestial things through celestial attributes. He is a Divine Offering, mirroring the Sin Offering of the Jewish Temple cult, shedding *magic blood* in perpetuity as an everlasting sacrifice, as portrayed in arduous detail in the New Testament book of Hebrews.

Philo of Alexandria, who popularized the synchronization of Jewish ideas with Greek philosophies and introduced the *logos theory*, also introduced the notion of a celestial Jesus who defeats Satan in the heavens. Perhaps the pen of Philo is the place we should be looking for the gospel's origins, and not within the rabbinic tradition.

All I knew at this point in my journey was that my head was spinning, and I was done with trying to shoehorn these pagan ideas into any form of Judaism that I was to encounter.

Chapter 20

WILL THE REAL MESSIANIC
JEWS PLEASE STAND UP?

"As long as the Jewish spirit is yearning deep in the heart
With eyes turned toward the East, looking toward Zion
Then our hope – the two-thousand-year-old hope – will not be lost
To be a free people in our land
The land of Zion and Jerusalem"
- "Hatikva" Israeli National Anthem

IT IS OFTEN assumed that Christianity emerged out of a sect of Jews who originally were Torah-observant, Jewish followers of Jesus. In fact, this was the perspective of the people in the Messianic Jewish movement. The idea presented was that the original disciples of Jesus were practicing an early incarnation of Pharisaic Rabbinic Judaism just like the Orthodox today, except they had been "enlightened" as to Jesus being the awaited Messiah. But I have learned that the actual *Messianic Jews* of the Second Temple period were not like this at all and had nothing whatsoever to do with any individual named Jesus or his followers. In fact, there were grave doubts as to whether the gospels even portrayed a historical person.

When I still lived in Vermont, I had started a small home fellowship Bible study which transitioned into a weekly online teaching session over Zoom with various students from around the country. At one point, one of my students, thinking it would be a good idea for me to address the seeming contradictions between Paul and James in the New Testament, encouraged me to teach the book of James, and I agreed. While I never did get around to teaching James, (and never will) I did do a very deep dive into Jamesian scholarship while I prepared myself to do so. I collected and read numerous books and PhD dissertations on James, and this personal study was transformative for me, ultimately giving me the confidence to reveal to my peers that I was no longer a believer in, or follower of, Jesus. I lost many friends and followers when I revealed this, which was expected, but also gained many others. It turned out that there was an entire community out there of people like me who had found the claims of Christianity deeply flawed, and had left off from belief in it altogether.

My James research became focused on a couple of issues I was wrestling through in my mind, which pertained to the conflict between Pauline "grace-based faith" and Jamesian "works-based faith" (the obvious conundrum hashed out *ad nauseum* by Christian apologists throughout recent history) and more subversively, how Christians and Jews traditionally understood the concepts of personal righteousness, meaning, how one attains a right standing before God. There was one scholar, Chris VanLandingham, who has a PhD in Judaism and Christianity in the Greco-Roman World, whose book, "Judgment & Justification in Early Judaism and the Apostle Paul" (Hendricks Publishers, 2006), I eagerly absorbed. It was incredibly well-researched, citing many apocryphal works of the period surrounding the Roman-Jewish War in the First Century, and served to challenge the Protestant understanding of Pauline doctrine in the modern era, particularly regarding the doctrine of "justification by faith alone", as articulated by Luther and Calvin and which still, today, informs the Protestant Christian world. This book was hugely important to me, as I had, around the same time, become familiar with the work of E.P. Sanders, who had challenged some of the same presuppositions among Christian theologians, albeit from the opposite angle. Sanders argued that Judaism, as well as Christianity, operated from a "grace-based" perspective, undermining the well-worn Christian trope of "Law vs. Grace". VanLandingham, on the other hand, also argued against the "Law vs. Grace" presumption within Christianity, but from the alternative perspective that early Christianity, with its attachment to Jewish apocalyptic messianism (such as is found in the Dead Sea Scrolls) was far more legalistic than modern Protestant expressions would have conceived. Citing such rarely studied works as Jubilees, Enoch, Apocalypse of Abraham, Sirach and the Qumran Scrolls, VanLandingham made a clear and compelling case for the presence of a radicalized messianic Jewish, militant sect which drove a militant contingent of apocalyptic messianism based upon covenant fidelity, with a focus upon a "Last Judgment based on Deeds", and which has echoes in various points within the New Testament quite prominently in Matthew, James and, as the author displays, portions of the Pauline writings. This was really the first exposure I had to the religious and political environment of the Second Temple period, during which time religious zealots within the Jewish world were the sandwich-board-wearing alarmists of the culture, proclaiming imminent doom and apocalyptic judgment upon the Nation should they fail to rise up against the iniquities and shortcomings of the generation.

I added to my reading another PhD dissertation by scholar Mariam Kamell, who authored "The Soteriology of James in Light of Earlier Jewish Wisdom Literature and the Gospel of Matthew" in 2010, (University of St. Andrew). She argued, in similar fashion, for a new reading of James which accepts the letter as teaching that salvation and judgment are not based on "free grace" alone, but upon covenantal faithfulness and behavioral righteousness. Again, the book of Enoch features prominently in her analysis. The crux of her argument centered upon a reimagining of James's epistle completely divorced from any considerations of Pauline doctrine regarding "faith and works". With this approach, James is quite consistent with ancient Jewish thought, and Paul is revealed as being in error. Her argument inferred that James was representative of the same radical messianism detailed in the apocryphal sources cited by VanLandingham, which she cited as well. These resources had revolutionized my thinking, and I thought I was ready to teach James. But, since I was not yet finished with the series I was currently teaching, I kept collecting more related material, and that's when the proverbial lid blew off the can. It turned out that there was a very simple cultural and religious reality, "hiding in plain sight", which essentially rendered such theological debates secondary.

I had begun, at around the same time, a deep dive into Jewish mysticism, and began my study with the great Jewish scholar Gershom Scholem, and a collection of his most famous essays published under the title "The Messianic Idea In Judaism" (Schocken Books, 1971). Scholem spoke directly to my questions of Pauline and Jamesian understanding, as it relates to conceptions of messianic redemption in the Second Temple era. As he explains, Christianity and Judaism have entirely different understandings and conceptualizations of "messianic redemption". Christianity snubs its theological nose at the idea of war, the exertion of force, or any notion of nationalism in its view of redemption, but rather views the idea from the Pauline lens of personal atonement in a spiritual and "unseen realm", which would be Paul's idea of "Jesus in me," based largely upon rather Gnostic conceptions. The realities of the physical world are largely irrelevant to this metaphysical paradigm. However, within Judaism, the concept of redemption cannot refer to such ambiguous and theoretical concepts. No, in Judaism, messianic redemption is *apocalyptic*, and refers to a re-ordering of the physical reality experienced by the people, as a *community*. It is a transformative event accomplished before everyone and is unmistakable to both the religious and the non-religious alike. It doesn't require "belief". It is a self-evident, observable circumstance. The massive importance of this distinction is easy to underestimate, but is the clue, as it turns out, to understanding the truth behind the concept of "Messianic Jew". Scholem brings the idea home with a simple, but powerful, observation:

"(Messianic apocalypticism) concerns the catastrophic and destructive nature of the redemption on the one hand and the utopianism of the content of realized Messianism on the other. Jewish Messianism is in its origins and by its nature – this cannot be sufficiently emphasized – a theory of catastrophe."

As I understood it, this Jewish form of messianism highlighted by Scholem fueled the war effort with Rome, and the later Bar Kochba rebellion. However, in the Pauline letters and certainly in John, this apocalyptic notion was largely replaced by the more Gnostic ideas which envisioned Jesus as resurrected within the *individual*, through *personal belief*, as Scholem observed in his accurate analysis of Christianity. Paul communicates these ideas in full throughout his letters. In fact, according to Church historians, most of the Gnostics of the early centuries credit Paul as the founder of their movement. Further, Paul's conceptions of morality and personal conduct are not, as is often imagined, primarily Rabbinic, or Talmudic, but are quite synonymous with those of the Roman philosopher Seneca, who was a Stoic, so much so that early Church fathers forged a supposed correspondence between Seneca and Paul, elaborating upon Seneca's Stoic philosophy and appropriating his ideas to Paul. This is perhaps why Pauline theology is very congruent with Platonic Stoicism and is perhaps a significant clue as to the origins of later Christian thought.

This left a problem, however, which I still needed to work out. If the messianic idea in Judaism was a catastrophic concept of physical transformation which involved the entire community, then it followed that the Jews who would have attached their hopes to Jesus (if he existed) would not have been following the Christ of Christian, or more specifically, of Pauline imagination, but rather, *a military leader*. The

Bar Kochba-led rebellion, in the mid-2nd Century (132 CE), proves this point quite convincingly. Any messianic leader in the Second Temple period or after would have been considered a *failed* leader if he died without leading the people to an overthrow of Rome and a reinstitution of a sovereign Jewish state. In fact, Jewish law is *explicit* in stating that this is one of the exact conditions which the Messiah must fulfill. This is further supported by the fact that the Romans reserved the penalty of crucifixion exclusively for political dissidents which dared to threaten Roman authority. Therefore, if Jesus was a real person who really was crucified by the Romans, as the gospels suggest, then this fate signified his crime; *political rebellion*. Whatever neat theological teachings he may have delivered was not central to his expected role, and really were of no consequence. Therefore, any attempt made to synchronize the statements of Jesus with later Talmudic idioms was an exercise in novelty but irrelevant to the core issue at hand. The same holds true for any "miracles" which may or may not have been performed by him. Again, these are not necessary or expected of any messianic candidate. In fact, if anything, they do nothing but arouse suspicion that he is a fake.

This realization of the disconnect between the reality of Jewish messianic expectations and Christian conceptions of what I had been told that Jesus accomplished (atoning for the sins of the world through his death) created in me an urgent sense of imbalance. I had to resolve it satisfactorily or I would be in a full-blown theological crisis. There was another book on James, which Professor Kamell had recommended in her bibliography, which I had purchased but never read, because it was so imposing. At over a thousand pages, Robert Eisenman's "James the Brother of Jesus" (Penguin Books, 1996) proved of monumental importance to my understanding, once I read it. One of the world's renown experts on the Qumran Scrolls, Professor Eisenman identified the Qumran community, not as peaceful Essenes, as many Christian scholars had assumed (those scholars had not read the scrolls, obviously), but as the very Messianic Jews that were waging war against

Rome. Whether or not Mr. Eisenman was correct on his dating, he was spot on with pointing out the perspective driving the resistance. The ideology of the Qumran sect was consistent with what Gershom Scholem had identified as the "messianic impulse" within Ancient Israel. They saw themselves as fighting a holy war against an evil enemy, and the victory which would result (with the aid of the heavenly host for whose assistance they were living such purified, ascetic lives) in an idyllic utopia called the "Messianic Age", in which all of Israel's oppressors and opponents would be laid waste and the Jewish state would not only be reborn anew, it would even be the head of all the nations of the world. This same expectation colors the apocalyptic framing of both Christian, Jewish and even Muslim conceptions of the end-goal of their religious hopes today. Suddenly, a whole collection of otherwise unfathomable mysteries of the gospel story began to snap into clear focus. If Eisenman was correct, there was a militant, hyper-religious extremist sect of Jews who had rejected the corrupt leadership that ran the Temple, as they were "in bed" with Rome (and were connected to the Herodians, of whom Paul was a member, according to his own testimony in the letter called "Romans"), and this sect operated, not two hundred years prior to the gospel timeline, as many assumed, but *at the same time*. And their leader was a person named, not Jesus, but *James the Just*. Eisenman deduced that this James was none other than the James who makes a strange and sudden dramatic appearance from out of nowhere as the head of the Jerusalem church in Acts fifteen. Eisenman believed that Acts was a pseudo-historical rewrite of actual people and events, with the names and sequences and import all garbled and jumbled and inverted to throw the inquiring reader off the scent of the true history behind the fiction. I was deeply intrigued, because it made sense of the religious and political history of the period in a way that the New Testament, or mainline Christian scholarship on the New Testament, never had. Another key ingredient to Eisenman's hypothesis, and which got him in trouble with mainstream scholars (oh well), was that he believed that the Apostle Paul was the "wicked liar" fingered in the Qumran Scrolls repeatedly as the antagonist of the messianic movement and the enemy of James. It just so happened that the early Church writings substantiated and backed up Eisenman's claims, particularly the Clementine Recognitions.

One key element of this was that it provided a clear political, social and religious explanation for why Nero would not have been bothering with "Christians", as we understand the term today. Most Christians and Christian scholars know that Nero persecuted Christians during his reign. *Or did he?* Just *who* were the people Nero was persecuting? Why would he persecute peace-loving, self-sacrificing Christians who were "turning the other cheek"? It didn't add up. After all, it was Nero who appointed Vespasian to lead the war effort against Judea. Nero was deeply concerned about the unrest in the Middle East and wanted it dealt with. Unfortunately for him, Nero would not survive long enough to witness Vespasian's victory in the hotly contested and brutal war, which ended finally in seventy-three CE, some four years after Nero's death, nor hear of Vespasian's son Titus's destruction of the Jewish Temple (with Philo's nephew as his chief general!). Nero would not have had any interest in persecuting Christians in Rome, even if there *were* Christians in Rome to persecute, which is extremely doubtful in the sixties. No, but there *was* one pesty group that Nero would *most definitely* have persecuted if given the opportunity, and that's the *militant, violent, Messianic Jews* who had positioned themselves as the enemy of the Roman State.

Eisenman's book was a tour-de-force and my head was reeling with new conceptions of the Jesus story when I was done reading it. Shortly thereafter, in my quest to find corroborating information about the sociopolitical state of Judea during the late Second Temple period, I discovered three other books that informed me about the identity of the Messianic Jews, or "Christians", of the First Century. The first was Joseph Atwill's "Caesar's Messiah" (2011), which showed the parallels between the events and sequences in the gospels with Josephus's accounts of Vespasian's campaign against the Jews. It was almost an exact match. Atwill concluded that the gospels represented nothing less than a dark political satire by the Romans, designed to lampoon the defeated Messianic Jews and mock their messianic ideals after the end of the Roman/Jewish War. While Atwill's theory met with derision from many, I found his ideas very compelling. After all, his theory matched the historical practice of the Romans in their dealings with conquered territories. The next book tied even more things together, since it provided solid archeological evidence, and not just textual evidence, for its claims, and that was James Valliant's and Warren Faye's "Creating Christ: How Roman Emperors Invented Christianity" (2016). These two books opened the floodgates for me, because they placed the gospel story squarely into the socioreligious and sociopolitical context of the day, something that almost no other scholars were doing. Once things were put into this light, I suddenly could understand why the gospel story appeared on the scene when it did, and why it was brought forth in Greek. Josephus, who was a former Qumran disciple and Jewish general who became a turncoat and Vespasian's court historian, would have had both the financial means and the inherent motivation to help create the story, as would Philo of Alexandria, another Hellenized Jew of the period.

Another book also helped me to think through this concept, called "Operation Messiah" (Valentine Mitchell, 2008), which elaborated and built upon Eisenman's work, positing Paul as a Roman/Herodian intelligence operative attempting to undermine the Messianic Jewish resistance effort from within, and who ultimately needed to be rescued and "air-lifted" off the scene by Roman soldiers. The New Testament backed up the book's theory convincingly.

The situation in Judea in the late sixties and early seventies of the 1st Century was dire. Rome was coming down hard on Israel; harder than any regime ever has. And the resistance to Rome was embodied and carried out by *Messianic Jews*, and no other. It included the *Zealots* and the *Sicarri*; dagger-wielding political assassins who were feared by the people. These were the *real* Messianic Jews, and not the imagined proto-rabbinic actors of Hebrew Roots and Messianic Christian fantasy, or of modern scholarship. The notion that Christianity "evolved" as a separate sect of "Orthodox Judaism" is so unsubstantiated and unhistorical it boggles the mind that it has been accepted by so many. There was no such activity during the time period in which the gospel story supposedly transpires, unless you are going to include the movement towards the Hellenization of Jews in the Diaspora, which is counterintuitive to the argument. From a Torah-observant Jewish perspective, anyone against the Jews, and in favor of Rome in this conflict was a traitor, *period*. The idea of a "Jesus" character, who was supposedly a "Messiah", telling the people to "render to Caesar what belongs to Caesar" would have been met with violence and outrage. It was beyond the pale of common sense to even consider such a scenario. Let alone the notion of the people chanting in unison, *"Let his blood be upon us and our children."* (Matthew 27:25)

There was going to be no more "Judaizing Jesus" for me. The actual political climate in the First Century made it clear; The New Testament was *literature*, not history. What's more, it was likely no more than religious propaganda which was no longer relevant to our modern world.

Chapter 21

AT THE FOOT OF THE MOUNTAIN

WHAT IS THE logic behind our beliefs? Is it even a fair question? I'm not talking about what's true or what isn't true. I'm talking about how we arrive at a belief, specifically, the presumption that a subjective theological concept, dogma, or religious perspective is true. What's the process? I'm not a psychologist, but it seems to me, as someone who has left the world of childlike confidence behind and embraced the liberating freedom to be not entirely sure of some things, that adopting religious convictions has more in common with the chemistry of a man and woman falling in love than it does with logical, rational deduction. Of course, anyone who has studied marketing knows this already. We make most purchase decisions through a combination of our drives, our egos, and pure emotion, and once these aspects lead us to a point of decision, only then do we seek to justify our decisions with rational analysis. Naturally, I am generalizing, but all normally functioning humans, from brilliant to dumb, are subject to the same ingrained neuronic pattern. The faster we learn to apply this to our religious lives, the more coherent our worldview will be, because our allegiances to our religious beliefs (or lack thereof) are among the most diligently defended parts of our thinking.

The heart informs the mind, like a jockey instructs a racehorse, every bit as much, if not more, than the other way around. This is clear to see in children, especially infants and toddlers, who cannot manage their emotions very well. One of the marks of maturity is the ability to overcome emotion and control it, at least to a point, to function and accomplish necessary tasks.

Rational, logical deduction is an essential tool in reevaluating our paradigms. But, for most of us, there is a price point at which we leave off from this process. What is that price? For many, it is the threat of a loss of relationships and community. Any attempt we make to change a person's mind on the issue of religion must take these factors into account and we must respect the importance that the need for relational security plays in people's responses to our arguments. Why do people fight against logic? Simple. When our logical arguments could potentially threaten their relationships with people in their security network, meaning (in this context) in their religious community, or their family, they would rather either attack or dismiss our arguments than engage with our ideas, because our ideas aren't going to defend them in the dark of night when the village has assembled in front of their house with pitch forks and torches.

I have learned the hard way, through much difficulty, that I am very unusual in this area. My daughter, who is addicted to personality profiles and analysis, tells me that my personality type is one of the rarest on the spectrum. Part of my profile is that I'm not afraid to blow up my world if I feel it's warranted, and in fact I've done so on numerous occasions. It's not desirable, but I'm willing to go there if necessary. Unfortunately, my wife is not wired that way, and she has had to suffer much loss of both relationships and security as I've chased the ever-elusive truth across the spiritual landscape. Neither are most other people, as it turns out.

I can try to tell people that the Trinity is a made-up doctrine, for example, and they will tell me I'm a heretic, without taking the time to investigate whether what I have claimed is true. They truly *don't want to know*. And I can try to tell people that Christianity talks out of both sides of its mouth concerning grace and works, but it won't matter because they want to believe that it all washes out somehow, and that there's a way to explain it. *Here, listen to John MacArthur explain why you're wrong.* I can try to tell people that Jesus cannot be the Messiah because he died without fulfilling a single expectation of the office, but they will just mock me, block me, slander me or dismiss me, without spending as much as a minute thinking further. Heaven forbid I suggest the possibility that Jesus never even existed. They will never listen to me again, regardless of what I say from that point forward. Why is this? Because we don't think logically. In general, *we don't think*, period. We *emote*. We *project*. We respond to ideas, images and theories that feel right based on our sympathies and biases. Sure, we can think at our jobs. We can solve puzzles and analyze data. But we tend not to do this when it comes to things like our religion. We don't like to *think* when it comes to that. The details and logic of the matter are backfilled after we make the decision as to what and who we are going to believe in. Facts rarely can move us off our spot once we've made a decision to believe in something. For many, that decision is made for them when they were young children, and they never found a reason to question it.

In like manner, though rational arguments can clearly be made for theism, most atheists won't often allow themselves to entertain questions or arguments which support belief in God, for the same reason that theists won't allow themselves to entertain questions or arguments from atheists which undermines their beliefs; because the decision to believe or to not believe is made at the emotional level of the ego and the drive, and then the information is backfilled to assert and underpin the bias. That's just how human psychology is. If this were not the case, you could never convince a soldier to charge into enemy fire, or a man to take on the obligation of marriage and its life-long vows, not to mention the threat of losing half of one's possessions to alimony should divorce happen. Something besides logic is motivating these, and other, decisions. However, in terms of theists and atheists, there is an interesting common ground to be found. The Christian who adopted Christian faith as an adult and the atheist who lost belief in God as an adult are brothers who share the same intellectual parentage. That's because both of these groups of people made both an emotional *and* rational decision to either believe or to cast off belief. This emotional element causes their perspective to become baked in, like a woodburning pen scars letters into balsam wood. Washing this scar with soap and water will do nothing. It must be violently sanded down to remove it. Therefore, when debating with a committed religionist or a committed atheist, the experience is largely the same; you get pretty much nowhere.

Again, I'm speaking of *how* we arrive at our beliefs, not *what* we believe. Many atheists, particularly, immediately dismiss any person as unsophisticated if they cherish belief in the supernatural or in a Divine Being, but they fail to acknowledge that they are trying to force the other person to operate in a framework of analysis that they personally subscribe to but that the other person probably doesn't. Nor are they obligated to do so. And who is to say who is right? After all, is science the only way to explain the world? If I consult with people such as the late Christopher Hitchens, he will suggest that all religion, as well as people's adherence to and promotion of religion, is the biggest problem mankind faces. He believed that all religions needed to be aggressively denounced and gradually removed from society, and that we would all be better off if this were accomplished. However, I disagree strongly with that view, because I don't see any evidence which suggests he was correct, and if he was wrong (as I believe he was) the results would be disastrous should such a world be achieved. While I share strong agreement with many of Hitchens's insights, I nonetheless depart from him regarding his bottom-line conclusions. There is much strong evidence for the notion that religious people tend to be the most generous, altruistic and civil of neighbors, and that religious people have also been the point persons for most of the greatest acts of humanitarianism and of compassion in the world throughout recorded history. Of course, it's also true that many millions have suffered and died needlessly in the name of religions and their imperatives. Yet and still, I've yet to see a successful, thriving culture that didn't have a strong religious ethos among a significant share of its population. Ever. In world history. Now, maybe Hitchens is right. Certainly, he is a hero of many atheists today.

All I know, concerning whether there is a God or not, is that my belief in God (at the least, I can say I believe in a form of transcendental consciousness, more akin to the Kabbalistic idea of *Ein Sof* (transcendent infinity) and hold loosely certain dogmatic declarations of the concept of "God") gives me a worldview which satisfactorily explains the origin of all things, the progression of humanity and its spiritual evolution as well as a plumbline for my sense of morality and mankind's connection to conceptions of personal worth and existence. I've also yet to find an atheist worldview which can account for mankind's existential sense of consciousness or otherness, or one that explains the question of origins. Emerging quantum physics theory appears to support intelligent design and is also in line with the Kabbalah at many important points. If ever I encounter an atheist argument which can explain the origins of the world, the universe and of why man is, by nature, seemingly constructed psychologically to look beyond himself for meaning, then I'll be all ears, but I've yet to hear one which can do that. Atheist arguments appear to exist in the physical plane and draw their strength from that which can be observed and measured. A good starting point, perhaps, and obviously necessary for scientific inquiry, but this approach is quite limited in its ability to explain the full spectrum of human experience. It is also unsatisfying at the deepest of levels, and due to these factors, I keep myself from getting too close to their worldview. Atheism, more than anything, is a mindset that, once adopted, makes it increasingly difficult for the adherent to avoid being cynical of any aspect of human existence which transcends empirical observation.

So, what could motivate us besides logic? Lots of things. *Love, duty, brotherhood, fear, lust, hunger, anger*, and this list could go on and take up an entire chapter. Clearly, while logic and rationality are important factors, they don't appear to be what motivates most of our decisions. Further, a truly rational person would not go out of their way to destroy another's sense of security just to prove that they are right, because doing so destabilizes their relationship with that person, and this aggression is just as inappropriate as what they accuse religionists of promoting. Atheists are still driven, it turns out, by emotional factors (in spite of protests to this idea) just like everyone else, and often seek out other atheists for community and friendship, just like religious people do. Birds of a feather flock together.

No truly rational conception of human life can ignore the human need for belief, community and emotional support. For many people, a good deal of this comes from their religious beliefs and the people they associate with through the expression of those convictions. You must rely in something to live a life that has meaning and a sense of purpose. You may not believe in God, but if not, you will believe in *something else* that takes the place of God. You still *believe*, in a generic sense, because belief is the natural progression which one arrives at through choosing to attach to a concept and trust in it. Even if you believe that mankind is merely an organic life form that has evolved to have intelligence and existential thought, then that belief was embraced emotionally at some point before it became concretized in your mind. You still had to choose it over and against other perspectives. Even religious agnostics are still believers in other areas of their lives. They aren't uncertain about *everything* in life. We all know, I think, that the sun rises in the east, and we can be rather certain of this.

One fallacy that is commonly repeated is the notion that atheism is the natural state of mankind, and that we only become religious because of manipulation by false belief systems called religions. This view portrays all religious practices and dogmas as inherently abusive and harmful. However, this position betrays both common sense and empirical evidence. If we are going to say that man has a natural state, it is not atheism but *paganism*. This is proven by the fact that people have participated in the worship of deities and have embraced religious mythologies for as long as human history can be traced, whereas the rise of atheism is a relatively recent phenomenon which is directly tied to the period of the Enlightenment. People naturally want to believe that there is something beyond this physical world which gives additional meaning to their frustrating lives, and this behavior has marked the human experience for as long as records have been kept.

Further, for mankind to live together, there must be moral codes that most of the people in the culture can agree upon to maintain peace. Religion provides this. Is it perfect? Of course not. For example, look at how the Church has treated the Jews over the centuries, or how radicalized Islamists have treated both Christians and Jews in recent times. But understand, neither Christianity nor Islam nor Judaism did anything to anyone. *People* did those things. People persecute other people. People hurt other people. Religions don't do that. People also build orphanages, hospitals, schools and seek to rehabilitate drug addicts, alcoholics, and provide charity to widows and other disadvantaged people. People do this, not religions. They may do these things in the name of a religion, but it's still the people doing it, of their own volition. It is simply wrong to assume, for example, that because you don't agree with a certain religious worldview on a particular subject, let's say transgender identity for example, that a religion is therefore abusing people by teaching that view which you disagree with, simply because you disagree. And you can't rightfully demand they stop teaching their view (whatever that belief is) because if you do, you have become guilty of the same thing you are accusing the religionists of doing. You are being a totalitarian, by trying to impose your will and your values upon them. Who establishes the baseline for that conversation? Is it mob rule? The whims of the day? If religion has no role in informing us as to those codes, or morals, then who gets to decide? The government? The richest among us? The mainstream media? Our athletes and entertainers? It is dangerous for any group of people to assume the right to determine the moral and behavioral standards that are acceptable for a culture of their own volition, independent from a higher power or set of transcendent laws that supersede the power of the individuals who are exercising that power over others. It is well known that the creators of the American Constitution were theists who patterned their conceptions of a representative Republic with a separation of powers squarely upon their understanding of the Jewish Bible. All sets of standards must draw upon perceived higher authority to have lasting impact. Otherwise, such standards are arbitrary and too easily modified for the sake of convenience. Religion is the equivalent of a "celestial court", which is (hopefully) able to overrule fallible men and women. Even if the God of the religion is not real, the *perception* of that God being real in the minds of men has proven invaluable towards the stabilization of the greater human experience, and this empirical fact alone is, by itself, evidence that God may in fact be real, since this ethos is shared by all people in every culture throughout history. Where does this impulse derive from, if not some transcendental consciousness that we all share deep in our DNA?

I believe that we need to think before we choose to denounce and offer to build before we choose to destroy. If I've learned anything about the true nature of humanity, it's that people will not usually follow rational lines of thought when left to themselves to establish codes of morality but will ignore science and observable reality in order to push an agenda which suits their own worldview. How is this rational, or based on objective truth? It isn't. Critical Theory proves this. It isn't based on observable reality or science at all, but on purely subjective, agenda-based methods of analysis. It is the type of thinking that often arises from a worldview devoid of religious underpinnings. Nonetheless, Critical Theory, in all its applications, is most definitely a form of religious thinking. Worse, it is a form of *fundamentalist religious thinking*, based upon an anti-theist ideology rooted in materialism. Yet, it is being taught and promoted to elementary school students today, right now. Who made this decision? On what moral grounds? It wasn't Christians, I can tell you that. Nor was it religiously observant Jews or Muslims. The ideology of Critical Theory proves beyond doubt that mankind is not naturally atheist apart from religion. *Mankind is naturally religious*. And in the absence of a "higher power", man appoints himself as God, and develops ideologies that are not rational at all, but categorically *religious*.

Additionally, religion provides stability and security for well over three-quarters of the world's population. There is more to evaluating life than through the principles of raw data and science alone. You may not believe in God. But is it wrong for another to believe? What makes you so confident you are right? If not for my discovery of Judaism prior to my deconversion, I may have become an atheist like so many others once I left Christianity. I study the Kabbalah, and I study Talmud and many wonderful Jewish books on philosophy, ethics and law, and have found, to this point, many satisfactory answers about life through these avenues, including answers to some of the hardest questions which used to flummox me in years past. Not perfect answers, mind you, as I don't believe such an idea as "perfect answers" exists, but reasonable, workable answers; the kind of answers that can keep my mind occupied wrestling with them until I'm considerably past caring about such things. I am happy with my choice. But I still have doubts and questions about many things which transcend my current knowledge base. Ultimately, perhaps I, too, will be left shrugging my intellectual shoulders at the futility of knowing any of it, and I will just try to enjoy the sound of the birds outside my window as my vision and hearing fade and my life force ebbs away.

However, there is an important caveat to my argument. We who are theists must realize, at least, that religion, on its own, isn't a solution to much of anything. Whatever solutions we are going to provide our world are going to come from *us*, as living, breathing people who physically inhabit the earth, and not from the constructs of religions, because we are living in the world, and if God is real in a physical sense than he, at best, lives in the world only through us, because as far as anyone can tell God doesn't have a street address. We carry the ideas of God and of our worldview wherever we go, in our speech, our actions, and our convictions. We must therefore, if we are part of a religion, decide what that representation will be, for us. There is no magician's wand which can be waved or applied to the ills of the world. There is no *magic blood*. There is only this: *Life is hard*. For everyone. Life disappoints. Life is a struggle. Sometimes, a person never gets what they want. *That's life*. If religion helps people counter that reality successfully and gives them the stability and strength to be happier, more at peace and to be more productive, despite the inherent physical limitations which war against religious belief, who is anyone to complain? The problem occurs when we fail to parse out the valuable aspects of our belief systems, such as moral values and ethics, and become extremists, foisting superstitions and irrational judgments upon people based merely upon our dogmas, and attempt to control them based upon those presumptive ideas.

These are all, in my opinion, important philosophical and psychological factors that we need to understand when we are trying to figure out why a person leaves one religion and joins another, or even leaves the world of religion and faith altogether. We must know, sociologically, that there are both emotional and rational reasons, as well as irrational reasons, for the beliefs we cherish, the ones we've chosen to abandon, and the direction in which we want our lives to go. While it's tempting to ask a person such as myself questions like *what was the key thing that made you give up on Jesus?* we must realize that such a question cannot be answered adequately, even by the person who attempts to answer it honestly. Even if the person answering makes their best attempt, as I am doing in this book, none of us fully know all the reasons why we have done anything in life or believe in anything at all. We are always discovering those reasons as life unfolds, and hindsight always provides greater clarity, though not always greater understanding, as convoluted as that may sound. Sometimes the answers we are seeking are only found within ourselves, and sometimes what we find when we stare into our own souls is scary and even a little disappointing, if we are honest.

For me, I spent the better part of forty years at the foot of the mountain, the one that leads to the spiritual Promised Land. For a long while, I was waiting for the invitation to climb and enter in. But the invitation never came. I had to just start walking up the trail. It was *my* journey, and it was up to me to make it. Neither Moses nor Jesus ever stood behind me and pointed the way. Each time I was able to make a breakthrough of some sort which enabled me to see further into the nature of what I was chasing, I experienced a feeling that I had crested the mountain, finally. But, just like when I used to climb the peaks of the White Mountains in New Hampshire, often the experience of cresting a new peak merely provided a view which showed me how much farther I still had to go to reach my destination, and there were, before me, descents into more valleys and more hills to climb after that one, and some of them were bigger than the one I had just ascended. This is a problem that restless hearts and minds encounter all the time. We never quite get there. But it's okay, because once we reach the top of the highest hill, there's nowhere we can go but down.

Chapter 22

THE GOLDEN ROAD
(TO UNLIMITED DEVOTION)

EVERY FAMILY HAS problems. It's the rare child that is so infatuated and impressed with their parents that they want nothing more than to imitate them in every way. It's not relevant whether the parents have been loving, considerate, responsible or hard-edged, severe, and smothering. I had left home a long time ago, but I still could not tell my father directly about my decision to convert to Judaism. Throughout my life, my father had expressed disdain for the way I made decisions in life, whether about religion or otherwise. Nor did I expect him to understand. My father, despite his lack of outward religious observance, was still a loyal Catholic and he loved Pope Francis. When we went to visit them in Florida, he had a package of hot dogs on the counter. I discreetly checked the package for a *hechsher* but before I could really inspect it my father ripped it out of my hands.

"It's not kosher! I paid for the food and you'll eat whatever I put in front of you, got it?" He said, in a threatening tone. That's how he rolls. I had left Catholicism as a young man, despite his disapproval.

Now, far worse, I was leaving Christianity itself. I could understand his defensiveness.

For a long time, I had believed that Christianity was a type of step-child of Judaism, at least, if not a direct descendant. Most Christians held to the Church-enforced opinion that Jews had "scales" on their eyes and therefore could not understand the gospel or see Jesus as their Messiah, because God had "blinded" them due to their initial rejection of him. This idea came from Paul's letter to the Romans; it was what he termed a "partial hardening". Dispensationalists at least believed that Israel would "wake up" in the latter days and lead a great revival of Christian faith, bringing many Jews along and evangelizing the Gentiles in the process. This was the singular motivation of all the many missionary attempts to convert Jews in Israel and in America to Christianity. Most evangelicals eagerly anticipate a day of mass Jewish conversions as the sure sign of the immanent return of Christ. In truth, though, Christianity's origins were no more rooted in Judaism than Hitler's Third Reich was rooted in humanitarianism. Further, I had reached the conclusion by this time that the whole Messianic Jewish movement was an unfortunate mistake. Perhaps some of them had good intentions, but the religious syncretism was not doing anybody any favors. It created awkward compromises for both Christianity and Judaism, which operate from entirely different paradigms on nearly every important theological topic. I believe, today, in the old saw that "fences make good neighbors". Jews needed to be in traditional Jewish space, and Christians needed to be in church. Couples from two different traditions needed to decide which religion they were going to belong to and raise their children in it. As the old saying goes, you can't have your cake and eat it, too. If they thought Jesus's *magic blood* rectified them to God, then drop the play-acting and rest in "his finished work". But if you have become infatuated with Judaism and Torah, then follow that. Don't drag Jesus into Judaism and don't drag Judaism into church. Neither needs nor wants the other.

I had concluded that, while resurrecting "Rabbi Jesus" sounded enticingly romantic, and speculation about Paul as a radical rabbi leading a movement of "grafted-in goyim" sounded vigorous and equally exciting to the messianic mind, none of it was based in truth. In fact, both notions were essentially impossible. The texts of the New Testament were not written in code. They had been properly interpreted according to their plain reading for nearly two thousand years. The impression you get reading Galatians, for example (that the law has become passe because of Jesus), is exactly how Galatians is meant to be read and interpreted. Fancy eisegesis aside, it was rather straight-forward. I had concluded that if I could not read Galatians or Romans as being consistent with Judaism unless I was adequately armed with a thousand pages of messianic commentary from radical, fringe scholarship which provided a lens which reconciled them, that I was on the wrong path. Christianity and Judaism were plainly different religions, I was convinced, by *design*. Every major element of Judaism which distinguished it in practical ways was turned on its head in the pages of the New Testament. Every single one. To spin it differently was to deny the plain reading of the text. What Hebrew Roots and Messianic Jewish groups were doing, therefore, was attempting to create a new religion, one which was neither Christianity nor Judaism.

I had gone to the Conservative synagogue in Atlanta to find out if I could fit in Jewish space. After I wiped my eyes, I entered the Torah study room, where a host of Jews were seated around a long executive table, and another twenty or so people seated around the edges of the room, among whom I lodged myself. It was an older crowd. I was told to feel free to share my thoughts if I had any. I didn't expect to say a word, but as the discussion progressed on the Torah portion, I remembered passages from Talmud which I had studied, as well as essays by some of my favorite rabbis. With trepidation, I shared a few thoughts. At the end of the session, during the kiddush (meal after the service), the President of the shul approached me and informed me that many people assumed I was a part of a yeshivah. I told him no. He then told me that what I shared in the Torah study was amazing and encouraged me to come back and maybe even lead a session. Uneasy, I informed him that I wasn't Jewish. He said they didn't care. If I had the knowledge, that's all that mattered. Well, *that's refreshing*, I thought to myself.

"Come celebrate Shabbat with us. We'd love to have you." He smiled and patted me on the arm. Within a month, I had been added to the Torah teaching team at the shul, even being listed on their website. However, it turned out that my wife wasn't quite ready for the Jewish shul and returned to the Messianic space. She didn't believe in Jesus anymore, but she felt comfortable there. I met with the rabbi at the Conservative shul to discuss it with him and ask his advice. He decided to push me off to another rabbi in his denomination but outside the perimeter, slightly, of Atlanta, and a little closer to our home. I exchanged emails with this rabbi, but instead of setting up a meeting with him, I accepted an invitation to attend a new Chabad shul that had just opened only twenty minutes from our house.

We became, ultimately, founding members of this new Chabad shul. I even started plugging into the men's group and was building friendships there. But when I brought up the topic of conversion, I hit a wall. The Conservative rabbi at the other shul had encouraged me to convert. Said I was a good candidate. With this sentiment in tow, I spoke to the Chabad rabbi, and, unfortunately, the obstacles to conversion through Chabad seemed enormous if not downright impossible. My friend had converted through the Conservative movement without much trouble. I needed advice. It appeared suspicious to me that I was being allowed to be a founding member of the Chabad shul as a non-Jew (which meant paying monthly membership dues) yet they would not work with me towards conversion. In other words, my money was certainly welcome. That was my impression. Is that fair? Perhaps not, but life isn't fair, so that's the way it goes. The classes offered by Chabad through the Jewish Learning Institute, however, are a great value in Jewish learning and I highly recommend them to anyone.

I consulted with an Ultra-Orthodox rabbi in New York City I had befriended a few years prior. He was a kindly, if not eccentric, old soul who was incensed at the way conversion to Judaism had been politicized in recent decades. There were several issues he railed against, and one of the chief ones was the consolidation of power that the Rabbinical Council of America wielded over the Jewish world in America, stripping local rabbis of their authority, an issue he felt strongly about. This man was a certified *posek* (a legal halachic scholar, able to decide in cases of Jewish law) in a couple of key areas, having received ordination in Israel, and I trusted his view. He agreed to talk with my wife and I over the phone.

"Well, you guys are going to have to do what you feel is right for your family. Here's the law…if you go before a Beit Din which is made up of Jewish men, preferably, but not necessarily rabbis, that are all keepers of kashrut, and shomer Shabbat, and you agree together to strive to learn the laws and to honor and respect your Jewish identity and stand with the Jewish people in times of distress, you are Jewish immediately after being circumcised and being immersed. It doesn't even need to be in a kosher mikveh. It can be in a river. A big part of it is intent. Contrary to what people are telling you, you don't need to be fully observant to do this. Hillel would convert people on an oath and then teach them the laws after conversion. I can send you the citations, it's all in the sources…" He paused, "Of course, Jewish law is generally not accepted anymore on this subject. It's all politics today." My wife was confused. "What do you mean?" She asked. He sighed so loud we heard the distortion in the microphone.

"If you find a Beit Din that qualifies under those parameters outside of the Orthodox community, I'll be surprised. The Conservative Movement used to be more Orthodox, and had mostly Orthodox rabbis decades ago, but nowadays it's moved more and more towards Reform. Most of the Jews who gravitate to these movements seek to maintain their ethnic identity but are not Torah-observant. They are all about social justice and civic activism now, and they support all kinds of causes that are highly questionable and frowned upon in the Bible. That's what *tikkun olam* is to them; marching for causes and protesting. As a result of this massive shift to the left of center, not only politically but in halacha, the Beit Din of Israel no longer recognizes non-Orthodox conversions. If you convert through the Conservative movement, neither Chabad nor any mainstream Orthodox will recognize you as Jewish. You will still be non-Jewish to them, and they will treat you as such. Honestly, I think you guys, since you have children who are of age, should just remain Noahide and attend Chabad and be happy to be non-Jews learning in Jewish space. You'll appreciate the spirituality a lot more than what you will experience in a more liberal environment. But you have to make the best decision for your family, of course."

"But you don't agree with their policy, right? The Beit Din of Israel?" Again, he paused before answering.

"I understand it. It's complicated. Don't quote me by name on anything I'm telling you. I don't need any trouble." I assured him I wouldn't. He continued, "My issue is that we should follow the halacha. Rabbis should not be judged by association. They should be treated individually and respected for the unique relationship they have with their congregants. I've seen Orthodox rabbis lose their jobs because they were spotted talking on a street corner with a Reform rabbi. It's sickening how political it's become." He seemed ready to end the conversation there, but I urged him to continue. "Well, I'm not going to tell you what to do. I'm not in Atlanta. Chabad won't convert you, at least not on any timeline that you'd put up with. It would probably take years. But they will allow you to attend. And you'll be able to learn and have some semblance of community. Some Jews will keep their distance from you, obviously, because you aren't part of the Tribe. If you convert through Conservative, you'll be accepted as Jewish among them, of course, and if you're happy there, great. But I don't think you'll be happy there, from what I know of you. You are not of the same mind as they are, generally. But, there are still some good ones…"

"So, basically, conversion is a bad idea. We should just remain as we are." Said Chana, interjecting.

"Again, it's your family. Your choice. I'm just giving you the lay of the land."

"Okay, last question," I said, "If there is a Conservative Beit Din here that *does* fulfill the halachic parameters, would we be Jewish then?" I knew for a fact that the Conservative Beit Din in Atlanta fulfilled the parameters he laid out. He paused for what seemed a long time. I wondered if we had lost the connection. "You still there?" I asked, nervously.

"I'm here. Yes, you would be legally, halachically Jewish if that were the case. I would consider you to be Jewish. Others? Can't speak for others. But it's unlikely you'll find many like me, I'll be honest."

"Okay, thanks so much. We really appreciate your time."

"No problem." With that, he hung up.

Some time after this, we left the Chabad shul and plugged into the shul that the rabbi at the Conservative shul in Atlanta had recommended to me. The rabbi there, a self-proclaimed "progressive", though ordained through the Jewish Theological Seminary, which is the seminary of the Conservative Movement in America, encouraged us to convert to "get the identity issue out the way" and learn the religion as we went along. We had been attending faithfully for nearly a year, and he saw no reason to prolong it. This advice was consistent with what the Ultra-Orthodox rabbi had told me. The rabbi gave us a couple of books to read, walked us through a few counseling sessions and then made arrangements on our behalf with the local kosher mikveh. I would have protested the speed of it and the lack of training and instruction, but after my Breslov rabbi had explained the halacha to us, I had no real objections. The mocking words of the Chabad rabbi rang in my ears, however. *They'll probably just have you attend a couple of classes, read a book and then dunk you.*

The morning arrived for our immersion, and we were both nervous and excited. It was a rainy, chill day in late winter. The Rebbetzin gave us a tour of the facility and explained how the mikveh worked. I had studied it some and she was amazed that I knew what a *se'a* was.

The rabbis questioned Michelle and I separately and read our statements which we had prepared. After the questioning process, and after they approved us, we each, in turn, left our dressing room and entered the mikveh alone. I had already done the *brit milah* (rite of circumcision). The rabbis stood outside the door and waited for us to audibly recite the Hebrew blessings after each immersion. At the end, they proclaimed, in unison, and joyously, *"yasher koach!"* There were tears and hugs all around when we emerged back into the lobby after getting dressed. The rabbis were thankful to have participated in the ceremony and congratulated us for joining the Tribe. This felt extremely significant to us. There was a tangible reality that my wife and I could wrap both our minds and physical selves around now. We really did feel different. We were Jewish. A week later, we renewed our marriage vows at the synagogue, with a true Jewish wedding. Our girls and some of our friends (the ones we still had), our oldest daughter and her family, as well as numerous members of our new Jewish family which we had now inherited attended and helped us celebrate. We had a ketubah that the rabbi and one of his *Gabbais* signed for us. Our Jewish friends from shul gave us lovely *mezuzahs* for our front door and bedroom. My daughter helped us professionally frame our *ketubah* so we could hang it on the wall. We had official paperwork, signed by the rabbis and by us, proclaiming us to be part of *Am Israel*. Today, this is now recognized by the State of Israel. We can make Aliyah to Israel now and claim our citizenship if we ever desire to do so. It's all true. It was the happiest two weeks of our entire marriage. We had never been so joy-filled or full of peace in all our thirty-plus years together. Finally, after all these many years of pain and trauma, of loss and disappointment, we had found a home that we wouldn't have to leave. We had also found a religious expression that made sense to us, and that didn't require extremism or cultic behavior or attitudes. I wore my *tallit katan* proudly to the marriage ceremony, with my *tzit-tzit* visible under my suit jacket. I was extremely proud to be Jewish. Michelle cried when she recommitted to me under the *chuppah* in front of the *bimah*, and my girls smiled from ear to ear. My daughter Jane let her mostly evangelical Christian friends know that she was Jewish and "didn't believe in that Jesus crap". We all laughed. Her friends laughed, too. Tara was mortified when her Sociology teacher asked her to give a Jewish take on the Holocaust when they studied it together. Our identity had changed. The following Shabbat, Michelle and I went forward to read from the Torah for the first time. People clapped for us as we retook our seats. We had done it, and we felt a measure of satisfaction. But all was not rainbows and Skittles.

As I said, every family has its problems. We had not stepped into a religion. We had stepped into a family. And now, I was coming face to face with some of the internal problems that the Jewish family faced, and these problems were neither able to be easily explained, defined or solved. I was learning that everyone had a story. Every family within the Tribe was unique. There were numerous families in our shul who had lost relatives in the Holocaust just a generation or two earlier. They were not uncaring or oblivious as to their identity. They cared deeply. Yet, it hurt us to know that the Orthodox barely considered them to be Jewish. Many had been encouraged by their parents and grandparents who immigrated to America to focus on being successful in America, and not to try to be stubborn about religion. Many of these people viewed the Orthodox as part of an Old-World mentality that had outlived its usefulness in the New World. This is one of the reasons why so many Jews in liberal expressions are so well-educated and successful professionally. Education is the prime value of most American Jewish families. For the Ultra-Orthodox, this means Torah study and yeshivah for the young men. For more secularized Jews, it means a Masters Program at Harvard or Columbia after their Bar Mitzvahs and a professional psychiatry, lawyer or medical practice, for both men and women. Others loved the old ways but had married a more liberal spouse who wasn't as committed to the tradition, so they reached a compromise, and found themselves at home in shuls like ours. Still others had been jettisoned out of organizations like Chabad, as if shot out of a cannon, denouncing them as a cult, and would discourage anyone they could from participating in their classes or services. But when it came time for the High Holidays, these same "non-committed" Jews would have tears streaming down their cheeks as they belted out *Ha-Yom!* at the top of their lungs on Rosh HaShana. Despite whatever strained relationship they had with the religious side of Judaism, they were *proud* to be Jewish. Nonetheless, there was something missing, for us. Something we needed. We were people of faith. Many of these people did not self-identify in that way.

Chana attended her first Sisterhood meeting and was greeted with a cold-shoulder that left her feeling like a leper. Most of the women were driving Mercedes and BMW's and didn't give Chana the time of day, and when the round-table discussion happened, led by the Rebbetzin, some spent all their time complaining about Christians. Chana looked down. She was not a Christian anymore, but most of her family was, still. When she was asked to share, she said simply, "Faith is very important to me." Only the Rebbetzin smiled in return. The rest looked down or away. Chana felt crushed.

"Most Jews here don't think in terms of having faith," the Rebbetzin tried to explain to her afterwards. Chana had no words. She couldn't even begin to understand what this meant, or where to put herself, in context. All she knew was that she would never have treated others the way she had been treated. And there was little that could be done to fix it, despite the Rebbetzin's efforts, least of all telling her that "Jews don't think in terms of having faith".

We had befriended a couple in the shul, but when we went to their home for the first time, the husband explained to me that I made him nervous because I wore a kippah all the time. He said to me, matter-of-factly, that, 'If you are going to be religious, we just aren't going to be able to be friends.' I told him that I converted to Judaism on purpose and that learning the tradition was important to me. He said, "Suit yourself". We aren't friends today, predictably. This was highly ironic. I remembered a time several years prior during which I was on a video conference call with several Messianic Christians about a writing project. At the start of the call I was asked, "Where's your headcovering?" They all sported caps or kippahs except for me, even though none of them were Jewish. Yet, now that I was Jewish, none of the Jews I dealt with wore a kippah except during services at shul. When I attended a men's event in public, at an arcade, I was the only one who had a kippah and tzit-tzit. I got many strange and suspicious looks. From Jews, mind you. The Ultra-Orthodox rabbi had been right. These people were not really in touch with the faith side of things. A good percentage of them (though certainly not all) didn't really care about observance all that much and seemed mildly irritated by Jews who did. One of them bemoaned to me that they needed to get a new "lobster pot", since the one they had been using for twenty years had cracked. Pity. On the other hand, there was something positive to be said for their approach, in that the Conservative shul was far more accessible to us than the hardliners in the Orthodox world, especially the Haredim who wore those big, round, fuzzy hats on their heads and those crazy long black day robes. Sorry, but I was never going to be *that* guy. *That was just weird.* I simply wasn't interested in expressions of religious extremism anymore, from any religion or any of their followers. Those types of approaches to religion had destroyed my life to that point. I appreciated the *Hasidim* on a conceptual level because they were passionate, they taught Kabbalah and liked to drink vodka every time they studied Torah. I liked vodka. But no, that was not the life for us. I could study their writings, sure, but *live* with them? With my wife? My daughters? It wasn't going to happen. As much as I was flustered and discouraged by the limp attitude the Jews of our shul had towards the religion, there were aspects about their approach I had to admit were a good fit for me. I was more like them then like the *Haredi*, with their long, curled locks hanging by their cheeks. I had a lot more *Heschel* in me than *Schneerson*. I was a philosopher. I was infatuated with the philosophies and spirituality of Judaism. The way that life was broken down and analyzed within Judaism was of never-ending interest to me.

I studied Talmud because it was a master class in critical thinking and deductive reasoning. I couldn't get enough of it. But the strictures of Torah living according to halacha were proving inaccessible to my family. The people who could teach us how to do it wouldn't let us into their world, and the people who were willing to let us in didn't want to teach us. We had reached an *impasse*. When the shul closed down because of Covid-19, my wife began to wilt like a flower that wasn't getting watered. Her lifeline to the faith was her time spent with people. *No people, no faith.* Slowly, she lost interest.

I was encouraged to contact the Atlanta Scholars Kollel for continued learning. It is a local yeshivah based out of the oldest Orthodox shul in the area, but it was open to all Jews in the region who were serious about study. It seemed a perfect fit for me. I was also deeply concerned about where Chana was at, and I felt that if we didn't connect with some people soon, that I would lose her forever and she would be done.

I enjoyed a Zoom meeting with the junior Rabbi of an Orthodox congregation in Atlanta associated with the Kollel. He took notice of the Talmud volumes behind me as we spoke and could tell that I was serious. After an hour-long conversation, we scheduled another meeting that my wife could participate in. Chana, recently, had accepted a management job in retail, largely motivated by financial insecurity about our future, and had to work two Saturdays a month now. But she was willing to go with me to an Orthodox shul if it meant being around people of faith, provided they weren't going to judge her or make her feel small in the process. This second meeting, which she participated in, went well, and led to the rabbi giving me the contact information for his uncle, the Senior Rabbi of the congregation. We felt encouraged. Perhaps the Orthodox would welcome us and help us learn and provide a sense of family for us that was desperately needed. We would see. I quickly called the Senior Rabbi of this congregation, as I had been told that he was eager to connect with me and was caught a bit off-guard when he was excessively stoic on the other end of the line.

"So, I've heard a bit about you. How can I help you?"

"Well, as you may know, we've been through quite a journey. I'd like to join the Kollel and we'd like to be able to celebrate Shabbat with you and your community."

"Tell me about your family. Where are you guys at?" He asked. I told him the state of our clan.

"Well, I'm afraid we won't be much use to you in that case," he said. I was a bit stunned.

"What do you mean? I know we have a lot to learn and all, but we are sincere. I love to study. We just need a community, you know?"

"I understand. But here's the problem...your daughters didn't convert with you, for one thing. It's against the halacha to live with non-Jews. No Orthodox Beit Din would have ever entertained converting you and your wife in your current situation. When you live with non-Jews, well, it creates insurmountable problems in the practice of Judaism. You can't *kasher* your home."

I explained to him about our counsel from the Breslov rabbi and assured the rabbi that we understood the halacha regarding conversion to Judaism. I told him that the Beit Din we went before was Shomer Shabbos and kosher.

"Well, if it was such a satisfying experience, why are you talking to me?" That was an excellent point. I tried to explain my disappointment we had experienced with the liberal social agenda taking priority over teaching us Judaism in the community we had been a part of.

"Well, aside from all that, there are reasons why we don't recognize conversions from liberal forms of Judaism. They pick and choose what they feel is important. It's not really Judaism, you see. Judaism hasn't changed. The law is the law. But they seem to think they don't have to respect it."

"Right, well we were hoping that my wife and I and our youngest could stay with a family for Shabbat so we could learn."

"No, that won't work. Listen, here's the deal. Chabad is happy to have people drive to shul and attend services. They are very outreach oriented. Even if you aren't Jewish. But that's not how it is in most Orthodox communities. If you and your wife started attending, the people in the community would either assume you were Jewish, or that you were working with me towards conversion, and then, yes, they'd happily help you. But that's not where you are at. You aren't Jewish and I can't help you towards conversion because of your daughters. More than that, I wouldn't even consider working with you unless you were willing to move into the Eruv. You cannot commute from north of the city. We don't have commuters. People walk to services. Now, if you want to get a divorce from your wife, then that's a different story. I could help you then. But unless you're going to split from your wife… how old is your youngest again?"

"Almost fourteen".

"Right. So, if you aren't going to get a divorce, I won't be able to help you for six to ten years, or whenever she finally moves out. I'm sorry."

I was stunned. We would be nearly retirement age by the time Tara moved out. I changed tactics, though by now I was discouraged.

"Well, what about the other part of this…what about the Kollel? Can I study with you guys?

"No. That's for Jews. I'm sorry." This ticked me off a bit. Not just a bit. I was suddenly hot.

"Wait a minute. If I had not been up front and transparent with you and just told you I was Jewish and wanted to plug into the Kollel, or if I was a secular Jew that wanted to do *ba'al teshuvah*, you'd accept me, right?"

"Well, yes of course."

"Rabbi, can I speak plainly?"

"By all means."

"I told you that our conversion fulfilled the requirements of Jewish Law. But yet, you don't accept me as Jewish. So, are you critical of the Conservative rabbis because they don't follow the halacha or because it's political? It seems political to me. Because if we followed the halacha and you don't recognize it, then that means your problem is not with the way they pick and choose about the law. Isn't that right? I'm just trying to figure out why I'm not Jewish in your eyes." He sighed.

"Well, technically, by a literal interpretation of the halacha, you fulfilled *most* of the basic requirements, but due to today's circumstances, no Orthodox rabbi would accept your conversion as valid, religiously. Now, maybe it would be recognized by the State of Israel for citizenship someday, but never by the religious leaders of the tradition. I'm sorry, no. I don't consider you to be Jewish. I'm not trying to be harsh. But this is the way it is. Like I said, if you get a divorce, feel free to call me. But otherwise, if I were you, I would put these crazy ideas of your Jewish identity out of your mind and enjoy being a Noahide. It's much easier. You'll have much less stress. Your wife can work her job. You can enjoy your family. Okay?"

"Thanks for your time, rabbi."

"Of course." He hung up the phone.

I wasn't sure where to put myself anymore. And I had seen a spark of hope flash in Chana's eyes when we spoke with the rabbi's nephew on Zoom. *What would I tell her now?* How would she react to all of this once I told her that we would not be allowed to attend their services and meet the people? Converting with me had been such a healing experience for her. She had climbed a mountain of mammoth proportion just getting to the point where she could do that, after everything we had been through. Now, though, she did not want to climb any more mountains. Her climbing days were over. Honestly, I was wondering if mine were, too.

The Jewish family had some internal problems, like all families, and they were problems I couldn't fix. I poured myself a drink. I called my friend in Pennsylvania who had converted through the Conservative movement also and vented on him. I was very down in the mouth. He offered what encouragement he could. He could relate and had been through similar struggles. It's hard to change your entire identity and the structure of your life when you're middle-aged and you're recovering from years of maladjustment, both emotionally and financially, as a result of your involvement in religious extremism. We agreed, ultimately, that the rabbi did me a favor by pushing me away. I didn't want to be the guy that escaped religious extremism in one religion only to dive headlong back into it within a different religion. I decided that my family's freedom was more important than impressing the elites within Judaism. Things weren't all bad. We had survived. We were still married. I owned a business. I had a community of folks online that were in similar straights, and we hung out together in classes through Netiv, the organization I was teaching for. I decided to be thankful for what we had and not frustrated for what we didn't. Some problems were beyond my reach. And the rabbi was right…our daughters were not Jewish. And what's more, they needed my attention at this stage, not my religious fervor. They had lived through enough of that craziness over the previous twenty years. It was time to get in step with where my family was at. They needed my time, not teaching. Love instead of lectures.

Chapter 23

——◆◆——

THE FASTER WE GO, THE ROUNDER WE GET

FOR AT LEAST a day after my disappointing phone call with the Orthodox rabbi, privately, I seriously considered, and visualized, what it would be like to say goodbye to my wife, who felt so alienated by the Jewish community and was rapidly losing all interest in religious devotion of any kind, and replacing my family with a new, Jewish community, potentially even a new Jewish wife, and rebuilding my life. I tried to imagine what that would look like, and how it would feel. I pictured myself wearing a broad-brimmed black hat, sporting a wild, unkempt beard, dressing in a black suit and white button-down shirt conceal-ing a starched *tallit katan* and wearing black shoes every day. I would put my shoes on just so...right foot, then left, tying the left laces, then the right. *Or was it the other way around?* I would be practicing fully observant Judaism within an Eruv community in Atlanta. I even pic-tured a crazy scenario, of a widowed, middle-aged Jewish woman that I would be matched with, eventually. Then, I nearly threw up in my mouth. *Who was I kidding?* Mind you, my wife and I have had serious marriage troubles over the years. But we kind of need each other. If I were twenty-five, with no children, and she was able to support herself easily, and we had simultaneously grown irreconcilably distant from each other, *maybe*. But at fifty-three, with a sub-standard retirement plan and children and grandchildren in the picture? To walk away from them just so I can call myself a "real Jew"? Nope.

My wife had tolerated many years of disappointment, unfulfilled desires and relationship heartbreak, only to have been brought into a foreign religious tradition and separated from her grandchildren and her blood family by over a thousand miles. She had happily entered the *mikveh*. She had happily become Jewish. She was now to be summarily dismissed as so much unfortunate collateral damage of the border war between the religious Orthodox and the various parts of the Reform movement? There had to be a better answer for me than *divorce your wife so you can be legitimately Jewish*. There just had to be. However, I needed to face reality. My teenage daughters, who were not interested in practicing Judaism, were a stumbling block to having a kosher home. I knew it.

It may be quite difficult for a person reading this, who has no depth of understanding of what it means to be Jewish, to understand. It's not like Christianity. The rest of a person's family does not need to be Christian for an individual in that family to become a Christian. A person's Christian faith is a private affair, ultimately. Not so in the Jewish tradition. A person is born Jewish, through a Jewish mother. That's not the mark of a religion, but an *ethnicity*. That's why the rabbi would not work with me unless my entire family was going through the conversion together. My girls chose not to do this. The Judaism that I could participate in was never going to be good enough for the Orthodox. Not now, not tomorrow. Probably not ever. Unless I no longer lived with my family, which would "free me" to do so. A big part of this also was a commitment to moving to a home inside the Eruv. This was absolutely required, or no dice.

The laws of Eruv, which were entirely rabbinic in origin, were a classically ingenious invention within the Jewish tradition. They were part of the laws of domains regarding the prohibitions of Shabbat observance. In Jewish Law, there are private domains, public domains, and neutral domains, or intermediate domains, called *karmelit*. The rabbinic establishment of domains on Shabbat and of an Eruv demarcated an established area in which Jews can move about without violating Shabbat prohibitions, and represented a form of leniency, rather than forcing Jewish families to be stuck inside their homes waving at each other through windows during Shabbat. Now, they could walk down the alley with their pot of chicken soup and share it with their neighbors, and study Torah and enjoy time together. It was a brilliant innovation. Unfortunately, for my family to join the community overseen by the Orthodox rabbi I spoke with, I would need to purchase or rent a home that fell within his community's Eruv. Not going to happen. The average home price in his community is over $500,000. We don't have that kind of money. Nor will I likely *ever* have that kind of money. I'm fifty-three years old and ramping down the back side of my working career. I'm looking to downsize, not upsize. I'm looking for *less* stress, not *more*. Of course, this is not what the sages intended by the rules of Eruv, mind you. The rules were meant to accommodate and make things more accessible, not more difficult. But here we are. And my lack of convenient circumstances doesn't constitute an emergency on Judaism's part. Like the Orthodox rabbi told me; *We don't seek converts. If you are ready to convert, the way will become available to you. We don't change the law to fit you in.*

Judaism is always one generation from extinction, every day. There are strong reasons for Jewish hardliners to hold their positions. They are not trying to control people, in most cases. They are trying to preserve something that they hold of precious value. Like the Fundamentalist Baptists, they are *preservationists*. But also, like them, their crowd is mostly unyielding. You must toe the line, or you won't last among them for very long. Is this unreasonable, though? On Memorial Day in the United States, we honor our veterans who fought, and often died, on foreign soil to help preserve the "American way of life", yet literally millions upon millions of Jews suffered and/or died through attempts by others to make the Jewish people extinct. And such attempts at genocide are not unique to the Holocaust under Hitler, but have been attempted by many throughout Jewish history, all the way back to biblical times, and continues today through attempts to destroy the nation of Israel. It isn't for nothing that the Orthodox and the Ultra-Orthodox are passionate about maintaining the traditions. Yet and still, for all my criticisms of secular Jews, and leftist, "woke" rabbis that promote Marxist ideologies, identity politics and anti-Torah values, it's hard not to cringe while watching a video of Hasidic Jews bouncing up and down *en masse* to some ridiculous *niggun (wordless melody)*, all dressed exactly alike as though they are collectively in the witness protection program. I must ask: *That's spirituality? That's what we are fighting to preserve?* This is the type of fundamentalist, extremist nonsense that all of us can do without, quite frankly. Preserving the Torah is one thing. Preserving nonsensical, even embarrassing rituals and traditions that serve no meaningful role in our lives is another. In a recent Reuters article, it was revealed that over 55% of Israel's *Haredi* population (nearly 10% of the nation's total) is unemployed and dependent upon the State and charity for sustenance. There's something severely wrong with this approach to Torah, in my view. While I applaud the *Haredi* for taking their tradition seriously, their type of unyielding extremism is unsustainable on almost every level. If your approach to Torah observance requires less-observant members of the community to support you financially, then you are not actually practicing Torah, despite your zeal. There's a reason why so many Jews, after their families successfully immigrated to America, unplugged from such madness, shaved their beards, and pursued Ivy League degrees in Social Sciences and Law. Holding the line hasn't proven to be a winning play for many Jewish families. Then again, to the opposite extreme, bemoaning a cracked lobster pot, as a Jew, doesn't work for me either. That's a bridge too far. There had to be some suitable real estate between the extremes. And I meant to find it.

Jews can be weird. That's because Jews are *people*, and people, in general, tend to be weird. But I'll tell you what else is pretty weird: Thinking that your eternal life is secured by the *magic blood* of some guy that died two thousand years ago as a political dissident in a half-forgotten conflict of power. Or buying into the notion that he subsequently resurrected from his grave after death and floated into and beyond the atmosphere to sit at the "right hand" of the Creator of the Universe somewhere in space, whispering sweet nothings to Him about Johnny's sex life. That's *really* weird. So, we all have our problems to work out. Jews don't seem quite so weird in light of Christianity and its claims, if we are going to be frank and honest here. And the fact that Jews still exist, and have survived the destruction of their worship center, expulsion from their land and many centuries of harsh treatment at the hands of Christianized nations and governments, and yet still thrive as a people today, is something to notice. And it hasn't happened because they "controlled the banks". The added fact that many people from around the world continue to be drawn towards Judaism, and its ethical monotheism, is also something to behold. Perhaps the strongest argument one can make for the validity of the Jewish Bible and the notion of the existence of the Jewish God is the continued existence of the Jewish people. It's not unreasonable to say that Christianity would have surely met the same fate as other, similar pagan religions of its day, if not for the fact that it hitched a ride on the Jewish Bible for its claims of authority. It's almost as if God allowed it to flourish just to preserve his good name; what Judaism would call a *kiddush HaShem*. Like I've said, every family has its problems. And like Jerry Garcia famously once quipped, "The critic is always wrong."

Our family is spread up and down the East Coast now, not unlike many other families. Keeping a family together and maintaining positive relationships with them through the ups and downs and changes in life is perhaps the world's most difficult job. The target must be intentionally chased with love and humility and, I think, a predilection to laugh at oneself and not take oneself so seriously all the time. Life is too short to do otherwise. I had decided to attach myself to the Jewish train, but it was okay if others in my family didn't. I love them exactly as they are. I suppose I'm unusual for leaving the faith of my upbringing, or maybe it's not so unusual.

My wife and I, and our girls, are not entirely sure where we truly belong today. We would love dearly to belong somewhere, but I'm not overly stressed about it anymore. I would not step foot in a church, of any denomination, unless it was to attend a funeral or something. And though the Orthodox do not consider me to be Jewish, I am not going to denigrate my own Jewish journey based soley upon modern political circumstances that have nothing to do with me. I don't agree with their assessment. It's my life, and my journey. Is progress needed within the Jewish community? Of course. When is it not? I wait, like everyone, for something to change. Some things are beyond any of us to control directly.

I do realize, now, the challenges that converting to Judaism without participation from every member of your household creates. Everything is more difficult. You work to provide proper kosher separation of items in your refrigerator, only for your teenage daughter to come home with her fast-food leftovers which she places in the fridge on top of the yogurts. You drive to the city to purchase kosher beef at seven dollars a pound and make a Shepherd's pie with it, forgetting that there is heavy cream in the mashed potatoes. Shabbat is interrupted by a need to drive your daughter to her job because she doesn't have her car. It's a hot mess a good chunk of the time. I shrug my shoulders. I love them. They try to love me. It's never going to be perfect. Fortunately, Judaism isn't about being perfect. You do your best. My best, unfortunately, isn't good enough to live in an Orthodox community. But you know what? It's okay. Because *life* isn't about being perfect, either. I've learned that if there are people who don't accept you, work at finding the ones who do. You'll be a lot happier doing that than by trying to impress the ones who don't.

We find ourselves having Jewish friends, Christian friends, and even atheist friends. There's no pressure. We can be ourselves. I fly my American flag proudly from my porch, cheer for my favorite football team, read Jewish books, study Talmud, and argue with people on social media. I hang out with whoever I want. I drink bourbon before I go to bed if I want, or, I drink tea. It's my choice. I don't worry about "ministry". I'm free from that duty-bound, fundamentalist lifestyle. I'm free to love and be loved and even to experience anger, hate, longing, and joy, without shame or guilt or obligation or apology. Today, I'm not trying to *become* something anymore. I'm simply being *me*, which means a lot of different things at the same time, and I'm hopefully a better, more loving, and more sane person as a result.

During my journey out of Christianity and into Judaism I discovered the teachings of Rebbe Nachman of Breslov. I really enjoy studying them. A key teaching is the concept of *bittul*, or self-nullification. I needed to remember this idea if I was going to move forward successfully. I had spent so much energy pushing and pulling my family, and specifically Chana, along the path of the discovery of truth, with many changes along the way. It was time for me to practice *bittul*. My ego wanted to win the game called religion, you see. I wanted to be the committed guy who did everything, who learned everything and helped everyone. But it was time for me to slow down and help the people closest to me, even if that meant nullifying my own personal ambitions. I learned that the faster I tried to go, the rounder I got. I became like a ball rolling downhill, crushing things in my path. It was time for me to stop doing this and to become a tree that simply held its ground. My wife is tired and has experienced deep, soul-crushing disappointment in her life. She has never enjoyed yearly vacations, bucket-list trips or adventures, fancy wardrobes or expansive shoe collections. She has lived for her children. She has spent the lion's share of her life's energy serving her family; trying to keep the clan together against all odds. She no longer has the emotional stamina for another massive life adjustment, or another massive rejection from another people group. There was a flicker of hope in her eyes when

THERE'S NO SUCH THING AS MAGIC BLOOD

we had the Zoom call with the Orthodox rabbi, but when they shut us out, that flicker died. Now, slowly, it's returning, but not in the same way. It's about being with people, for her, and loving our family. She's no longer tolerant of extreme religious expectations. And I'm getting tired, too. The children are almost all grown. My oldest is over thirty now. The grandchildren are growing fast. Currently, none of them are Jewish. I have books to write, and this takes a lot of energy, too, if you are going to do it well. I'm not sure I have it in me either, to tell the truth, to reinvent myself anymore, at least in a religious sense. Faith has become something very personal and has shaped itself to our needs and our station. What Chana needs from me is love and support, not for me to force her into a religious box. Life is so short. And so very fragile.

Once, a long time ago, I sat in a hotel penthouse suite at two in the morning and heard a billionaire say that *life is that thing that happens to people while they are trying to figure out what they are going to do.* And I've learned that he was right. If I had internalized anything over the previous forty years, since I lay in my father's overgrown field near the crashed airplane contemplating my future, it was to *pay attention to your life*, and to live it intentionally and with clear purpose according to the most important values you hold dear. That meant, at this juncture, that I needed to become *less*, not more. On a personal level. I needed to lay some things down, such as strict observance of the Jewish faith, so that I could focus on loving my family. I needed to practice *bittul*. If I didn't, I would lose what I cherished the most. The Orthodox rabbi did me a favor. I should say, rather, he did my wife and children one. He put a firm hand up and stopped me in my tracks. He didn't accommodate my addiction. He pointed me back home. And the faces looking back at me when I turn in that direction have different ways of measuring my success than the people in the religious hierarchy. I've learned to stop judging myself and others harshly. Life is hard enough. No one appreciates the zealot wagging his finger in their face at their shortcomings, and this includes one's own finger in the mirror at oneself.

After weeks of depression caused by my being rejected by the Atlanta Kollel, I suddenly realized the obvious: I had spent my life, largely, pursuing the depths of my religion, whatever it was, whether the many forms of Christianity I had been part of, or now, Judaism, to achieve a sense of purpose and identity. But when I took stock of who I was after all those years, I discovered that I was no longer the same person who had started the journey. The insecure, intense, and lost young man that was stuck repeatedly reenacting his dysfunctional relationship with his father; beating his head against reality, trying to force people to acknowledge him and affirm him and validate his existence, had grown up. I knew who I was now and was okay with it. I had survived religious extremism, yes, but more importantly, what I had really survived was my own battle against myself. I had been afraid to face *me*. I was like Jacob wrestling with the angel of Esau, but the limp that I walked away with was from fighting against my doppelganger. And once I came to terms with who I was, which included accepting who I *wasn't*, I discovered that the idea of the *magic blood* of Jesus was ludicrous and entirely unnecessary. *I didn't need a redeemer.* I was a human being and my inadequacies were part of the package of my design. I was not ashamed of myself anymore, nor did I need to be. The only redemption I needed was to redeem the time I had left. But along with this fundamental discovery, I also realized something else: that extremism in any expression of religion is dangerous and unhealthy. Apocalyptic messianism, particularly, was incredibly dangerous to yourself and the community at large, whether you are a Christian, a Jew or a Muslim. I had learned that I am responsible to the people around me to interpret my beliefs in such a way that I did not run roughshod over others or trample their dignity. I also could no longer ignore *reality* in favor of a vision of the future that may never materialize, particularly during my lifetime, such as the apocalyptic messianic transformation envisioned by Evangelical Christians and Ultra-Orthodox Jews. I believe in the thirteen core principles of Jewish faith, which includes belief in the resurrection, but I'm not in charge of the big red button that initiates it. Nor do I have any inkling of the manner or form in which it may transpire. *I'm not in charge.* And neither are you. And neither, for that matter, are any of the religious or political leaders we look to. My job is to *live*. Period.

When I converted within the Conservative Jewish movement, a saint of a Jewish brother, a black man, who was raised Orthodox in New York City, and who is part of the Conservative movement today as well, gave me a precious gift: a set of *kosher tefillin*. It came with a proper, full-length *tallit* as well. In the morning, when I daven *Shacharit*, and I'm wrapping the tefillin, making sure the strap is wrapped tight around my middle finger, I recite the blessing;

"I will betroth you to Me forever;
I will betroth you to Me in righteousness and justice,
Lovingkindness and compassion;
I will betroth you to Me in faithfulness;
And you shall know the LORD"

My faith has become personal, precious and private. It's not a show, or a performance that others see. It is *bittul*. I have been reduced to a shadow that disappears under the *tallit* and becomes nothing. And in this simplest of actions, I am as much as I ever could have hoped to be.

CPSIA information can be obtained
at www.ICGtesting.com
Printed in the USA
LVHW032143030921
696926LV00001B/27